A Beginner's Guide to Tibetan Buddhism

Notes from a Practitioner's Journey

A Beginner's Guide
to Tibetan Buddhism

Notes from a Practitioner's Journey

Bruce Newman

Snow Lion Publications
Ithaca, New York
Boulder, Colorado

Snow Lion Publications
P.O. Box 6483
Ithaca, NY 14851 USA
(607) 273-8519
www.snowlionpub.com

Printed in Canada on acid-free recycled paper.

ISBN 1-55939-211-8

Library of Congress Cataloging-in-Publication Data

Newman, Bruce, 1950-
 A beginner's guide to Tibetan Buddhism : notes from a practitioner's journey / Bruce
Newman.
    p. cm.
 Includes bibliographical references.
 ISBN 1-55939-211-8 (alk. paper)
 1. Spiritual life--Buddhism. 2. Buddhism--China--Tibet. I. Title.
BQ7805.N348 2004
294.3'923--dc22
                              2004006388

Contents

Dedication   vi

Preface by Chökyi Nyima Rinpoche   vii

Acknowledgments   viii

Introduction   ix

  1   Buddha-Nature: The Ground   1

  2   The Teacher   11

  3   Finding a Teacher   19

  4   Empowerment   29

  5   Centers   39

  6   Path Buddha-Nature: Instruction and Practice   51

  7   Getting Started   61

  8   Getting It Wrong   71

  9   Systems and Stages of Practice   87

10   The Four Noble Truths   95

11   The Four Thoughts   105

12   Ngondro: Refuge and Bodhichitta   119

13   Ngondro: Vajrasattva Practice and Mandala Offerings   131

14   Ngondro: Guru Yoga and Devotion   137

15   Kyerim   147

16   Rituals   159

17   Dzogrim and the Body   173

18   The Path of Liberation   187

19   Fruition   195

Appendix: The Future   207

Notes   211

Dedication

The book is humbly and devotedly dedicated to the long life and enlightened activities of my two primary teachers, Venerable Chökyi Nyima Rinpoche and Venerable Gyatrul Rinpoche.

Preface

Bruce Newman has been my close student for almost thirty years. Having resided in both India and Nepal for many years, Bruce spent many years seriously studying and practicing Tibetan Buddhism with a number of well-known, highly qualified Buddhist meditation masters.

Being a diligent practitioner, Bruce successfully completed the traditional four-year retreat at Samye Ling in Scotland and thus qualifies for the designation of "lama." Presently, he resides at Tashi Chöling Retreat Center, founded by H. H. Dudjom Rinpoche, in Ashland, Oregon where Bruce has been teaching meditation and guiding others in general Buddhist practices for almost a decade.

Given Bruce's exceptionally kind nature, stable disposition, and innate intelligence, I am confident that he will be able to share his insights with others and help them on the Buddhist path. I am pleased that his new book will soon be published and wish him all the best.

Chökyi Nyima Rinpoche

Acknowledgments

This book would not be possible without the help and inspiration of a great number of people. Foremost are my teachers. I've been very fortunate to have many, but my two primary teachers are Venerable Chökyi Nyima Rinpoche and Venerable Gyatrul Rinpoche.

Many people suggested that I write a book. Most importantly, my wife, Susan Bosworth, and my root teacher, Chökyi Nyima Rinpoche, who basically ordered me to write it and wouldn't let me quit!

Also, many people read the various drafts of the manuscript and offered suggestions. Here, the two most helpful have been my dear friends Gaea Yudron and Barbara Caselli.

I also extend my heartfelt appreciation to the patrons and sponsors, both past and present, whose generosity and trust has made it possible for me to devote my time fully to the Dharma. I won't mention any names, but you know who you are. Thanks again.

Thanks also go to my agent, Jimmie Young, who showed up seemingly out of nowhere and to all the good folks at Snow Lion who have made so much of the precious Dharma available to us over the years.

Lastly, to all my friends and students along the way. Through our connection, I have learned a great deal about the manifold ways that buddha-nature unfolds in different practitioners; the lessons have been invaluable.

Introduction

I wanted to call this book *Tantra for Dummies*. Unfortunately, the *...for Dummies* name is trademarked. Nevertheless, this is going to be that kind of book.

When you buy a computer, it comes with an instruction manual. It is usually too brief, obtuse, and never talks about the stuff you're really interested in. So you go buy a book like *Windows for Dummies* or *Macs for Dummies*, and it leads you through everything you have to do, step by step. It doesn't assume you know anything, and it leaves nothing out.

When you study Tibetan Buddhism, either by reading books, listening to teachings, or participating in a center, a lot goes unsaid. A great deal of background knowledge is assumed by the author, the speaker, the older students running the center. It takes awhile for the neophyte to gather this background and to learn the ropes, and by then, who knows? You may have become discouraged and quit.

I don't want you to quit. Tibetan Buddhists have a system of wisdom and technique that is just amazing. The more I learn about it, the more impressed I am. Also, I'm sure your interest is sincere—you really want to better yourself and perhaps attain a level of realization. So in this book, we'll try to make the pieces match.

Perhaps it would make things clearer if I begin by talking about myself and how I got involved in Tibetan Buddhism and how I've struggled and persevered, zigged and zagged, over the years. I feel some reservations about talking too much about myself, that as a Buddhist I should be more anonymous and self-effacing and make the presentation more traditional and less personal. However, when I was struggling at the beginning of the task of writing this book, my primary teacher, Chökyi Nyima Rinpoche, advised me to make the book more personal and autobiographical. When I took his advice, the material seemed to just pour out of me. With time I've come to believe that as much as anything else what we older students have to offer is our own personal story of practicing the path. Tibetans have been enthralled by the stories and songs of Milarepa for centuries; they've served as models and guides for countless followers. I'm no Milarepa, but perhaps the reader will be able to learn and benefit from reading about my limitations and the errors I've made along the way. I strongly feel that by sharing experiences that are unique to Westerners in our modern age, we are offering support to all Western practitioners.

With that said, here's my story.

I was never a very good sixties person. In many ways my heart wasn't in it. In some ways I didn't believe the jargon. And I was just too shy and withdrawn to truly participate. But in any case, that's where my story starts.

I went to the University of California in beautiful Santa Barbara from 1968 to 1972. My major field of study was theoretical chemistry, that is, applying quantum mechanics to explain chemical phenomena. I truly fell in love with quantum mechanics with its paradoxes and seeming parallels to Asian thought.

I also began a major love affair with drugs, especially smoking marijuana, but whatever positive or consciousness-expanding effects drugs may have had on me were soon overshadowed by the increasing numbness, depression, dullness, and withdrawal that smoking caused me.

My first exposure to Buddhism was through my best friend's older brother who began an involvement with Buddhism that led him to a center in Scotland (where twenty years later I did a four-year retreat) and a monastery in Thailand. I developed both an interest in Buddhism and a fear of it. It just didn't seem like something you could do in your spare time. If one truly believed its premises, that we are suffering in illusion, then it seemed that one would abandon everything and commence intensive practice immediately, which is, of course, what many have done over the centuries. Buddhism seemed to demand a little more than going to church on Sundays and being a nice person. Nonetheless, its analysis of phenomena in terms of emptiness seemed to agree with the insights of quantum mechanics with one major difference: Buddhism offered a path to experience these truths rather than just speculation about them. No matter how profound the insights of scientists, science doesn't claim to offer a path of personal transformation.

By the time I graduated in 1972, I was really torn. My involvement in drugs made continuing my education problematic and rendered my social life disastrous. Also, my interest in Asian spirituality made Western science seem irrelevant to a life bent on understanding reality.

Since I had some money from my family, I decided to follow the footsteps of a couple of friends and travel in the Third World. I was hoping that a change of environment would give me the opportunity to change my personality and break my drug habit; as well, I was sincerely interested in exploring Buddhism and Hinduism in their countries of origin. I traveled about a year and a half and unfortunately only deepened my dependence on cannabis. I did, however, make a connection with the Tibetans in India and Nepal.

In order to meet a traveling companion, I went to Dharamsala, India, the residence of His Holiness the Dalai Lama and home to many Tibetan refugees. As soon as I got off the bus, I immediately felt a kind of inner bliss, a unique experience for me at the time. I began attending classes at the Library of Tibetan Works and Archives at a school for Westerners established by His Holiness. I was deeply impressed by the rigor with which the lama, Geshe Ngawang Dhargyey, taught the class. The material was all systematized into outline form. I reasoned that with a structure like this, any errors in their system would be quickly revealed. One must be very confident of one's system to organize it like this.

My father, Samuel, was an extremely brilliant man. He excelled in any intellectual pursuit to which he applied himself. I grew up having to debate him about everything. Along with my scientific background, this made it impossible for me to trust anything that could possibly contain any loopholes, articles of blind faith, or any items that simply contradicted logic or common sense. I had approached my earlier studies of Asian religion deftly afraid that I would eventually turn up some discrepancy or contradiction that would completely unravel my faith and force me to abandon my commitment. When I heard Geshe-la speak so authoritatively, clearly, systematically, and logically, it was more miraculous to me than a human flying, and I knew that I had found my path.

Unfortunately, I still had a lot of ordinary things to work out. I had my drug problem and all the unresolved emotions behind the problem. Suffice it to say, it took me another year and a half of tortured soul-searching before I returned to Dharamsala in early 1975 at the age of twenty-four to begin my spiritual path in earnest.

The training in Dharamsala emphasized philosophic studies as a preliminary to meditation. As someone who had already studied scientific views of reality and was used to getting into altered states through drugs, I never felt completely at home with that approach. While there, I did, however, learn the basics of the path very well, and I'm very grateful; it's provided a very firm foundation for all my subsequent study and practice. At the same time, I was able to immerse myself in a Western community that was completely committed to the path; many were ordained, and many were doing long solitary retreats. There was a real sense of adventure for me and a feeling of escape from all that I had been involved in up to that point.

At the same time I began studying in short retreats with two Theravadan masters, a Burmese master named Goenka-ji and an English monk called Longpe. They taught meditations that are now popularly known in America as *vipassana*. Their instruction gave me my first taste of meditative experience, an awareness of the body's energetic processes, and simple techniques that I could and would fall back on for decades. I still teach mindfulness to my students; I don't feel its value can be overemphasized.

After ten months of study at the Library, I began craving a more meditative approach within the Tibetan tradition. A couple of Americans recommended that I visit Kalu Rinpoche in Darjeeling, in northeastern India. I did and was immediately impressed by his powerful presence and obvious meditative qualities. He seemed to hold the whole valley in his meditative absorption. From Kalu Rinpoche I received authorization to begin the *ngondro*, the preliminary practices of the Vajrayana.

As I began my prostrations, the first of the ngondro practices, my health collapsed. So began a pattern of weakness, lethargy, and dullness that persisted right through to 1995, when the brilliant doctor Shandor Weiss diagnosed me as having cannabis toxicity and was successful in detoxifying me. In the twenty years in between, I had wonderful opportunities to practice but was always hampered by my physical condition.

After leaving Kalu Rinpoche, I could no longer stay in India because of visa problems, so I went to neighboring Nepal. I settled near the famous Great Stupa of Bouddhanath outside Kathmandu. There are many monasteries there, now more than twenty, and I introduced myself to the abbots of a large white monastery called Ka-Nying Shedrup Ling, where His Holiness Karmapa was about to begin a series of empowerments to consecrate the new monastery.

Since then, that monastery has proved to be my spiritual home. The abbot of the time was Tulku Urgyen Rinpoche, one of my most important teachers; his son Tulku Chökyi Nyima Rinpoche has become my principal teacher and root lama.

Under Chökyi Nyima Rinpoche's guidance I completed most of my ngondro in Nepal in 1976. I returned to Dharamsala in 1977 and did about five months of retreat. Because of family problems, I returned to California later that year.

In California, I worked some odd jobs, tried to get healthy, watched my father die, and began studying under Gyatrul Rinpoche, His Holiness Dudjom Rinpoche's West Coast representative. Along with Chökyi Nyima Rinpoche, Gyatrul Rinpoche is a lama to whom I owe more than I can ever conceivably repay, and I've maintained my connection with him to the present.

I returned to Nepal in 1980 and spent the next eight years either practicing near my teacher or in Manali, a very lovely spot in the Himalayas in northwest India. I also worked in Kathmandu as an English teacher.

At my teacher's order, I went to Scotland in 1988 to do a four-year retreat at Kagyu Samye Ling, where my friend's older brother had studied in the sixties and where I had visited during my hippie travels in 1969. We first had to build the retreat center, and then we actually began practicing in 1989. I will be mentioning this retreat frequently in this book; it's a constant source of stories and examples.

At the conclusion of the retreat, I made a brief visit to Nepal and then returned to America with a little money from my generous retreat sponsor to get me started. I was very lucky to be able to settle first at Gyatrul Rinpoche's retreat center south of Ashland, Oregon, and then close by. After about a year, Rinpoche asked me to begin teaching, which I had wanted to do, both to earn a little money and to experiment with some ideas I had about teaching, and I started my teaching at his center in San Francisco. Not long afterward, I began teaching in Ashland and fell in love with my first serious student, Susan Bosworth, whom I have subsequently married. We're now living in town where I am teaching, practicing, and writing this book.

So why am I writing this book? The short answer is my lama told me to. Also, several friends felt it would be a good idea to put some of the things I say while teaching into book form. The longer answer is that I perceive a problem with how Tibetan Buddhism is being transmitted to and in this country, and I want this book along with my classes to do as much as possible to ameliorate what I perceive to be a problem.

Whenever Buddhism has come to a new country, there has been a transition period from when the old traditional form is accepted and practiced to when it is transformed into a form more accessible to the new host. For instance, Buddhism was introduced into China by Bodhidharma, who is called the First Patriarch of Chan or Chinese Zen. But it wasn't until Hui Neng, the Sixth Patriarch, that Buddhism evolved into a form that was accessible to more Chinese and had truly become a Chinese rather than a foreign religion.

Often, when Buddhism travels from one country to another, it comes as part of a "package deal" with many other aspects of the original country's culture. For example, when Buddhism spread from China to Korea, it brought with it the arts, literature, and so on of a larger, more civilized country. This perceived superiority of one culture over another made it easier for the new hosts to accept the new religion.

This is hardly the case with the spread of Tibetan Buddhism to America and the rest of the West. We have very little interest in other aspects of Tibetan culture. Besides, our scientific background makes it difficult for us to accept anything new without a lot of investigation.

Tibetan Buddhism is a truly astonishing system. The more I study it, the more overwhelmed I am by its depth and profundity. But Tibetan Buddhism obviously evolved within the Tibetan situation. Its system of practice is perfectly designed to bring ordinary Tibetan lay and ordained people from their present state to complete enlightenment almost like a car on an assembly line in Detroit. So how does their situation differ from ours? In almost every way imaginable.

Let us look at some of these differences to try to understand how they may influence both the presentation of Buddhism and our understanding.

First, in Tibet most Dharma material was presented for ordained monks and nuns—in other words, people who were full-time Dharma practitioners. For the most part, they were the only ones who could read and were interested in the more advanced topics of tantric Buddhism. We Westerners, on the other hand, generally come to the Dharma at an older age and often with too many commitments to spend a great deal of time studying and practicing; however, we are literate and intellectually sophisticated. We often find the teachings that are intended for the Tibetan laity too simple and unsatisfying, but the teachings that are presented for the ordained too time-consuming to practice.

Second, Tibetans grow up with a deep sense of reverence and respect for the Dharma and for the lamas who teach and represent it. Although the teachings always advise one to question the Dharma with an attitude of sincere investigation, the very success of Buddhism in Tibet made most of that questioning seem irrelevant and often disrespectful. We, on the other hand, haven't grown up within a Buddhist culture. On top of that we are taught always to question and demand proof. Some teachings are presented in the West without a question-and-answer period. A Tibetan may feel that since the lama is a buddha, the presentation must have been perfect, so how could one even begin to question? However, we as Westerners might feel alienated or confused by the lack of questions and might sense that the teaching was more a ritualized affair than an exchange of information.

Third, Buddhist practitioners in Tibet were supported both emotionally and materially. Here in the West they generally are not.

Fourth, because of the harshness of Tibetan life, people were accustomed to hardships and were more willing to take them on for the sake of their practice. Here, we just buy more stuff. We're also definitely willing to take on some hardships, but what we consider to be hardships would be seen as luxuries in Tibet. One lama living in America has said that if he were to teach about the correct posture for meditation and insist that his students use it, he would be opening himself up to lawsuits.

Fifth, also because of the simplicity of Tibetan life, their minds were also much simpler. They had fewer distractions, less to think about. Among the Tibetans I have known, I have observed that even when encountering difficulties, they deal with them and then move on without looking back. Therefore, when they meditate, they are able to remain undistracted and progress through the practices. We, on the other hand, are almost never able truly to quiet our minds, and the very profound techniques of Tibetan Buddhism never seem to work as advertised. It can make us feel let down, like failures.

Sixth, and perhaps most importantly, most of us come to the Dharma with a kind of psychological woundedness that would be almost unheard of in Tibet. Tibetan lamas were just stunned when they first heard that many Westerners hate their mothers. This woundedness results in two major problems for us as Westerners: First, we have to go through a long process of healing before we are stable enough to meditate properly, and second, we have many hidden agendas that can make our practice go astray. (This will be discussed in later chapters.)

So, on the one hand, we have this wonderfully pure and profound Dharma with these incredibly high and realized lamas, and on the other, we have us, perhaps confused, but genuinely sincere, intelligent, and interested. But because of the newness, the language and cultural problems, and the abovementioned differences, there's still a gap. We're not quite getting it. Western yogis give up on retreat; Western monks and nuns often abandon their ordinations. Dharma centers are rife with politics, and many people get very hurt in these places. New students wonder why the older students don't seem more together.

This book is my attempt to fill this gap—to make a bridge between the traditional teachings and the person you really are. I find most teachings and books idealize the listener or reader. They seem to assume that the reader has lots of leisure and will easily be able to practice the techniques that are taught, and that once he or she practices them, results will come quickly.

If you're one of the lucky few for whom progress has been rapid and smooth, this book isn't for you. It's for those of you who are new to Tibetan Buddhism and feel overwhelmed by its complexity as well as for those of you who have been practicing awhile but whose experience hasn't lived up to your earlier expectations.

This book is not a substitute for more traditional teachings. There are many great lamas who are teaching and incredible books that are available in your bookstore. You will need to have some previous exposure to these teachings in order to follow my discussion here. This book is to help you make sense of and apply those already perfect traditional teachings, rather like the ...*for Dummies* books I mentioned at the beginning of the introduction.

The first text I received teachings on and studied extensively was Je Gampopa's *Jewel Ornament of Liberation*. It was written in the twelfth century in Tibet, just as Buddhism was beginning to spread and flourish there. In this text, Gampopa gives a complete overview of the Buddhist path from the very beginning to the attainment of complete buddhahood. Although I am not claiming in any way to have any of his qualities, I am taking his book as guidance and inspiration for this, especially in the progression of material from chapter to chapter.

The are four major orders of Tibetan Buddhism—the Gelug, Sakya, Kagyu, and Nyingma. Although I've received instruction in all four, my primary focus has been with the Kagyupas and Nyingmapas. Therefore, my presentation will reflect the perspective of those two traditions. I don't feel the differences between the four are very major; I feel that most of what will follow will be applicable to any student of Tibetan Buddhism. However, you should note that if your interest happens to be in the Gelug or Sakya traditions, you might notice some minor differences or change in emphasis.

Also I use the first and second person a lot in this book. I hope you don't mind. I talk about myself because I feel that since I've spent almost twenty-five years practicing, I've made twenty-five years' worth of mistakes. Where I've erred, so might you. By sharing these mistakes with you, it is my hope that some readers will be able to avoid them. I was lucky and lived in Asia with much leisure; when I erred, I had the opportunity to correct myself. If you, with your busy lifestyle, multiple distractions, and competing spiritual paths, err, you might very well abandon Tibetan Buddhism for something more initially rewarding. Also, with my use of the second person, it might seem I feel the reader must be a fool who will make every possible mistake. That's not my intention at all; it's simply the most natural way of writing for me. Mentioning all the pitfalls as I have done might also make the book and the material it represents seem bleak and foreboding; that again is also not my intention. I sincerely hope that by applying the advice, warnings, and hints in this book, you will find that your exposure to the wealth of Tibetan Buddhism will be as rewarding as you would wish.

CHAPTER ONE

Buddha-Nature: The Ground

I just got married. My fifteen-year old stepson, Nate, has recently been talking with his mother and me about his feelings that life is meaningless. He is obviously fascinated by the adult toys of fancy cars and the like, but he is also intelligent and sensitive enough to realize their limitations and that a life of working hard to buy things and then dying is not all that appealing. Susan and I can definitely empathize with his plight and feel pleased with his maturity; we also long to "sign him up" for some deeper involvement in our Buddhist path. However, we mostly sit back, listen, and hope and pray for the best.

We have all had that yearning for meaning in our life. We might give it other names—truth, value, love, cosmic consciousness, ecstasy. But it is inevitable that when our stomachs are full and there's a roof over our heads, we begin to question and long for something deeper.

In Buddhism that yearning is in itself proof of the existence of something deeper within us. If there weren't something there, how could we be aware of its absence? Do we have any desires for completely nonexistent things? Some of us will dismiss that yearning; others will be consumed by it.

Let's examine this a little more deeply. The foundation of the spiritual life is called *zhi* in Tibetan (Skt. *alaya*). These words both mean "ground." If we want to build a house or plant a garden, the first thing we need is a plot of land to build them on. Without this land, it is impossible. No matter how brilliant our plans, what quality our materials, or what diligent workers we are, without this land we will get nowhere. This is something we all know.

So in Buddhism what is this land, this ground? It is called, among other things, buddha-nature. All beings possess the potential to become enlightened, to be buddhas. It is not as if only the Buddha and a select few have it and they teach us through their pity. Nor is it that some of us have buddha-nature while others don't. Nor is it that humans have it while animals don't. As long as there is sentience, there is buddha-nature.

We may feel like the most miserable people in the world. We might feel we have neuroses and depravities that others can barely imagine. We might think of ourselves as the lowest of the low, completely unworthy and totally unlovable. Believe me, I've spent a considerable part of my life feeling these very same things. No matter how you feel right now or what you think about yourself, you still possess this buddha-nature. No matter how rotten the house is, it's still built on the ground.

At the present moment, this buddha-nature is concealed from our awareness, like the sun being completely concealed behind clouds. Yet just as we can sense the presence of the sun even on the cloudiest day, we sometimes have some sense of our buddha-nature, some sense there's something more to life, some capacity beyond our normal way of thinking, feeling, and perceiving. And please remember what I just said: This yearning is proof of the existence of this ground. Don't be too harsh with yourself; listen and respect this great need within yourself.

Some have this strong longing. Others have had some initial experience that has opened them up to a richer view of their life.

My teacher, Venerable Chökyi Nyima Rinpoche, is the abbot of a large monastery in Nepal. He tells me that many Westerners come to him to learn something about Buddhism after trekking in the Himalayas. He says that the vastness of the mountain panoramas gives these trekkers some sense of the basic vastness of their own minds. This experience inspires them to take the next step.

I remember reading many years ago about a very strict Chinese monastery north of San Francisco. The monks there even slept in the full lotus position. The newspaper article featured three Caucasians who had made this incredible commitment based on experiences they had had while surfing. Again, some sense of vastness, perhaps oneness with nature, and the proverbial "being in the flow."

Others have found their initial inspiration through the religious upbringing they had when children. They experienced their religion of birth as something powerful and meaningful but found that they lost connection with it as they grew up. However, they always longed for that inspiration and meaning.

Because I was a person of the "sixties," many of the people I knew got their initial inspiration from taking psychedelic drugs. These drugs gave us a new perspective, or at least some sense that there was a different, more profound way of perceiving the world. And although I am in no way advocating their use, probably much of the initial interest in Asian spirituality came from people's involvement with drugs.

People can get this initial glimpse in many ways. Some might get it listening to beautiful music, others by being in nature. Many have powerful experiences while making love. Still others find that the insights of modern science compel them to investigate more deeply into the nature of reality. Perhaps your work with your therapist has brought you to the very boundaries of your ego, and now you're looking for a way beyond those boundaries.

So whatever the cause, we have had some experience, some glimpse, some understanding that reveals new vistas of human potential and forever changes how we see the world. One problem though: These experiences do not last. Eventually, we return to being the same person we were, with the same thoughts and perspective.

One thing has changed, however; now we know better. It is as if we have seen through someone's disguise and can no longer believe their façade, even though they still appear the same. Actually, that is exactly what has happened. We have penetrated the disguise of our ego.

We now have some sense that there's a better, vaster, more profound way to deal with life. Our old habitual patterns, which we have taken for granted for so long, now seem so constricting. It's like returning to a prison after a brief but glorious trip outside. It can be painful and depressing; we might even want to run away and hide from our new insight.

It was like that for me. As I mentioned in the introduction, I was incredibly inspired by my initial contact with Tibetan Buddhism. However, upon my return to my family in America, I felt a return of all my very deep emotional problems. I feared returning to India because of the risk of more serious drug addiction, and I feared studying Buddhism because I thought it might simply be an escape. I was completely torn— it was as if two armies were doing battle inside my head. I was hardly aware of the outside world during this period, though I was somehow able to hold down a job as a research chemist. However, my yearning for a life in harmony with my initial insights eventually prevailed.

Before I returned to India and began practicing, I used to follow my thoughts and feelings blindly, completely believing in my self-images and in the socially constructed reality around me. When there were gaps—anything that could possibly threaten this fabricated world—I would lose myself in distraction. Unfortunately, this is a common experience for most of us, since we have no system for understanding those glimpses and no societal support for following up on them.

A friend of mine, when she was in college, was sitting on a knoll looking up at the sky with two of her girlfriends. They all saw the most wonderful sight, a group of female deities frolicking in the sky. For my friend it was transformative and was instrumental to her beginning a search that eventually led her to become a very committed Buddhist practitioner. Years later, she happened to meet the other two girls. They denied any memory of the experience. It reminds me of the story of Darwin, who reported some islanders were unable to see his sailing ship because they simply didn't have the conceptual system to apprehend it.

In a very real way, our society is structured around denying these experiences and feelings. Spiritual seekers do not make good consumers. We live in a culture of addictions, from substance abuse to workaholic patterns. It's always sad for me to see how busy some of my old friends are; I frequently speculate that they, too, are trying to escape the logical conclusions of their own insights.

Some of us will spend our lives compulsively ignoring that gnawing feeling, that deep yearning. But for some, this is no longer possible. We are no longer able to fool ourselves completely and are no longer completely satisfied with who we are. *This is the discovery of buddha-nature as the ground.*

Frequently, this newfound commitment will accompany an experience of death—that of a friend, a parent, or possibly the discovery of a terminal illness within us. It may also come with a lesser kind of death—the loss of a job, a divorce—experiences that help us pierce through the bubble of our self-satisfaction. In all these experiences we discover that the ego is not doing an especially good job of managing our lives.

When we acknowledge the importance of our new or renewed insight, when we feel inspired by our discovery, we start to take some steps, however tentative, to learn how to return to the ground, how to experience it more and more often and with greater intensity, duration, and clarity. We probably begin by reading and sharing our insights with our more sympathetic friends. If we are fortunate, we find a teacher, receive his or her instructions and blessings, and begin and sustain a meditation practice. *This is taking the buddha-nature as the path.*

When, through our diligence, our experience becomes stable, and we reside effortlessly in our own ground, *this is the buddha-nature of fruition, complete buddhahood.*

Tibetan lamas like to explain subjects like this in terms of these three: *ground, path,* and *fruit. Ground* is the basis, the foundation, as I discussed earlier in the chapter. *Path* is what you do with that foundation. You might have a seed, but you still have to plant and water it. Finally, the plant grows into maturity. That is the *fruit.* This book will be discussing all three, ground, path, and fruit, in terms of buddha-nature. As in the example, we all have the seed, our buddha-nature, but we also must plant it and nurture it to fruition.

Tibetan Buddhism is called Vajrayana. A *vajra* is an indestructible weapon, something like a diamond scepter. It refers to this buddha-nature, which is indestructible, always residing within, and able to destroy the enemy, which consists of the obscurations, discursive thoughts, and disturbing emotions. *Yana* means vehicle. Vajrayana is the vehicle, the spiritual path, where the whole approach is centered on the concept of this buddha-nature.

Let's explore the ground in a more formal, traditional way. In the Tibetan tradition the main teaching on buddha-nature, the root text is the *Mahayana Uttara Tantra Shastra*, which has been translated into English as *The Changeless Nature*. This teaching was given by the future Buddha Maitreya to the great Indian yogi and scholar Asanga almost two thousand years ago and is still studied in Tibetan monasteries and Buddhist centers around the world. So to expand on the topic of buddha-nature as the ground of our being I will quote from the text, from the words of Maitreya Buddha himself:

> The buddha-essence is ever present in everyone because
> the dharmakaya of perfect buddhahood pervades all,
> the suchness is undifferentiated, and they all have the potential.[1]

In this oft-quoted but difficult to understand passage Maitreya gives three reasons why all sentient beings possess the enlightened essence. The terms *dharmakaya* and *suchness* refer to the ultimate truth, the truth of emptiness. Emptiness can be clearly established through logic; indeed, this is the main task of philosophic studies in Tibetan monastic colleges. Thus, simply put, we possess buddha-nature because it is true; it is our personal experience of emptiness. It is just the way things are.

Our own ego-centered perspective can be logically and experientially shown to be defective or false, and as the above anecdotes demonstrate, we ourselves can see the faults and limitations of our present point of view and have some trust in a higher reality. Since emptiness is the truth of our world in general ("suchness is undifferentiated" and "the dharmakaya ...pervades all"), it is not the possession of a limited, select few. We don't have to worry if we're among the select. We are. We're sentient. Discovering our buddha-nature means understanding the absolute truth of the entire world in which we live, not merely a soul within our being. We speak of our buddha-nature as our essence, something that can be discovered with us, but it's not like finding a pit in an apricot. We may find it by looking within, but what we find is all-pervasive. This is probably something most of us have sensed—that a deeper truth pervades the world in which we find ourselves.

It might be easier to understand this important point if, in the place of *'absolute truth,'* I substitute the term *'unconfused truth'* and instead of *'relative truth'* I substitute' *'confusion.'* Then it's easy to see that confusion can always be clarified or removed to reveal the unconfused truth. If we think of Lord Buddha as the 'Awakened One,' then we can understand that we as sentient beings are asleep. And sleeping beings inevitably awake.

This quote from Maitreya is not meant to be a rigorous logical proof. The bottom line is that our fundamental potential for enlightenment along with one or two other premises in Buddhism, such as in the law of karma, cannot be logically demonstrated but must be accepted as either an article of faith or, perhaps more precisely, a basic starting assumption. All systems of thought begin with a few basic axioms and then go on to build a logical system based on them. If a system is logically self-consistent and leads to no contradictions with experience, then we can trust the validity of that system. For example, in geometry we start with *point*, *line*, and *plane*, These elements are undefined; nevertheless, we intuitively grasp their meaning. Based on these three, a wonderful system was built that has remained valid for twenty-five hundred years.

Likewise, the Buddhist system starts with a few fundamental core elements that are then developed into a complex system. The validity of this system is demonstrated by its logical consistency and, most importantly, by the confirmation given by countless practitioners over the last 2,500 years. Thus, although the concept of buddha-nature cannot be strictly proven, it can at least be demonstrated to be reasonable, sensible, and worthy of further consideration and investigation.

I'm also trying to demonstrate how the formal study of Buddhism corresponds to our initial insight and inspiration. Remember your own experience, ponder what you've heard and read, and try to reach some firm conclusion. It's very important to work gradually and systematically to resolve all doubts regarding buddha-nature. In a sense, it's a lifetime project—our doubts slowly become more and more subtle.

I remember some of my own process. I studied the theory of quantum mechanics and tried to understand the deeper philosophic issues it revealed. My experience with drugs convinced me of the existence of a deeper reality. I read some of the books that were available then, such as the *Diamond Sutra* and the *Sutra of Hui Neng*; I thought deeply and tried hard to reconcile these different perspectives. I spent a great amount of time and effort on this task, and I feel much of my later diligence was based on this effort. Practice is always more productive when not hampered by doubt and by the hesitation it creates.

What is this buddha-nature? Once we have cleared up most of our doubts regarding its existence, we must still be convinced of its value. Is it really worth pursuing? Maybe we'll be disappointed when we become enlightened:" "Hey, that wasn't worth it. I want my money back!" Lord Maitreya says:

> Like the purity of a jewel, space, and water,
> It is always undefiled in essence.
> Its qualities resemble those
> of a valued gem because it is powerful,
> of space because it is unalterable
> and of water because it moistens.[2]

Maitreya explains the qualities of our essence. It is undefiled by the usual garbage of our minds—our incessant thinking, our turbulent emotions, and our erroneous self-centeredness. No matter how neurotic or upset we may be, no matter how debauched or evil we may become, our buddha-nature remains our buddha-nature. It never loses its purity. No matter how dark and stormy the clouds may become, they never affect the sun. They might decrease our ability to perceive it, but the sun doesn't lose its luster. If buddha-nature is simply the true nature of things, how could it possibly become defiled?

The positive qualities of our nature are indicated by the metaphors of a jewel, space, and water. The gem refers to the mythological wish-fulfilling jewel that can confer any boon on its possessor. Likewise, our nature is beyond any suffering. Suffering comes from not knowing the truth, from abiding and acting in error or misapprehension. On the other hand, realization of our nature will satisfy our deepest needs and aspirations because we will no longer be separated and alienated from our world with all the ensuring attachment and aversion. Therefore, it is likened to a jewel. Realization of our buddha-nature is more precious than any jewel or any imaginable wealth.

Not only will its realization be completely satisfying, but once perfected, it will be unalterable like space. Space can never be changed. You may fill your room with clutter, but the space itself is unaffected. Our buddha-nature may be obscured by our negativities, but it is not polluted by them. And because buddha-nature is unalterable like space, when we do attain realization, the realization is permanent. It will not be a glimpse that fades, a "high" from which we come down. When stabilized, it's forever.

The metaphor of water has always been more difficult for me to understand. I have requested clarification and what I have learned is this: When a cloth is wet, the moisture permeates the cloth; in the same way, buddha-nature pervades all phenomena. Every aspect of our own experience will be pervaded by it.

Maitreya goes on later to explain that were there no buddha-nature, there would be no discontent with suffering, nor would there be desire, effort, and aspiration for nirvana. Maitreya shows how buddha-nature manifests in ordinary beings like us. As discussed earlier, some people can be fairly successful in propping themselves up and satisfying their desires. Some are miserable with gaps and holes in their self-image all over the place. But who is completely happy? Who doesn't feel at least some discontent, some mild paranoia, some ill-defined malaise? This discomfort is the sun of our nature patiently burning through the thick clouds of our habitual patterns. My own metaphor is a slumbering animal awakening in his cage—our discontent is his yearning to be free. Sometimes we're lucky, like those trekkers and surfers, and our nature shines fairly clearly, if only for a short while. We're forever transformed, and we aspire to strive to integrate this experience until it becomes our reality—the realization of nirvana.

≫ CHAPTER TWO ≪

The Teacher

Having glimpsed the ground, we desire to repeat the experience. We might try to recreate the original circumstances, but even if we are successful, it becomes clear that we can't spend our whole lives trekking in the Himalayas or surfing in Hawaii. If our initial glimpses were chemically aided, we might find ourselves descending into pretty dangerous territory as we strive to repeat or hold on to the original experience. I know that from my own experience—the more I tried, the lower I descended. We may reach the conclusion that although we have stumbled onto something of paramount importance, we have no idea how to proceed.

Sooner or later, however, we discover that our glimpse has been described by all the major contemplative traditions of the world. It dawns on us that we are far from alone; rather, we have joined an old and dignified club. From the beginnings of history, men and women have asked the same questions and have felt the same deep stirrings and longings. Beyond that, many have ventured further and have discovered a path and, finally, a fruition that has brought them complete satisfaction. Some of them have then gone on to found traditions, some of which are still with us. Furthermore, these traditions have mapped out the path from our present state of consciousness to the goal, provided techniques for following that path, and continue to have living teachers who can guide us along that path.

At this point, we may try to read as much as we can, talk to our friends and acquaintances with similar interests or experiences, and perhaps visit some centers or listen to talks by various teachers. We are searching. Either we find a tradition that we feel inspired by, that seems sensible and true, or we meet a teacher who embodies everything we have been searching for. For example, we could meet a great Sufi teacher who really blows our minds and so then decide to become a Sufi. Or we could, say, believe Zen Buddhism is the tradition that makes the most sense and start to check out various Zen masters.

I was initially exposed to both Hinduism and Zen, but I was won over by the Tibetan Buddhists, by both the earthy warmth and joy they manifest and the rigorous intellectual system they maintain. In this book I will not discuss the relative pros and cons of various traditions, try to convince you of the superiority of Vajrayana Buddhism, or gloss over the very real differences between different religions. I will simply assume at this point that for whatever reason you have decided that Tibetan Buddhism warrants a closer look and so will continue on based on that assumption.

It is likely that your reading and other preliminary research convinces you of the necessity of finding an appropriate teacher. If that is the case, in the next chapter I will offer some guidelines to simplify and expedite that search. On the other hand you might feel that a teacher is unnecessary or perhaps even detrimental to the path; in that case I will try to demonstrate the necessity of having one.

When I first became interested in Eastern spirituality in the sixties, we were all quite naive. Also, many teachers or gurus were making the most extravagant claims. Everyone seemed to be the avatar or messiah for our age. It seemed that if only we could meet this person, find our guru, all our problems would be over. We would be given a simple practice that we could effortlessly accomplish giving rise to cosmic consciousness.

I remember having a feeling that finding a guru was the culmination of the path, rather than the beginning of it.

We're all a little older now. We've lived through fourteen-year-old avatars, messiahs with fleets of Rolls-Royces, and gurus who have given their students AIDS. We certainly have a right to be hesitant and skeptical.

So why are gurus necessary? I will give you my personal reasons, what I've learned from experience, and hope that I haven't left out anything important. Also, from now on, I will be using masculine pronouns to refer to gurus and lamas, primarily for the sake of simplicity but also because all my important teachers have been men. I hope this doesn't offend anyone. As time goes on there are more and more female teachers appearing in the west, both Tibetans and Westerners. However, I haven't had the good fortune to study with any of them. I feel, however, that with time, there will be a parity between male and female teachers here.

First, the lama gives meditation instructions. Not only does he know the myriad of techniques, but also through his clairvoyance, he knows the ones that are most appropriate for us. We might have spent the last nine lifetimes practicing the deity Vajrayogini. A truly qualified lama will know this and will guide us correctly. Our own choice of practice would most likely not be as accurate and could be based on fantasies and wishful thinking. As a teacher myself, I really appreciate this; I feel that I am able to help a student with his or her practice but that I have no real guidelines regarding which kind of practice to recommend to them. I don't have the slightest idea with which practices they are karmically connected, and most students are usually either uninformed or overwhelmed by the various choices available. So the guru will know what kind of practice is right for you and will be able to instruct you in its techniques and meaning. He'll also know when you're ready to move on to something new.

Also, when we have difficulties or obstacles in our practice, our teacher will know the techniques for removing them. Believe me, some really strange things can happen when you begin to meditate diligently. It is not always obvious what to do about these experiences, or even whether they're good or bad. I've talked to a couple of people just recently who get hot when they meditate. Is this good or bad? Typically, we take anything that's different as a positive sign. It's easy to understand that rationale: If we hadn't been meditating, it wouldn't have happened; therefore, it must be a sign of progress. But it takes a certain degree of experience and perhaps study to put these experiences in their correct context.

When unusual experiences happen, if we are without guidance, we may become discouraged and quit if we feel that the experiences are negative. Even more likely is that we become puffed-up and arrogant if we believe our experiences to be extraordinary. Someone I know once had a series of the most amazing experiences I've ever heard—the kind of visions and realizations for which I've been secretly longing for decades. The problem was that in the absence of a close relationship with a qualified teacher, he sincerely believed that he was realized and able to begin teaching. He occasionally got himself into some jams. Luckily, he straightened himself out through meeting real teachers.

The same thing happened to me. Twenty-five years ago, I attended a short retreat after only a few months of practice and had the most extraordinary experience of my life. I really thought I had made it! I was seriously pondering how I was going to teach my disciples. Either the leader of the retreat was not all that qualified, or more likely, I didn't communicate with him thoroughly enough. Imagine my chagrin when the experience faded and I returned to my normal, neurotic self.

Experiences like this are one thing; recognizing buddha-nature is another. By its very nature it's ineffable. We can easily fool ourselves into believing we understand when, in fact, we don't. Only a deeply realized master can clarify these points for you. We would consider someone foolish who tried to teach himself medicine or a foreign language. How much more difficult is the stabilization of buddha-nature!

Second, the guru acts as a role model. He embodies everything we strive for. If he did it, so can we! Whenever I'm feeling really sorry for myself, I remember that there once was a time when my teacher was as confused as I am. This thought always gives me encouragement. Also, since Buddhism is centered around the concept of egolessness, it is daunting, paradoxical, or outright absurd to dedicate oneself to a life of seeming psychological suicide. Meditation often feels like a process of dissolution and can feel confusing, chaotic, and threatening. The teacher acts as an example of someone who has actually given up his ego, his self-centeredness, and has proceeded through the dissolution process without becoming a martyr or a vegetable. In fact, he is a highly functioning human being who seems to be having a lot more fun than I am.

Many of my students fear that if they stop identifying with their thoughts, they will become somewhat dysfunctional. They feel that they need to indulge in their usual discursiveness and that it is necessary to have an ego or self-image around which to structure their lives. The presence of the lama is living proof that this is simply not the case.

Third, the lama is a source of blessings. Although it is impossible to demonstrate in a laboratory the nature and existence of these blessings, I'm sure any sincere practitioner feels from the bottom of her heart that she is indeed being blessed. I feel that this blessing takes three broad forms. First, things may go smoother in the outside world. Money may be there when you need it. You may get the last room in a hotel at two in the morning. Situations that maximize your growth and learning spontaneously happen (unfortunately, such situations may seem quite painful and confusing at the time). None of these things can be counted on or predicted, but one recognizes them intuitively as signs of grace. Then there is the transmission of energy that is also the blessing of the teacher. One feels currents of energy awakening in one's body releasing blockages and becoming the basis of deeper meditative experience. This could be experienced as something like an electric shock when being touched by a lama, or we may feel it more continuously when we practice. However we experience it, it is a great aid in our unfolding. Lastly, the teacher transmits the experience of buddha-nature, either in his presence through a formal empowerment ceremony, or in the solitude of one's own practice. This transmission is, of course, the most profound meaning of blessing and in and of itself makes a lama indispensable. Since this point is of crucial importance, I will speak more of it later.

Fourth, the lama is a source of unconditional love. It's truly amazing and deeply touching to be loved in that way. No matter how poorly I follow his instructions, he's there. No matter how much doubt or negativity I have toward him, he's there. If I'm seething with arrogance or hatred or ashamed that I've just masturbated, he still loves me. As meditation can and will reveal the most negative, despicable things about oneself, it's easy to fall into a pattern of self-condemnation. The unconditionality of the lama's love can be a life-saver pulling one out of that kind of swamp. Being accepted on such a deep level by another human being gives me the strength to accept myself and gently let go of these shortcomings rather than continue to condemn myself without having the strength or courage to change. As we all know from our ordinary relationships, being loved threatens and ultimately heals the most negative of self-images. How much more so when one is loved by an enlightened being! It gives you a firm, healing ground to stand on. (When I talk about devotion in a later chapter, I will mention how that love also creates a sense of strength and independence within us.)

Fifth, the lama is a source of authenticity. Buddhism, and in particular Tibetan Buddhism, is a system where teachers are rigorously trained before being authorized to teach. Once they become teachers, they regularly report back to the lamas who are their superiors or who authorized them in the first place. Students can have some sense that their own training is being monitored not only by their teacher but by the tradition as a whole, the same tradition that has been cultivating highly realized beings for centuries. I myself, as a teacher, check back regularly with my own teachers, explain what I'm doing as a teacher, share my problems, difficulties, or insights about my students, and petition for feedback, guidance, and support. After a conference like this, I return to my students confident that what I am teaching is of benefit to them.

Sixth, the lama is an object of surrender. Having such an external referent, one can begin to let go of one's ego. It may seem paradoxical or contradictory to speak of surrender and independence both coming from relating to the teacher, but later I'll try to demonstrate how that can be so.

Lastly, without a teacher, one has no choice but to rely on one's ego as the mediator of one's spiritual life. This is something like putting the prisoners in charge of the prison. We may tend to give ourselves advice that protects rather than dismantles the self. We may feel we are listening to our heart when we're simply listening to our desires. Perhaps even more dangerously, one may rely on visions or inner voices. While such visions may be valid, you might also be cultivating schizophrenia—schizophrenics often get guidance from inner voices. I've seen it happen even to the point where the external teacher was rejected in favor of the voices in the head. If you feel you have a disembodied teacher of some sort, check with an embodied one. If your spirit is a valid guide, the master will confirm it. If not, he can save you from major problems.

I'm suspicious of people who say they don't need a teacher. Is there anything of value we've learnt without one? Is there anything we've ever attempted that has been more difficult than attaining enlightenment? So why are we resisting? Perhaps it's better to look at and understand the resistance than to find fault with a teacher.

Longchenpa, the great Nyingma master of the fourteenth century, poetically summarizes the need for a teacher:

Just as a patient is in need of a physician,
People of a ruler, a lonely traveler of an escort,
A merchant of a guild-master, a boatman of a boat,
So in order to calm the emotions, to make evil harmless,
To overcome birth and death…and
To cross the ocean of fictitious being, you must rely on a teacher.[3]

Longchenpa goes on to praise teachers:

If someone were to praise only partially such a person who is a
    helper of living beings
And whose qualities are so vast [he would have to say]:
As he makes them cross safely over the ocean of fictitious being he
    is a steersman,
An incomparable leader of those who have started their journey…
He is the bright lamp dispelling the darkness of the loss of pure
    awareness.
He is the wish-granting tree from which comes the happiness of all
    who are alive.
He is the auspicious jewel by which all desires are spontaneously
    fulfilled.
He is the countless rays of the sun of great kindness.
He is the moon with its white light of prosperity and happiness,
    removing afflictions.[4]

As the great Indian yogi Naropa quoted to his Tibetan disciple, Marpa the translator:

> Before any guru existed
> Even the name of Buddha was not heard.
> All the buddhas of a thousand eons
> Only come about because of the guru.[5]

CHAPTER THREE

Finding a Teacher

Some people are lucky: They find their teacher almost by magic, like something out of a spiritual storybook. Others aren't: They flounder from teacher to teacher, never really connecting, sometimes getting burned-out, sometimes getting very hurt or becoming bitter and angry. Or perhaps they always dwell on the periphery of a Dharma scene, vaguely knowing that they're missing out.

A friend of mine was living in a small refugee community in northern India when she heard a certain famous lama was passing through. She immediately knew he was going to be her teacher and wept excitedly in joyful anticipation. She became his student and spent many years in strict solitary retreat. She is a most amazing person.

I was lucky, too. I met my teacher after I had been practicing about a year. Chökyi Nyima Rinpoche was the opposite of any images I had of the archetypal guru. He's a little younger than I am and about a foot shorter. Hardly the old wise man with the white beard. When I met him, I didn't know anything about him, his credentials, or his lineage. He hardly spoke a word of English. What I did find, however, was that the advice he gave, in the most basic, broken English, seemed to have a most deep and profound affect on me. He would say something simple, and after a month I would discover that his words had reverberated inside me and had changed me on some fundamental level. I was very moved, and after several months of this, I clearly felt he was my teacher. As soon as I determined this, I was filled with a deep joy and have not had a moment of doubt since.

I sincerely wish that you have this great good fortune. Some would say that such an occurrence is due to karmic connections from past lives. Perhaps there's not much we can do about it. But until this kind of connection ripens for you, I will offer some advice about finding a teacher. I don't believe we can be too naive or fatalistic about this. Perhaps you are destined to meet your guru, but there are a lot of teachers you can learn from in the meantime, and this learning can only hasten your eventual reunion.

Many, many Tibetan lamas are coming to the West these days. They represent a bewildering number of lineages and bear an equally bewildering number of titles. Since it seems quite valid to examine these credentials before going further, let us examine these lineages and titles as a first step in establishing the bona fides of any particular teacher. Traditionally, we are supposed to examine a teacher carefully before taking Vajrayana teachings and empowerments from him; in the modern world that may not be possible, and we' may have to judge more quickly based on credentials and reputation.

Tibetan Buddhism is divided into four main orders, or lineages. They are sometimes called sects, but that word certainly has a negative connotation that doesn't apply here. The four are Gelug, Sakya, Kagyu, and Nyingma. They are very, very similar! Their primary difference is historical. From about 800 to 1200 C.E. there was a strong flow of ideas from Buddhist India to Tibet, which had just started to develop its own Buddhism. Indians came to Tibet to teach; Tibetans went to India to study. The four major lineages arose from this spiritual commerce. For instance, the oldest lineage, the Nyingma, was founded by Padmasambhava, who brought Buddhism to Tibet around 800 C.E. The Kagyu order was founded by Marpa the Translator, who went to India in the eleventh century and studied under the Indian yogis Naropa and Maitripa.

All four lineages hold to an identical set of Buddhist beliefs and principles. They all teach Buddhism in the form of the three yanas while emphasizing the Vajrayana. They all teach renunciation, the enlightened motivation of bodhichitta, and the correct view of emptiness. The only real distinction I have discovered is in how the traditions balance meditation and study. Gelugpas emphasize study somewhat more, Kagyupas and Nyingmapas practice, while Sakyapas seem to fall in the middle. I would like to add here that is far too simplistic to say, for example, that Gelugpas are scholars while Kagyupas are solitary yogis. Monks and nuns of all four lineages engage in study for many years and then gradually shift to a more contemplative lifestyle. All of these orders have produced centuries of highly realized beings. It is quite a serious fault to belittle one tradition at the expense of another. You should follow the tradition to which you feel closest while retaining respect for them all. Some people will feel comfortable studying more than one of these traditions; others will find this confusing and will feel better studying only one.

Within these four there are many subdivisions. These divisions are based on both the traditions of different monastic centers (called monastic lineages) and the mastery of various techniques of meditation (called practice lineages). In addition, there are some smaller lineages outside these four, such as the Jonangpa, who specialize in the practice of Kalachakra. You can find out more about these different lineages through reading or by talking to older students. Since I've studied mostly within the Kagyu and Nyingma traditions, this book will represent my feeble attempt to transmit a little of their wisdom. If you find' any contradiction with what you've studied in other traditions, I may be wrong, or you may have discovered an interesting fork in the road.

With respect to titles, we must start with the most ubiquitous, that of *lama* itself. *Lama* is the Tibetan translation of the Sanskrit term *guru*. To me it has come to mean someone who is completely qualified to guide me on the path, who can lead me to recognize buddha-nature, and who knows all the techniques to help stabilize that recognition. He should have all the qualities and capabilities that I mentioned in the last chapter.

However, the term *"lama"* has come to acquire a bewildering number of different usages. Some of them are as follows:

- Any Tibetan monk: This usage is common in many of the older books produced in the West—hence, the archaic term *"lamaism"* for Tibetan Buddhism. The word *lama* is rarely applied to Tibetan or Western nuns or Western monks.
- A term of respect for an older Tibetan monk: We would like to think that he has made it by now!
- Someone, Western or Tibetan, lay or ordained, who has completed a traditional three-year retreat. During that retreat, one should in theory have developed the qualities of a real lama. My teacher refers to me as a lama because I have completed such a retreat.
- A Dharma teacher, whether highly realized or not: This could perhaps be someone who runs a small center.
- A Nepalese family name used by many Tibetan refugees: A European friend of mine married a Tibetan in Nepal; she is now Mrs. Lama.
- A real, legitimate, fully qualified spiritual teacher.

Thus, you can see that the title *lama* has so many meanings that it can mean almost anything. Therefore, the title should have very little weight in your search.

The next most often used title is *tulku*. *Tulku* is the Tibetan for "nir-manakaya," one of the three "bodies" or aspects of a buddha. In English it means something like "emanation being" and refers to a buddha or bodhisattva who consciously emanates or takes birth in our world in order to benefit us. The Dalai Lama is, of course, the most famous example of this, being the fourteenth consecutive emanation of Chenrezig, the buddha of compassion.

There now are literally hundreds of tulkus. On one trip to Tibet, H. E. Tai Situ Rinpoche recognized 160 of them. They come in all shapes and sizes. Some are very dignified and powerful abbots of huge monasteries; some are dashing young playboys. Some live their lives anonymously; after their death one may hear rumors that perhaps they too were incarnations. We see how we took their humble goodness and gentleness for granted. Many are being reborn in the West, which gives me great hope for the future of our culture and the role of Buddhism in it. Unfortunately, very few are being reborn as women, or if they are being reborn as women, they are not being recognized. Perhaps this will change with time.

Although most tulkus prove to be who they are supposed to be by manifesting more and more enlightened qualities as they train and mature, the system has some problems. There can be controversy regarding the recognition. The most famous example, and for me personally the saddest, is the contention regarding the Seventeenth Karmapa.

The First Karmapa, Dusum Khyenpa, was an incredible meditator who lived in the twelfth century C.E. It was he who started the tulku system by leaving a message where he was to be reborn. He was reborn as Karma Pakshi, another incredible being, who was teacher of Kublai Khan (Marco Polo recorded his miraculous powers) and is now known as the Second Karmapa. The Karmapas are always the supreme heads of the Kagyu order. The Sixteenth Karmapa, Rangjung Rigpai Dorje, made several trips to the West and was an extraordinary inspiration for all of us who were lucky enough to meet him. Since his death in 1981, his two closest disciples have maintained a running disagreement regarding the recognition of his successor, and there is much bitterness between their respective followers. They have each recognized their own Seventeenth Karmapa so now we have two youths with the same title. Many of the Western students of the Sixteenth Karmapa, myself included, feel very hurt and confused by the controversy. But problems like this, however painful, are the exception, not the rule. On the whole, the tulku system works remarkably and reliably well.

Some tulkus are quite amazing. I recently met the four-year-old incarnation of His Holiness Dilgo Khyentse Rinpoche and had no doubt regarding his recognition and no difficulty in seeing his predecessor in him. It is as if the older lama were superimposed on the child and somehow still accessible to his followers.

I once read a very profound meditation manual by the Third Khamtrul Rinpoche. In the conclusion he wrote, "If you wonder about my qualifications for writing this book, I first recognized my buddha-nature at the age of two and had completely stabilized that recognition by four." One can also read accounts of the amazing qualities and miraculous abilities of the various Karmapas: There are two books about his various incarnations translated into English. There is now even a website that shares the various miracles by the young Karmapa in Tibet!

Most tulkus, once recognized, get an early and thorough education and training. Some seem almost effortlessly and spontaneously enlightened; some develop through their training. One of my teachers told me that perhaps 30 percent of tulkus are not real; their recognition is politically motivated, perhaps to gain the support of a rich and powerful family.

As I mentioned earlier, Westerners are also now being recognized as tulkus; two of those that I've met, Lamas Wyn Fischel and Tsering Everest, appear to have exceptional qualities. Now that he has been legitimately recognized, I'm looking forward to see what kind of enlightened activity Steven Seagal will create. More and more tulkus from all four traditions are being recognized in the West. I both pray and anticipate that they will have a profound effect on our culture.

Although I'm quite unable to judge the realization of others, tulku or not, I've been quite impressed with the tulkus I've met, whether young or old, whether traditionally or more contemporarily trained. It seems like a wonderful system and an excellent way to insure the continuation of the teachings since these children are able to begin their training at such a young age and without becoming too corrupted by modern culture.

If, however, you do have doubts about a tulku, try to find out who recognized him. Was it an unequivocal recognition by one of the great lamas, or something a little more dubious? What was his training like? What do other lamas have to say about him? (Beware of subtle nuances here; no lama is ever going to trash another.) How do his older students respond to your doubts? A little caution or hesitation on your part is good; in fact, the traditional Vajrayana texts all recommend it. With time the enlightened qualities (or lack of them) will speak for themselves.

Other titles include *geshe* and *khenpo*. These are academic degrees, like a Ph.D. Whether or not a geshe or khenpo is realized is hard to say. They are generally strict monks who teach in a very thorough, methodical style.

Druppon means retreat master, someone with great meditative experience who oversees a long group retreat. Expect him to be very ascetic, to emphasize retreat, and to teach that if you simply practice more diligently, everything will be all right. (And he is most likely correct!)

All monasteries have "throne-holders," the most revered lamas of their monasteries. The larger the monastery or monastic system, the greater the fame and esteem of the lama. Most throne-holders are tulkus; for instance, the throne-holder of Palpung is always the Tai Situ Rinpoche. Some are based on merit, such as at Ganden Monastery, where the head is simply the most accomplished disciple of the previous throne-holder.

Kyabje is becoming more widely used these days. It means something like "source of refuge" or "noble refuge" and is almost always used for the most respected and revered lamas. The Western titles "His Holiness" or "His Eminence" roughly correspond, but these are certainly not literal translations. Also, there doesn't seem to be any standard in applying them. Who exactly determines who is or is not a kyabje, holiness, or eminence? When I started practicing Tibetan Buddhism, only the Dalai Lama was "His Holiness." The title then spread to the heads of the various lineages, such as His Holiness Karmapa and His Holiness Dudjom Rinpoche. "His Eminence" seemed to be reserved for throne-holders. But slowly we've experienced title inflation, and I feel that a little standardization would be useful. It's only normal to want to venerate and promote your teacher; however, most of us find it a little confusing and off-putting.

Guru Rinpoche, or Padmasambhava, the most important founder of Tibetan Buddhism, had twenty-five major, fully realized Tibetan disciples. Before he left Tibet, he entrusted them to reveal in their future lives teachings that he had concealed. The teachings are called "treasures," or terma, and the lamas who discover them are tertons. Some do not accept the validity of termas in general, and there are claims that certain tertons are bogus. However, a genuine terton is a most amazing of lamas, someone whose teachings have been formulated exactly for our times. Many centers in the West practice termas. His Holiness Dudjom Rinpoche was the most famous traditional terton to bless the West with his presence; Chogyam Trungpa Rinpoche, who did so much to plant the teachings firmly in America, revealed a very comprehensive and relevant set of teachings, known as Shambhala: The Sacred Path of the Warrior.

Many lamas are called rinpoche, or "precious one." It is a title of respect used for tulkus and other highly regarded lamas. Many newcomers think it is a family name and then mix all the lamas up! It is often used as a form of address; you might say to your teacher, "Rinpoche, please answer this question."

Titled or not, you might find a truly qualified lama and still not connect with him. It is often a matter of style.

You might find many of the older teachers quite traditional. They teach Westerners in the same way that they taught in Tibet. Kalu Rinpoche summarized this approach when he said, "Westerners have defilements, Tibetans have defilements." In other words, the teachings, as they are, are pure and perfect. There is no need to reformulate them for a different audience; in fact, it might very well corrupt the teachings and dissipate the blessings of the lineage. Younger teachers, exposed to Western concepts from an earlier age and perhaps even educated in the West, may try to make the teachings more relevant or accessible to the average Westerner. They recognize that Westerners have different backgrounds, needs, and attitudes than Tibetans, that a traditional approach might alienate them or at least play upon their fascination with the foreign and exotic. They may use scientific, psychological, or Christian concepts, or they may talk about the teachings in the context of work or relationships. It is very important to realize that in reality there is no fundamental difference between these two approaches: These teachers are simply taking the same pure teachings of Lord Buddha and making them accessible, comprehensible, and relevant for different groups of people. As time goes on, this Westernizing trend will only increase; Buddhism has always adapted to the culture of its new hosts.

Another stylistic distinction is in the lifestyle lived or espoused by the teacher. Broadly speaking, there are three main lifestyles: those of laypersons, of ordained monks and nuns, and of yogis. A layperson is one who practices with family and career; an ordained monk or nun practices in a monastic environment; and a yogi or yogini practices retreat in solitude. Gyatrul Rinpoche, our lama here at Tashi Chöling in Oregon, meditated in hermitages in Tibet for twenty years. He definitely encourages the yogic approach, and most of his more committed students aspire to a life of retreat. Some lamas encourage their students to become ordained, perhaps facilitating their finding of sponsors. In some centers monks and nuns have a much easier time getting interviews with their teacher than their lay counterparts. Trungpa Rinpoche always encouraged his students to develop realistic careers and to function and be successful in the world.

Some teachers emphasize study, including the study of Tibetan, saying that if one meditates without sufficient study, one can only go astray—a blind man roaming in the desert. Others emphasize practice, saying that life is too short to spend a considerable amount of time studying. Different teachers are masters of different systems of meditation and will encourage their students to do these practices. Many teachers have various projects that demand much volunteer labor such as building or publishing. Students of these teachers must be willing to delay or postpone their own aspirations or practice to participate in these activities.

Chinese students like their teachers fat—they feel it's a sign of vast merit. Westerners like theirs thin, perhaps a sign of desirelessness. Rich and poor teachers will also attract their respective followers.

There should be a good fit, therefore, between your aspirations and what the teacher has to offer. If you like to offer your services as a carpenter, find a teacher who has building projects. If you want to learn dzogchen, make sure that lama knows it well before committing yourself. When I met my teacher, I was interested in learning the yogic practices called the Six Doctrines of Naropa, and I wanted to meditate diligently in solitude. My teacher was a master of these practices and always sincerely encouraged me to practice, discouraging me from study or any other kind of non-meditative spiritual activity. It was a good match.

Also, you should consider the logistics. Four years ago, an incredible terton visited the United States from Tibet; since that time, however, he hasn't been able to return. I imagine that his Western students are finding it difficult to clarify their doubts and confusions and receive further instruction since he hasn't returned. So consider the teacher's accessibility: Does he live in your town, or does he visit once a year? If he's not around very much, has he left a representative? And if so, is he or she someone you can trust and with whom you can communicate? When your prospective teacher is around, how easy is it to get interviews? Does he speak good English, or does he have a competent translator?

Everything I have said boils down to this: Can you really communicate with this teacher? Can you really open your heart and trust him? Do his replies really touch you deeply—that is, does he understand the real question behind your question, and do his answers feel like someone has just illuminated a darkened room?

One of my closest teachers, Zigar Kongtrul Rinpoche, will always answer my questions by addressing the real issues behind them. If I ask him about retreats, for instance, he will read me like an open book and speak to my doubts about traditional methods of practice and their relevance for Westerners.

If your prospective teacher is unqualified, he won't be able to answer you skillfully. If you and he are not compatible, you will feel his answers or teachings miss the mark and are not really what you need to hear. If he is unavailable, your relationship will not develop any depth; you will feel he doesn't know you or understand you, and you might make mistakes or waste time in his absence. But when you find the right one, the magic begins.

CHAPTER FOUR

Empowerment

The gateway to the Vajrayana is what is known as "empowerment." An empowerment is generally a very elaborate ceremony wherein a highly respected lama will confer the blessings of a particular Buddhist deity, such as, for example, Chenrezig, the buddha of compassion. During an empowerment ceremony, the lama plants a "seed" in the student's mind that will eventually ripen in the student, through practice and devotion, manifesting the enlightened qualities of that deity. An empowerment marks a student's formal entrance into the tantric path.

We might hear that such a ceremony is going to take place in our community and want to go in order to learn a little more about Tibetan Buddhism. Or we might wish to meet the famous lama who is bestowing the empowerment. We might even travel great distances. A friend of mine recently traveled from Oregon to Australia to receive the Kalachakra empowerment from the Dalai Lama.

As we approach Vajrayana Buddhism, we will become aware of these ceremonies taking place. They may afford us our first opportunity to connect with Tibetan Buddhism in general or a particular lama about whom we have heard. Once committed, we may attend to deepen our connection, to receive the blessings of a great or famous master, or because we are interested in the associated practice.

When Tibetan Buddhism first came to the West, empowerments were called "initiations," a word we inherited from our Theosophist predecessors. The word is still used today and is completely interchangeable with "empowerment"; it is simply a different translation of the same Tibetan word. I will use both terms, although the word "empowerment" is the more literal and superior translation.

What is an empowerment? In this section I will discuss the ceremony of empowerment. I will not consider the spontaneous transmission of insight from teacher to student—that will come in a later chapter. In terms of the ceremony, an empowerment is almost always associated with a particular deity, or *yidam*. There are thousands of yidams in Tibetan Buddhism, and each one has its own initiation ceremony.

Each empowerment is also associated with a particular lineage. So a Manjushri empowerment in the Gelug lineage will be different than one from the Sakya lineage. Each of the different lineages of Tibetan Buddhism has its own set of empowerments, and each specializes in the deities it practices the most. For instance, the Kagyupas practice Chakrasamvara a great deal. Most people would feel it would be especially auspicious to receive the Chakrasamvara empowerment from a high Kagyu lama. Gelugpas also practice Chakrasamvara, but they are particularly famous for their practice of Yamantaka, the wrathful form of Manjushri. The Nyingmapas specialize in Vajrakilaya these days.

A lama, called the "vajra master" in the ceremony, always bestows an empowerment. He, himself, will have received it from another lama and on and on, backward in time. The lama should be qualified according to the guidelines already discussed, but as the teacher may only briefly be passing through our community, we might have to decide whether or not to attend based on reputation. Our teacher here in Ashland, Gyatrul Rinpoche, has brought many great lamas here to give empowerments. Some I have not heard of, but I do not hesitate to attend because I trust Gyatrul Rinpoche's integrity and judgment.

An empowerment is a ceremony. I will discuss empowerments in a general way from the point of view of purpose and structure. I will base my words in part on Tsele Natsok Rangdrol's *Empowerment*, perhaps the most definitive account available in English.

An empowerment is an authorization to do the various stages of meditation associated with a particular deity. Taking an Amitabha empowerment authorizes you to practice the meditation and mantra recitation of Amitabha Buddha. Also, it authorizes one to do any other practices associated with that deity. So along with the main practice of Amitabha, you can do Amitabha's long life practice and the transference of consciousness (*phowa*) practice to the Pure Land of Great Bliss (Sukhavati). Tsele Rinpoche says:

> Unless you first obtain the ripening empowerments, you are not author-ized to hear even a single verse of the tantras, statements, and instruc-tions. Unauthorized people who engage in expounding on and listening to the tantras will not only fail to receive blessings; they will create immense demerit from divulging the secrecy of these teachings.[6]

We need to receive empowerment so that our subsequent Vajrayana practice will be successful. If we aspire to do a certain practice, we should exert some energy in obtaining its empowerment. Sometimes we aspire to do practices that seem to have nothing to do with deities, for instance, the yoga of inner heat (*tummo*) or dzogchen. Nonetheless, their teachings will generally be contained within a particular deity's practice, for which it will be necessary to attain empowerment.

The empowerments have a ripening or purifying effect on the practi-tioner; in fact, they are often called "ripening empowerments." If our buddha-nature is likened to a seed, the empowerment ripens this seed and puri-fies the obscurations that prevent the seed from growing. Every section of the empowerment purifies a particular obscuration of our being. For instance, the vase empowerment purifies our obscurations of body and ripens our physical constituents into the body of a deity.

At the most profound level, the empowerment is a direct transmis-sion of the ultimate truth of Buddhism. As we previously discussed, we all possess buddha-nature, but it is obscured. Furthermore, we don't know how to recognize it. If we are ready and have a pure connection with the vajra master, the recognition can be transmitted through the ceremony. As Tsele Rinpoche explains:

> Free from platitudes and mere lip service and exactly in accordance with the master's words, the disciple should understand how the world and beings, everything animate and inanimate and comprised of the aggregates, elements, and sense factors, has, since the very onset, never been anything but the mandala of the deity. Right then, through the master's kindness and instructions, the disciple's obscuration of momentary delusion is cleared away. He is able to understand how the external world is in fact a celestial palace and its inhabitants are indeed a mandala of deities.[7]

Like this, each section of the empowerment introduces us to a different aspect of our true nature, purifying on the spot the various habitual tendencies that prevent our recognition. Perhaps this recognition will stick, and we will be realized from this point on. Or the recognition may only be temporary, but having seen, we will be able to access this awareness in subsequent practice. Either way, we are truly fortunate!

Although every empowerment is different, they all generally follow the same basic structure. More elaborate ones will begin a day early with a preliminary ceremony, called the *tagon*, that serves to prepare the students. Otherwise, the student prepares himself by washing and putting on nice, clean clothes. This is not a hippie event; an overly laid-back hippie mentality has no place here. These are the kinds of attitudes we are trying to let go of. Preparing ourselves like this purifies our body. Meanwhile, the initiating lama will also have begun his preparation , and when we enter the shrine room or auditorium, he will have already been there a couple of hours, doing the preliminary rituals and generating himself as the deity.

As we enter the shrine room, we will be given saffron water to purify our speech and a mantra to recite to purify our minds. It is appropriate to prostrate to the lama before sitting down; if that doesn't feel right for you, you may not be ready for Vajrayana. In some empowerments, the master will speak English or else most of the proceedings will be translated so that the student will be able to follow step by step and do (or at least try to do) the visualizations associated with each stage. In others, very little explanation will be given, and merely a general overview or brief introduction to each section will be explained. Remember, they didn't have any public address systems in Tibet; in public ceremonies people received the empowerment through the strength of their faith and devotion. As a sophisticated Westerner, you will probably find, however, that the more you know about the ceremony the richer your experience will be. By trying your best to follow the visualizations, you are more open to receiving the blessings and transmission of the ceremony. If you can't follow, I've heard it's best to relax the mind into a state of trusting openness.

The ceremony itself will start with the offering of a *gektor. Tor* is short for *torma* and refers to the sculptured ritual cakes that can be seen in all Tibetan shrine rooms. In this case, the torma will be small and painted red. It is being offered to the *geks*, that is, to the negative or obstructing forces. They can be seen either as external beings or as one's own negativities and dualistic thoughts. Here is a good chance to let go of all that internal dialogue that we always carry around and that we have most likely brought into the ceremony with us. In essence, we are saying, "Dear geks, please take this wonderful offering and leave us alone. Don't disturb or hinder our ceremony." For those that refuse the torma and still remain, wrathful techniques are used: *gugal*, a tree-resin similar to frankincense, is burned in a censor and mustard seed is scattered while the master recites wrathful mantras. The gugal and mustard seed appear to the geks as weapons. Now that the environment has been sanitized, a protective canopy, called a vajra tent, is imagined as encapsulating the proceedings.

The lama will probably give a short talk recounting the history of the empowerment and its corresponding practice. He might, for instance, mention how it originated in India, how it spread to Tibet, the vast number of practitioners who attained realization from doing the practice, the ease and simplicity of the practice, and the power and profundity of its blessings. All of this is to engender faith in the disciples. Students should feel that this event is something truly special, that they are very lucky to be participating; they should feel committed to what lies ahead.

At every empowerment you will hear how unique and special it is. Don't think, "But they said the same thing at the last one!" This praise is to meant engender the proper faith and openness; it is not really meant to be the basis of comparison.

Next, refuge and bodhichitta prayers are repeated after the lama. If you don't know what this means, I will be explaining each of these in a later chapter. These correspond to the Hinayana and Mahayana levels of practice and commitment. The *samaya* vows (explained at the end of this chapter) are given with some saffron water or alcoholic liquor to seal the commitment, along with a stern warning about what may happen to those who break these commitments. At this point, we have reached the point of no return and have committed ourselves to being tantric practitioners. The next section, "the descent of blessings" invokes the blessings of all the buddhas, bodhisattvas, and deities while music is played and the students meditate on a visualization that the master has just described, usually imaging countless buddhas in the form of the deity melting into them.

What is the purpose behind all this? Tsele Rinpoche explains it quite clearly:

In fact, it is necessary to purify our karmic perception of everything outer and inner, the world and beings, as being ordinary and solid. Consider the methods and auspicious coincidences necessary for this to occur. During any empowerment ritual, at the time of the descent of the wisdom beings, a blindfold is tied on the recipient in order to interrupt the thoughts that cling to visible forms as ordinary. Music is played to stop the thoughts that cling to sound as ordinary. Smoke prepared from substances such as incense and resin causing the wisdom to descend is spread to halt the thoughts of smell as ordinary. Consecrated nectar [the saffron water or liquor] is given to interrupt thoughts that fixate on taste as ordinary. The physical position of the sevenfold posture of Vairocana or the vajra posture is taken to stop thoughts that cling to touch as ordinary. Finally, the steps of visualization, emanating and absorbing are taken to interrupt the deluded clinging to our mind as ordinary.[8]

So, through these preliminary rituals, the student should feel more open and responsive, ready for the main part of the empowerment that follows.

Although empowerments follow many forms, they almost always have either three or four main sections, which will be described shortly. The bestowing of the empowerment consists of the master reciting the text, possibly translated so the recipients can also participate by visualizing the various stages taking place, touching the disciples with various blessed symbolic objects, and giving consecrated substances for the disciples to eat or drink. Since most empowerments involve many participants and it would be too time consuming for the master to do this for each student, often he personally bestows the empowerment on a few people close to him who then bring these articles through the audience. Or sometimes the various articles are left at the front of the hall and the students file through and make contact at the end.

If there are three main empowerments, the first is the body empowerment. This purifies the defilements of body, such as illness, and authorizes the disciple to visualize herself a deity. The speech empowerment purifies defilements of speech and breath and allows the student to recite the deity's mantra. The empowerment of mind purifies the mind and permits the students to dissolve the visualization and rest their minds in buddha-nature.

The empowerments for the higher levels of tantra have four main sections. They empower us to practice the systems of meditation to which we as Westerners usually aspire, and their sequence and structure should be studied and understood over the course of our involvement with Vajrayana. This same pattern of four will keep arising in different formats. When you understand it, it will help tie together for you seemingly unconnected aspects of the Vajrayana.

The first empowerment in this system is the vase empowerment, which is sometimes subdivided into five, representing the five buddha families. This initiation purifies our body and allows us to practice the development stage, the visualization of the deity and the recitation of the deity's mantra. As a result, the disciple attains the nirmanakaya, the emanation body of a buddha.

The second is the secret empowerment, purifying our speech. We are authorized to practice the completion stage, the practices using the inner energies of the *tsa, lung,* and *tigle. Tsa, lung,* and *tigle* refer to the inner channels, winds, and essences or drops. I will say more about them in the chapter on the body (see chapter 17). We attain a buddha's sambhogakaya, or enjoyment body, as a result.

Next comes the wisdom empowerment, purifying 'our mind. We are permitted to practice the meditations of union, which result in the dharmakaya, or truth body.

Last is the fourth, or word, empowerment. This purifies our body, speech, and mind together with the tendency to see them as separate. It authorizes us to practice the profound practices of mahamudra and dzogchen and results in the svabhavikakaya. This empowerment can directly introduce us to our *rigpa,* the self-cognizing awareness of our buddha-nature. Quite often this introduction takes the form of the lama holding up a crystal while he says a few words about the ultimate nature of the mind. This is a profound pointing-out instruction, and we should be especially attentive during this section. With faith and interest, we may be able to experience something of great importance.

At the end of the empowerment the disciples approach the master and offer a *kata,* the traditional Tibetan scarf, and an offering, often in the form of a cash donation.

What are the signs that one has genuinely received the empowerment? Tsele Rinpoche explains:

> The foremost disciple experiences the dawning of self-existing, coemergent wakefulness. The next best experiences pure perception with overwhelming and intense devotion while the manifestation of experience blaze forth, while the disciple of lesser caliber should at least feel slightly exhilarated.[9]

I think it's safe to say that we're all probably among the latter, so we can at least hope for some kind of energetic experience, perhaps a feeling of being "blissed out" or the kind of experience that Hindus call "*shaktipat.*" As the ritual is usually powerful and awe-inspiring, we may feel great devotion and reverence. And if we follow the directions carefully and with trust and faith during the fourth empowerment, we might glimpse our buddha-nature, the coemergent wakefulness.

At the end of the empowerment, the master might give us a commitment practice. That is, he will tell us to do a certain meditation every day.

It might be nothing or something very general, such as continuing to practice virtue or the Dharma; it might be a short recitation, such as one rosary of OM MANI PADME HUM; or it might be something rather long, such as a one- or two-hour daily practice. A dear friend of mine once had five hours of such practices to do every day. On busy days she was unable to sleep.

Since one has already drunk from the water of samaya at the beginning of the ceremony, one has no choice but to follow the lama's command. To ignore the commitment is said to have the direst consequences. Empowerments given to large groups in public, especially here in the West, generally have light commitments; however, it is the student's responsibility to determine beforehand if he is really ready for such a commitment. If you do not feel you will be able to keep the commitment, do not take the empowerment. As well, if you do not feel you can maintain trust and respect in the vajra master and pure perception and loving kindness toward the other participants, it is also probably better not to take the empowerment.

There are, in addition, other samaya vows that are implicit in the empowerment even though they will probably not be mentioned during the ceremony. Nonetheless, it is your responsibility to find out what they are and to try to keep them as well as you can. There are thousands and thousands of these vows, some clearly more important than others and many nearly impossible to keep. I will mention a few of the most important ones, but please try to study them from your teacher. Find out which ones he feels are the crucial ones, how to keep them, and what to do if they are broken.

In Vajrayana it is taught that our buddha-nature is obscured by our ordinary thoughts. In order to maintain a continuous sense of our underlying true nature, we vow to maintain pure perception or sacred outlook. We vow always to view our surroundings as a mandala with all beings as deities, all sound as mantras, and all thoughts as the expression of enlightened awareness. Not so easy! For my part, I at least try to cut strong indulgence in negative judgments and to see the pure and positive side of things. My teacher said that although people are always messing up, careening here and there as they go through life, they all have a good heart. I try to perceive or acknowledge this good heart and not get too caught up in reacting to the minor irritants of their quirks. I try to apply this to the other points as well. Not getting too irritated by my environment, but trying to see the beauty and vastness in all places. Not getting stressed by grating noise, but using it to open my mind. I can't claim to be very successful, but I'm trying, and at the least I am able to use these approximations as a starting point. So you see, pure perception is both the starting point and the central concept in both Vajrayana practice and in keeping the samaya vows and commitments.

There is also a set of fourteen vows that accompany any empowerment. A description can be found in many books but especially in Dudjom Rinpoche's *Perfect Conduct*. Three of these I feel are most important. First is to respect the officiating master. One should view him as the deity himself and certainly not let doubts and negativities pervert one's view of him. In particular, don't lose your temper and fight with him! Second, maintain pure view toward all the Buddhist teaching. Don't think some teachings or teachers are better than others. What possible benefit can come from thinking like this? Just consider that the wide variety of teachers, teachings, and techniques are available to suit the various needs of diverse beings; thus, no hierarchy is implied. They are like different medicines for different illnesses. Especially maintain pure perception and respect toward the Vajrayana. Some people think that it is an aberration of the Buddha's teaching or, at best, a merging of Buddhism with Hinduism and Bonpo. You should abandon this attitude. Third, maintain pure perception toward the other students, your vajra brothers and sisters. No matter how irritating and neurotic they may seem to be, they possess buddha-nature and are trying their best. Besides, they probably think the same of you! So don't fight, don't argue, and don't gossip about them behind their backs. If there's someone you really can't bear, simply avoid that person. In addition to these three, maintaining some kind of regular practice is essential.

As you can see, taking an empowerment propels you into a whole new world and, as you've probably gathered from all the above, assumes a willingness on your part to let go of the old one. There's no doubt that something powerful, awesome, and vast is taking place. No matter how thick skinned we are, there's an undeniable grandeur to the ceremony. Beyond that is the very real possibility of a glimpse into or an intuition about a mode of being well beyond our small world. We have reached the point of no 'return' on our journey, and in a sense our searching phase has come to an end. There's no turning back now.

CHAPTER FIVE

Centers

Tibetan Buddhist centers are all over the place now. Even small towns have them—Ashland, Oregon, where I live, has 20,000 people and three Tibetan centers. Sometimes someone will invite a lama to visit their community, and from then on their living room is the center for that lama. And why not? Seems like an efficient system to me.

Does your lama have centers in America? If he does, I would strongly recommend moving to a city where one exists. No matter what hardship is involved, your relationship with your teacher is the most important relationship of your life. I lived in Kathmandu for many years, and however romantic that sounds, I hated it. I had asthma several months a year when I've had it nowhere else. I've lived with levels of noise, pollution, and filth unimaginable in America. If I could do that, you can move to Boulder or Austin or wherever your teacher spends a lot of time.

At Tashi Chöling, where I used to live, most of Gyatrul Rinpoche's students have made many sacrifices to be with their teacher. They live in trailers. They commute on muddy roads in the snow during winter. They put in a lot of hours maintaining the grounds and buildings. People content themselves with lousy jobs, little employment, no medical insurance, and very little economic security. All of this, which I greatly admire and respect, is so they can be close to their teacher, do what pleases him, and help to make his teachings more accessible to a larger public. The opportunity to get regular guidance from an enlightened master is extremely precious to them. You've probably read stories of the hardships people in India or Tibet have gone through to be close to their teachers; Americans are doing the same thing right now.

If you haven't found your teacher, you'll probably still benefit by associating with a nearby center. Buddhism is still Buddhism; what you'll learn will be beneficial no matter who your lama turns out to be. Just remember some of what I called differences in style; your teacher may emphasize rituals or texts other than those you have just learned from someone else.

Also, it's perfectly fine to study at the center of a different lama if you already have one; just check with him first. My teacher lives in Nepal, as I've mentioned, but I've derived great benefit from studying with Gyatrul Rinpoche at his centers in California and Oregon. In any case, it's quite normal for people to have many teachers. However, I would recommend that once you feel you've found your teacher, stick with him a while to deepen the relationship. Later, it will again be appropriate to take teachings and empowerments from other teachers; it will enhance what you've learned from your main teacher. If your relationship with your main teacher hasn't matured yet, you might end up wandering here and there without ever making a real commitment. Of course, much of this will depend on circumstances. When I was living in Oakland and studying with Gyatrul Rinpoche, he went to India for a while. During that time I visited a Zen center under the English abbess, Kennet Roshi, and I learned things that I cherish to this day.

What happens at these centers? First, there will be teachings. If your teacher is in residence or if he has sent a representative these should take place on a regular basis. Otherwise, your center might have "events" where teachers are invited for short periods to teach, give empowerments, or lead short retreats.

If your lama is not in residence but has sent a representative, you may assume that this person may not be a completely enlightened buddha or as completely realized as the lama who sent him. These lamas, whether Tibetan or Western, are there to help you and are doing the best they can. Since they probably aren't at the same level as your teacher, you can't expect them to display the same qualities. As a beginning teacher myself, it's a constant challenge to set aside my own attitudes and needs in order to teach as purely as I can. I'm sure I make lots of mistakes. Luckily, I've been given no administrative responsibilities, which is where a lot of the problem can arise. The American invention of the separation of church and state was a brilliant idea. Someone can be a good teacher and genuinely care for his students; that doesn't mean he'll be skillful at running an organization. So learn what you can from these people but never completely surrender your critical facilities. You'll be able to learn a lot. Teachers like myself know the territory, speak your language, and have the availability and time to work with you over a long period of time, to really listen to you and hear you out. Then, when the high lama is there, he can give you more of an overview and direction. Answers to many questions and high teachings may come only from the high lama; many of the basics can very easily be dealt with by people like myself.

Centers will have a regular program of rituals. This program will follow the Tibetan lunar calendar (it's worth picking one up) and are usually *tsogs* (Tibetan) or *pujas* (Sanskrit), rituals centered around offering and sharing food. The most likely days are as follows:

- Eighth day of the Tibetan lunar month: Always a peaceful deity such as Tara or the Medicine Buddha.
- Tenth day of the lunar month: Guru Rinpoche Day. Guru Rinpoche, or Padmasambhava, the founder of Tibetan Buddhism, promised he would visit anyone who did his practice on this day. All Kagyu and Nyingma centers will do his puja on this day.
- Fifteenth day of the lunar month: Full moon. Another peaceful deity, such as Amitabha or Medicine Buddha.
- Twenty-fifth day of the lunar month: Dakini day. Dakinis are female emanations of the buddhas, either wrathful or semi-wrathful.
- Twenty-ninth day of the lunar month: Protector day. Protectors are the wrathful guardians of the teachings. You probably will not be allowed to attend unless you've had the empowerment for this one.
- Thirtieth day of the Tibetan lunar month: New moon. Another peaceful day.

Many Westerners, myself included, have a problem with Tibetan rituals. They just seem alien and strange. Also, when lamas teach, they very rarely speak about rituals, even though they are the main events at the centers. Furthermore, they are almost always done in Tibetan. Very few Westerners I've met have a really good sense or understanding about what these rituals are about. I'll speak more about this in a later chapter.

Nevertheless, rituals are very important. If you go to monasteries in the East, they're doing long, elaborate pujas all the time. The lamas aren't fools; they know what they're doing. In a later chapter I'll talk a little about the theory or meaning behind pujas; for now, see them as your entry gate into the center. In my retreat, I told our retreat master that I didn't like all the pujas. He told me to think of them as a social event. At the time, I thought that was glib and superficial; however, I've learned that there's a lot of truth and benefit to what he says. These rituals will present a good opportunity to meet the other students of the center. By participating in the ceremony and sharing the offering with people who share your deepest aspirations in a pretty alienating world, you are creating together a healing and bonding experience. As well, you'll learn skills that will come in handy if you ever do solitary retreat, such as making and offering tormas. So suspend your disbelief a little and make an effort to participate.

The other main activity of your center will be work. There are lots of things that need to be done, and all centers depend on volunteer work to get them done. That means you. This presents quite a challenge to us. We're already quite busy, and we didn't get involved in Buddhism to be, say, a bricklayer. We will be constantly tested regarding our commitment and priorities around this issue— how much to contribute, how much to pull back, how much to practice, etc.

There are also real personal benefits to these projects. Not all of us are ready for intensive meditation, no matter what our aspirations are. Work gives us a chance to surrender our concepts about spirituality, accumulate merit, and please our teacher. We will get to know the other students and form close friendships with them. Many of our most painful emotional issues will come up in these interactions; people will push our buttons, revealing many of our hidden faults. We will have a chance to heal and grow. If we're committed enough, we will be pushed to our limits, which is where some of our juiciest stuff will be found.

If we read the stories of great meditators of the past, we rarely hear of any that started right away as yogis or yoginis. Almost all of them spent some time in an apprenticeship serving their gurus. Milarepa spent many years building one useless tower after another for his guru, Marpa. Only then was he considered ready for meditation. If you recall from the story, he escaped and received instructions from another lama. He practiced diligently in retreat but with absolutely no benefit. He was forced to return to Marpa and continue building.

Milarepa is an extreme example of course—he had killed thirty-five people with black magic. However, this period of apprenticeship seems universal. Zen always talks about "chopping wood, carrying water." In monasteries, monks spend many years absorbed with their duties before they begin retreat.

When I arrived at Samye Ling, in Scotland, to start my retreat, they had just completed building their temple. It had been an eight-year project, but they had to hurry for it to be ready in time for the consecration. The abbot, Akong Rinpoche, put them on a schedule of working from 7:00 A.M. until 10:00 P.M. seven days a week for three months. Can you imagine what this kind of routine would do to you? How it would constantly test your commitment and trust? How your defenses would break down through your exhaustion and all kinds of negativity would come streaming to the surface of your awareness? I have incredible admiration for those dedicated students.

I personally feel I missed out on something by starting right out away with intensive meditation. I'm sure I would have benefited by a period of work. Perhaps many of the difficulties I later encountered in my practice might not have arisen so strongly if I had had a chance to work them out through virtuous Dharma activity and service. However, I probably would have rebelled against any teacher who might have suggested it.

What kinds of jobs will you be asked to do at your center? First are organizational tasks. There's the day-to-day organization of the center and the extra organization needed whenever your center is putting on an event. The latter will push you to your limits—don't expect to get much sleep at those times. Then there's secretarial and publishing work. Most centers transcribe and publish many of the teachings given at the center. Also, they might publish the texts used in their rituals. There's always a need for transcribers, editors, and so on.

Many important jobs are associated with community outreach. Centers need to extend themselves into the broader community for many reasons. In order simply to survive, a center might need more students offering assistance. Also, centers need to interrelate with the larger community in order to accomplish different objectives, such as getting building permits, non-profit status, and bank loans and grants. For these purposes, the center must present itself as professional, competent, and mainstream, and successful professional students are often best at accomplishing these tasks.

Country centers need construction workers. The need is generally unending: temples, lama's residences, retreat centers, monasteries, and just ordinary maintenance. If you have those skills and show up, you will be very welcome! You may have a difficult time leaving, however. Some country centers may have a work-study program: If you work so many hours a week, you may receive room and board and some retreat time.

The job that people typically like the most is serving the lamas, whether resident or visiting. You may be cooking, cleaning, or driving. This usually presents a wonderful opportunity to get to know the lama better.

There is also maintaining the shrine. This is a good way to learn about rituals and make friends with some of the more serious older students, the experts who can teach you what to do. You might learn how to make the tormas or play some of the traditional instruments.

Another activity that might be taking place at your center is Tibetan language classes. I suppose this is as good a place as any to discuss the various pros and cons of learning Tibetan. I've spent thousands of hours and have gotten almost nowhere with it. So you may want to call what I'm about to say "sour grapes."

Tibetan is completely different than English; it's not at all like learning German or French. As you know, Tibetan uses a different alphabet. The word order and grammar are also very different. There's nothing that exactly corresponds to our ideas of clauses, sentences, and paragraphs. They use words where we would use punctuation marks.

Also, written classical Tibetan and spoken colloquial Tibetan are significantly different from one another. There are dialectic differences in spoken Tibetan. Imagine learning English from an American for a short time and then trying to practice with a Scot or an Australian. As well, since many Dharma texts are written in verse, key words are left out for the sake of meter. Tibetans know what is missing, but we are left floundering for the meaning. All in all, becoming proficient in Tibetan is a daunting task.

In addition, consider what we're trying to learn—Buddhist philosophical, psychological, and meditational texts. Not exactly "Dick and Jane." So unless you're prepared to study until you attain a high degree of fluency, how will you use your knowledge?

With time, more and more of the younger lamas are learning English. Many of them already wonderfully fluent. Unfortunately, the great older lamas who never learned English are passing on. So once again, unless you develop a high degree of fluency, what are you going to talk about?

On the other hand, the reasons for learning Tibetan are also very strong. I'm very sorry I never learned it—things would have been much simpler. Having learned Tibetan, you can recite your liturgies, prayers, and pujas and know what you're doing. The words of all our prayers, etc., are believed to be blessed; they were written by enlightened beings, and there's a power and transmission contained within the very words. If we do our practice in English, we lose some of that blessing. If we do it in Tibetan, we don't understand what we're saying, and we're flying on blind faith alone. Learning Tibetan is extremely helpful here. Gyatrul Rinpoche has said that doing one's practice in English is like being deaf, while doing it in Tibetan when not knowing it is like being blind. Not much of a choice!

Few of the deeper texts and meditation instruction manuals have been translated yet. When you learn the practice of, say, Amitabha, there are commentaries on the practice that teach you everything you have to know: how to do it, the signs of success, and the remedies for obstacles. These texts are a wealth of precious information. Learning Tibetan would be like discovering buried treasure. In the case of many of the lesser known practices, it could be ages before they are translated.

Many Tibetan words simply cannot be translated into English. These words describe experiences that very few people in our culture have had, so we haven't invented the vocabulary to discuss them. Even if you never learn fluent Tibetan, it is good to learn what a few of these words mean, because the English translation will always be misleading. A good example is *rigpa*. *Rigpa* is the self-reflexive awareness that cognizes buddha-nature. Recognizing and stabilizing rigpa is the whole point of Buddhism. But how do you translate such a term? Often it is translated simply as "awareness," but if you heard the word "awareness" would you know that it was really referring to rigpa?

So, to summarize this discussion of language, what I would recommend is this: If you're good at languages, enjoy studying them, have the time, and would be committed to attaining a certain level of proficiency, then by all means go ahead and study Tibetan, especially if you are young; it will expand your horizons and options. If you're unable to, rest assured there's plenty of material already translated, and more is being published every day. Also, there are many teachers now who can speak English with you.

No discussion of centers would be complete without discussing center politics. Unfortunately, since I usually keep a low profile, I haven't had much experience. What usually seems to happen is this: We want access to the lama or to certain activities of the center but that access is denied by certain of the older students. We might feel very hurt and annoyed. We might also start doubting the wisdom of the lama who gave these people authority in the first place. Try to be cool. Be diplomatic. Examine your own unacknowledged needs for power, recognition, or mothering. These people usually become indispensable by doing the lion's share of the work, so they've earned their position. Consider it all "grist for the mill," and integrate it into your practice. So many of these problems, I feel, come from people projecting their unacknowledged needs and aggression onto others. Try to understand what is going on, especially your own behavior.

When you come to a new center, don't forget that everybody there is just like you—sincere in aspiration but still a little neurotic. Consequently, everybody's stuff gets played out in public view. It's like living a soap opera. I haven't heard of any center that isn't like that, and every one that I have been associated with has had its difficulties. We're all getting pushed from all sides—by our worldly commitments, by our teacher, by our practice, and by the other students in the center. Flare-ups are inevitable, and sooner or later you will be in the center of one. It just seems to be the nature of the path. A famous Korean Zen master said, "I put all my students in a big bag like potatoes and shake them until they rub each other's skin off!"

As a result, center difficulties can appear like small civil wars. People's tempers flare, people's egos are on the line and getting crushed, people leave feeling burnt out. But each episode ends, people learn from their mistakes and heal, and then move on to the next thing.

In group retreats, it can be much worse. So many people imagine that everyone will be blissed out and loving. This is hardly the case. In truth, it can be a war zone. In my retreat, I sometimes felt afraid of leaving my room! A lot of meditation time went into processing the previous unpleasant encounter and preparing for the next one. There seems to be no escaping the harsh realities of interpersonal dynamics.

You might also find your new center cliquish, with older students hanging out together and not being very friendly to newcomers. Usually this is not conscious behavior on the part of old-timers; they're simply happy to see old friends. If you're friendly and willing to work, you'll probably make friends and be accepted in no time. I've noticed it here at Tashi Chöling. People arrive with a positive, friendly attitude and a willingness to share in the chores, and all of a sudden there are no cliques, no old-timers, and all the doors are open.

Perhaps what we really get from centers is support. We're living in an extremely non-spiritual environment. Everything about our culture can be seen as a conspiracy against meditative awareness. It's so important to have friends with whom we can share our struggles and aspirations!

I often wonder about my students. People from the larger community take my classes because they sincerely want to learn something about meditation. But when the course is over, what happens to them? Many of them even have unsympathetic spouses. Meditation is difficult enough in the best of circumstances; it is definitely worth putting up with some of the problems of a spiritual community to reap the very real benefits. But without the support of a community, it is very difficult to maintain one's practice; it is always like swimming upstream.

I often run into former students who may have taken many classes from me. If they haven't joined a Buddhist community, they are almost never still practicing. The ones that have become affiliated with a Buddhist group are practicing regularly. This may appear counter-intuitive since center activities will decrease the amount of time one would have for personal practice, but that almost never seems to be the case. Participating in a center seems to be a time-efficient way of getting the support one needs to maintain a practice in an extremely materialistic culture.

One of the many things I really admire about my teacher Chökyi Nyima Rinpoche is his ability to make people feel part of a family. During his last retreat in California he married Susan and myself and used the occasion to create a very loving environment and melt everyone's heart. At the end of the retreat, we had a little talent show with retreatants putting on little skits or singing songs. Rinpoche was present, howling with laughter. These warm feelings make people feel connected and feel that they belong. These feelings will later fuel devotion and the discipline necessary to persevere in practice.

Sometimes, there's an "outer circle," a group of disgruntled older students who get together to bend or break the rules and complain about others, confusing cynicism and negativity with sophistication and insight. I would avoid them if possible; it seems like a good way to break your samaya vows. There might be another outer circle of more serious students who are more interested in practice than in center activities and who therefore keep a low profile. You might find what they have to say very insightful and useful.

An interesting situation that I've noticed over the years is that spiritual communities develop certain styles of ignorance. What I mean by this is as follows: A group of students hold a particular view of the teaching or the teacher that newer students assume is valid; consequently, the community grows with that view at its core. I've seen Buddhist communities that have a "wild yogi" ideal where drinking and promiscuity were an accepted part of the practice. Other groups believe that back-breaking work prepares one for intensive meditation. Another believes that the lama intentionally tries to keep his students confused and in conflict. While there may be some trace of truth in any of these views, I certainly did not hear the lamas themselves propagating these ideas; typically, these views just seemed to be accepted by the students as valid.

One problem I always have with centers is this: When lamas teach, they generally emphasize the formless aspects of practice, such as mahamudra. They also generally emphasize the importance of practice, usually advocating retreat. However, in the centers they establish, the main practices that people actually do are the rituals. Also, work rather than practice is needed in many centers. I would like to hear a high lama teach on the spiritual benefits of construction! A seminar on rituals would also be very useful. This contradiction forces us as fairly ignorant beginners to try to understand the demands of the center on our own, in our own terms with our own prejudices. I feel it would be very beneficial to the growth of centers and their members if this split were addressed.

So welcome to your new center. Don't think that becoming a Buddhist is like going to the movies, where you pay your six bucks for the seat and at the end you just walk out. There's no "just walking out" in Vajrayana Buddhism. Your commitment demands that you give more of yourself than that. From your involvement in your center, you can learn a great deal that's extremely precious even if sometimes very painful, you can make life-long friends, and you can deepen your connection with your teacher.

CHAPTER SIX

Path Buddha-Nature:
Instruction and Practice

A most extraordinary event took place at the Orgyen Dorje Den center in San Francisco in the summer of 1994. Venerable Gyatrul Rinpoche, a most accomplished meditation master, was teaching an amazingly deep and detailed meditation manual on how to recognize and stabilize buddha-nature. He was assisted by the translator B. Alan Wallace, a brilliant scholar and serious practitioner.

Rinpoche taught throughout the weekends, giving profound instructions. On Wednesdays we had a question-answer section, sometimes with a short sitting.

Rinpoche eventually canceled the Wednesday session. Very few people had been asking genuine, meaningful questions based on their own experience. It was a terribly sad missed opportunity.

I began teaching at the center soon after. Most of my students were people who had attended Rinpoche's teaching. I was appalled to learn how little my friends understood of the context of that summer's teachings or of the correct protocol for questioning and learning from a master.

The greatest advantage to living in Asia is, of course, the proximity and accessibility of so many great teachers. While living there, it is quite easy to form a close, ongoing relationship with a high lama and from him learn how to go about understanding buddha-nature. Since I had had that wonderful opportunity in Asia, and since it had become apparent that many Western Buddhists did not have a similar experience here in America with their teachers, one of my highest priorities as a teacher and Dharma friend has been to explain to students how buddha-nature is apprehended through the close guidance of a master.

In the first chapter, I talked about buddha-nature as ground, the basis of our being and the force that propels us into a spiritual life. In chapter 4, I talked about empowerments as a way to gain further or deeper insight into our true nature. But by now you may be wondering, "I never really glimpsed the ground before I started. Nothing much happened to me during the empowerment. What's he really talking about anyway?" Or you might feel, "Isn't understanding buddha-nature too advanced for me? Don't I need many years of strict practice, many years of philosophic studies, even to approach this subject?"

Actually, no. In fact, there are several traditions or styles for introducing the student to the nature of the mind. In one tradition, yes, lots of study is necessary. In another, deep meditative absorption is considered necessary. But there also is a third tradition where the introduction can be made early in the practitioner's career, and this one may be the most appropriate for the propagation of Tibetan Buddhism in the West. This tradition seems to be in accord with prophecies made centuries ago about the spread of the dzogchen teachings. It is in this tradition that I've been trained and it's from that perspective that I'm writing this book.

I'm not going to describe the nature of the mind to you. It's beyond my ability as a teacher. There are many excellent books in English on mahamudra and dzogchen. Great lamas are freely spreading these teachings. What I am trying to do is to help you relate correctly to your teacher. I hope to help you avoid a missed opportunity like the one I just related. Although I'll be writing in the context of receiving the pointing-out instruction, the teaching that reveals buddha-nature, what I will be saying will be of general use in getting instructions from your teacher on any topic. So please read the following with both purposes in mind.

How does this pointing-out take place? Sometimes a teacher will give you the introduction directly. That is, you'll be with him either alone or in a group, and he will do something to make you experience your buddha-nature on the spot. It could happen while taking an empowerment, especially during the fourth empowerment, as I've previously related.

There are more spontaneous, less ritualized ways for this transmission to happen. We've all read Zen stories of the disciple who attained satori when struck by his master. This has also happened frequently in the Vajrayana tradition. Naropa became enlightened when Tilopa beat him with his sandal. When this happens to an advanced practitioner, the experience could be permanent; the disciple is enlightened from that moment on. For the beginner the experience is most likely fleeting. After it fades, it is the student's life-long job to learn how to access and recreate that experience. As beginners we are granted these glimpses so that we can access them later in our practice so that we know what we are looking for.

We can't sit around waiting for the introduction to happen. The most common way for one to be introduced to the nature of the mind—that is, buddha-nature or rigpa—is simply through instruction, hearing teachings from your master on how the mind really is. It's up to you to clear away doubts and arrive at genuine experience.

For example, your teacher may say, "The nature of the mind is empty." Figure out what that means. Does it mean free from thoughts, blank? Does it mean nonexistent? Look carefully at your own mind. What does emptiness really mean? Try to experience it. Is it like space? Is it completely calm? Remember all the other teachings you've had on the nature of the mind, emptiness, or buddha-nature. What kind of experience are they pointing to? Do you have only an intellectual understanding? Even on that level, is your understanding consistent with all the teachings you've heard? If you've had some experience, is it consistent with all that you've previously been taught?

At this point in the process, one begins to form a mental image of what the experience might be like. Then, we try to actualize that experience. If we are able to do that, then we can see how it compares with what's been described. We have to continue checking and inquiring.

Are you starting to understand what's involved here? We have to assume that the lama didn't give this teaching just because he loves to talk or show off his own deep understanding. And I don't think you are any more stupid or less developed than anyone else in the audience.

So at this point one of two things may have happened: You've had some experience that you think or hope is *the* experience, or you haven't. If you haven't, you can report, "Rinpoche, I've been trying to meditate on what you said when you said, "Mind is empty." But nothing has happened. I don't understand—I have no idea what you're talking about! Can you give me one word of advice on how to proceed?" Then you take that advice and start all over. A word of caution: he may not answer you straight away. He might say that you have to do some other practice, such as the preliminary practices, to clear away obstacles to your understanding. Complete these practices to his satisfaction then report back for further clarification and instruction, for however long it takes. At this point you'll know that your practice is proceeding in the right direction.

If you had some experience, report back for confirmation. Don't assume you've understood. There are countless ways to get it wrong, and if you do, it will make the rest of your practice wobbly, since it will based on a wrong view. It would be like building a house on a rotten foundation.

When you report back, you can say, "Rinpoche, in your teaching you said that mind was empty. Since then I've been trying to meditate on your words and I've had the following experience..." It's very difficult to put these kinds of experiences into words, but please try; it's really worth the effort. Study helps here—it provides you with the vocabulary to explain yourself. So you might ask, "Is this really it?" He might ask you several questions, often to discern whether you're talking about a real experience or mostly mixing it up with what you've read or heard. If he says "no," "not quite," etc., then you go back to the beginning. If it's a definite "yes," then ask for further clarification, some instruction on how to proceed. Even if you have recognized and your teacher has unequivocally confirmed your recognition, there's still much more to learn. First are the techniques for repeating and stabilizing the recognition. (This is, of course, many lifetimes of work!) Second, there will be doubts, and you'll have experiences you're not sure how to categorize. "Was that last experience really rigpa? Perhaps it wasn't empty enough." This can go on for a long time. The doubting and questioning can start to become problematic after a while, but it's very necessary in the beginning to make sure you have it right.

There's a more elaborate and systematic form of introduction wherein the teacher asks the student questions and the student is expected to meditate until he reaches a definite conclusion. The teachings I mentioned at the beginning of this chapter were of this form.

The lama might ask, "What color is your mind?" You are expected to come up with an answer. You might say, "Blue," or that you were unable to find any color or whatever. The lama will then give you the next instruction in the form of another question such as, "Where in the body does the mind abide?" If you are diligent, eventually you'll begin to have experiences. This is the point. You can reply, "I was trying to ascertain the shape of my mind, when I had the following experience..." and then it's as described above. The questions are simply to get you to look deeply into yourself in a way that you probably never have; consequently, the questions, which were relatively straightforward at the beginning (I know that my mind has no color), become deeper and more difficult as you proceed.

Please don't lie to your teacher or try to impress him. What's the point? The worst thing that can happen is that he'd believe you. Try to forget what you've read. When looking at your own experience, formulate it using your own words; try not to use Buddhist jargon. Don't say, for example, "I've experienced emptiness," but rather something like, "I've had an experience in which my mind became vast and spacious." Don't assume anything. Don't assume you've understood. Don't assume the lama can read your mind and knows for sure what you've experienced, and so on. It is not that the lama doesn't understand or know what you are really experiencing; rather, it is that your assumptions make it difficult for you to be open and receptive.

This dialogue can go on with more than one lama, especially among those who have a similar approach to introducing you to your nature. This can happen in the West, where you are receiving guidance from various lamas as they pass through. Remember the three approaches to introducing buddha-nature that I mentioned in the beginning of this chapter? If you can, stick with teachers who share the same approach or you can become confused. If one lama says, "Mind is empty," and you meditate on his words and then later ask a lama who favors the philo-sophical approach, he might say, "You can't possibly understand the empty nature of the mind! You haven't studied enough yet. Learn Tibetan, study these texts, and this will lay the ideal foundation for you. Otherwise, you can't possible understand and you'll go astray."

The opposite can also happen. You can be developing deep concen-trative absorption under one teacher. He has said, "You can't possibly understand rigpa while you have a monkey mind. Your chaotic thoughts obscure your true nature, and if you try to understand, you will waste your time." When you report to another lama, perhaps a simple yogi, he might say, "Concentrative states are still dualistic and conceptual. They will only keep you in samsara. Go straight for the main point!" Very confusing, eh?

If you remember that there are these three main styles for introduc-ing the mind's nature, you won't get confused. When receiving teachings from a lama, ask yourself into which one of these three approaches his teaching mainly fits. If you recall, they were introduction through philo-sophical study, introduction through progressing through the stages of meditation, and the more direct style of introduction. Of course, this is a general guideline, and lamas are also capable of being quite flexible; they can often accommodate more than one style. In the beginning, how-ever, it's probably better to discuss the mind's nature with lamas who have similar approaches.

If you are receiving instruction from more than one lama, you can ask, "Rinpoche, when Lama A was teaching here last spring, he said that the mind was empty, and since then, I've been trying to understand, with little success. Can you help me?" or "I had such-and-such an experience during the empowerment last fall. What does it mean?"

As a matter of fact, this is what my teacher has recommended to me. "When you meet a great teacher, ask his help clarifying your experience of rigpa." Believe me, lamas really appreciate it when you ask sincere questions about buddha-nature that come directly from your own expe-rience. You'll make their day. They much prefer those kinds of questions to any other query. Sometimes my friends tell me that they feel shy pre-senting their understanding or experience to the lamas. While I respect their humility, there is really nothing better to discuss with them.

Of course, not all your interactions with lamas will be about the nature of mind. But the same protocol should apply. I've seen so much flakiness pass for real communication with a teacher. I'm not saying we need hours and hours to unburden ourselves completely in front of him. Perhaps a 15-minute interview will suffice. It should, however, be authentic. Use your time wisely; ask questions that come straight from the heart. Also, never confuse your fantasies and projections with what your teacher really said. As this is an important point and a mistake we all seem to make, I will give a few examples.

I first started studying Buddhism in Dharamsala in India. There was a class for Westerners at the Library of Tibetan Works and Archives founded by the His Holiness Dalai Lama. At the conclusion of each class, we would file out the door while bowing to the geshe who taught us. Sometimes he would smile at someone; often he would merely continue to prepare to leave. Among the students, this was taken as a form of divination. If you were thinking of, say, going to New Delhi for a break and he smiled at you while you were exiting, that smile would be interpreted as an approval of what you were daydreaming about—you could safely proceed on your trip. If he didn't acknowledge you as you were leaving, it was considered a "no"—sorry, no trip. I know it sounds silly (well, it does to me), but many people believed in this. The lama is omniscient; he knows what I'm thinking; everything he does is meaningful; everything is a teaching. Hard to argue against.

Recently, I heard a discussion between two long-time students of a certain lama. One student said that it's taken him twenty years to put together the pieces he's received from his teacher. He concluded that the lama intentionally only gives bits and pieces, leaving it to the student to put them together over time. I remarked that students traditionally studied many texts with their khenpos, doing nothing other than putting the pieces together. Is this something only for Tibetans and not for us? Do the lamas think that they don't want to make it too easy for us or something like that? Or is it that the student hadn't sufficiently communicated with his teacher, hadn't asked the right questions at the right time, and therefore hadn't made the necessary connections earlier? If I'm correct, then the student was projecting his own lack of skill in approaching the teacher onto the teacher and imagining the miscommunication to be some bizarre strategy.

Probably the strangest and saddest example of this kind of noncommunication happened to someone I knew in the East. He would ask his lama's advice, disobey it, and suffer as a consequence. He couldn't understand why his teacher was doing this to him! His logic: Because of the omniscience of the teacher, he would know my friend would disobey and had, therefore, advised him accordingly. That it ended in disaster was the desired result of the teacher. Why did the lama want my friend to be unhappy all the time? This logic was as unbreakable as it was bizarre. I always found it difficult to help him.

I suppose one could say that there are many subtle communications between a high being like a lama and his closest students. Students will report advice given through gestures, jokes, innocent comments, facial expression, etc. Maybe I'm just too dimwitted to pick up on them. But I've asked lamas many times about things like this, and they always express dismay at the way Westerners misinterpret their actions. My teacher Chökyi Nyima Rinpoche says it's frustrating for him to have to be especially vigilant not to say or do anything that a Westerner will interpret as a sign. If you think I'm wrong and that you are receiving subtle messages from your teacher, that he's teaching you something nonverbally, simply check in with him. Occasionally ask him if your interpretation of his actions are correct. You have nothing to lose.

One of the reasons I feel the material in this chapter is important is that most readers won't be able to spend all that much time with high lamas. Your one interview may be nothing more than a quick question while getting your blessing in a reception line. With the spread of Tibetan Dharma in the West, the lamas' time is becoming more and more precious; it is becoming more and more difficult to spend much time with them. So if the time isn't spent wisely, you may not get a second or third chance. Ask questions of high lamas that only high lamas can answer. Save your other questions for senior students, your therapist, or whoever you feel can help you.

One little trick I've learned is this: In teachings with question-and-answer sessions, word your personal questions in such a manner that they becomes questions of general interest. For instance, if I am seething with , I can request techniques for dealing with anger. If I feel my mind is opening up in some new and unusual way, I can ask a question, say, about the relationship of space to emptiness. Among other things, this has the effect of keeping other students from feeling that I am taking up the teaching time with my personal problems.

Basically, it's up to you to establish a dialogue with a good teacher. Never forget why you're there and don't lose sight of the goal—your recognition and stabilization of your own true nature. The lama is the only one who will be able to help you. Without him, you'll be completely lost.

☞ CHAPTER SEVEN ☜

Getting Started

Now that we've received instruction on meditation, it is up to us to get started with a regular routine. So in this chapter I will offer simple, straightforward advice on how to begin a regular practice of meditation. Sounds simple, right? But how many really do it? How many people really maintain a daily practice? Not that many.

I read an analysis of meditation instruction once. The author had compiled statistics on the percentage of students still practicing after a certain period of time. The figures were abysmally low, and he commented that no other field of instruction would find such a failure rate acceptable. Actually, I don't find it acceptable either. Many of my students tell me that although they started years ago, they were never able to maintain a consistent practice, so they eventually gave it up. Coming to my class was a new beginning for them—I can only hope they will continue.

I try to teach, and now I'm trying to write this book, in a way that warns students of the most common mistakes they might make and prepares them for as many of the difficulties, obstacles, and misunderstandings that can hinder or derail their practice. At times it will seem rather gloomy as I go through one thing after another that can go wrong, but I feel that the most useful thing I have to give my students and readers is the lessons I've learned from my own mistakes. If you can learn from these, your path may be smoother and more delightful. I hope the advice in this and subsequent chapters will help you avoid the pitfalls that have caught so many of us. I have included some advice that is specific to Vajrayana practitioners, but most of what is contained herein will be of use to anyone who is learning to meditate.

First, find a time to meditate. Morning or night, both have their adherents. Traditional texts generally recommend morning, although many of us are "night people." You should choose the time when your mind is most naturally clear and calm, your body fresh and rested, your environment relatively peaceful and quiet, and you're least likely to be disturbed. Don't be afraid to be creative—I just recommended to a student that he meditate during his work lunch hour.

Select a period of time for your meditation. Fifteen or twenty minutes is probably best for beginners. If you've read many books or heard many stories, you'll realize that the great practitioners of the past were extremely diligent and you might be tempted to emulate their example: "I'm going to sit in the full lotus position for three hours. Whatever happens, I'm not moving!" Forget it; that isn't going to work. No matter how strong, tough, inspired, or disciplined you feel you are, you'll quit. It'll just be too much for you. You won't necessarily say to yourself or your friends, "Gee, this is a little too much for me." You will probably just find yourself getting interested in something else.

I would observe the following so often in the East that I became sadly cynical about it: A newcomer would meet a high lama, receive some teaching, and then go gung-ho into retreat, frequently into some famous cave, full of inspiration and vowing never to quit. Without fail, after a while he would return to town, usually with some excuse, saying that he was now ready to practice tantra (meaning he wanted sex).

So think of meditation like a physical exercise. You wouldn't start off jogging three hours a day, would you? Follow the same common sense. Start slow, gradually increase, and build yourself up. Develop meditation muscles. With time you'll be able to sit for longer and longer periods. The problem is both physical and mental. If you force your body too much, it will simply be too painful—you'll spend your entire session coping with the pain. If you force your mind too much, either you'll feel burnt out or you'll find you've been daydreaming for the last fifteen minutes of your meditation session.

When I was first taught meditation, the instruction was that your meditation session should be like visiting a friend. When you visit, you have your cup of tea and you chat. If you're skillful, you'll end the conversation before you run out of things to say and feel awkward. If the meeting ends on an unpleasant note, you might feel reluctant to see your friend again. It is the same with practice—end your session before it becomes unpleasant. If you don't, you won't look forward to practicing again. Although meditation can often be difficult and challenging, view your session as a special time in your day, a time you look forward to with joy and anticipation. If you do this, your ability to meditate for longer and longer periods will develop naturally.

One way I've developed for monitoring my duration and exertion has been to ask myself, "Can I meditate like this every day for the rest of my life?" If I have doubts about answering "yes," then I know I am probably pushing myself too hard.

The next major consideration is place. Many people like to meditate in groups and that is fine. I know it is common for Zen practitioners to go to their center to meditate before work. I certainly admire that kind of diligence. For now, I'll assume that you'll want to establish a daily practice in your own home.

If you're lucky, you might have an extra room to set aside for meditation. That's great. If that's not possible, select a room that's already in use. Most people select their bedroom. Since we usually meditate either right before or right after sleep, it's a sensible choice. Also, since it's the room you've selected for sleeping, it's probably the quietest room in your house. Whichever room it is, it should be quiet, airy, and free of smoke.

If you really want to do things right, you can orient your house, room, shrine, or seat according to the traditional Chinese rules of geomancy, or *feng-shui*. You can consult books or find an expert. There are many, many rules, and some of the lamas, especially H. E. Tai Situ Rinpoche, place a lot of credence in them. His Eminence is the overseer of the Samye Ling Tibetan Center in Scotland where I did my four-year retreat. He made sure that both the building and individual rooms conformed to feng-shui. Doors were bricked-up and new ones built. A pond was dug. Shrines and meditation cushions were moved about.

One rule of feng-shui that I always try to follow is not to place my shrine in the direct line between my bedroom door and window. I try to put it in the last place I see when I open my bedroom door from the corridor.

Many people like to meditate with a view, perhaps looking out a large picture window. This sense of space can be very expansive and is especially appropriate for certain kinds of practices or to counteract certain hindrances (such as dullness or sleepiness) in your practice. Others will find this distracting and will prefer to sit facing a shrine or a wall. Of course, many people meditate with their eyes closed so that none of this matters too much. Lamas generally recommend meditating with the eyes open; however, my teacher says that for beginning practices it's acceptable to close the eyes. I personally find meditating facing my shrine too hectic, too overwhelming. But orientation is up to you.

Some people like to meditate on a special mat on the floor; others just sit up in bed. I've always meditated in bed; it's never seemed like a problem. Traditionally, of course, people generally didn't have enough room to meditate any place other than where they sleep. On the other hand, we can argue that the area normally associated with sleep and sex may not be the most conducive to meditative equilibrium.

I think you'll find that if you meditate in the same place every day, your seat will build up a very special feeling, some sense of power or positive energy. I usually don't notice it until I've been away for a while; when I return, my seat almost seems as if it were humming.

I strongly recommend having a shrine where you practice. If you're a Vajrayana practitioner, a shrine is a necessity; instructions for its layout are contained in the commentaries on your practice. A shrine creates a sacred space in your room—it uplifts you and reminds you of the spiritual dimension of life. It also becomes both a repository and generator of positive energy that will benefit your practice.

If you don't have the space for a separate piece of furniture, you can use the top of a bureau or chest of drawers. If you're doing a specific practice, the instructions will specify the shrine layout, but for now I'll give you the bare minimum. It's always nice to have the seven water bowls for offering. Traditionally, they should be made of the most expensive metal one can afford, but I've come to prefer the porcelain of Chinese teacups. You can also offer candles, incense, or flowers if you like. Next, place photos of the teachers to whom you feel closest. They will keep you inspired and motivated. And it's nice to have one nice image, either a *thankha* (Tibetan scrolled painting with embroidery) or statue of a buddha or deity, to remind you of your goal and to be a central focus for your practice.

The image should be clean and shiny; don't buy an old, worn-looking thankha or a dark, sooty statue. They might look like antiques, but they're not appropriate shrine objects. Our buddha-nature is not worn and sooty. Also, make sure it's a useful image for you. Is it a deity for a practice you've never heard of and probably will never do, or is it something more generic, like Shakyamuni Buddha, that will always be appropriate? The image must be iconographically correct or it cannot be blessed. If you're not sure, have it checked by a lama before you buy it. Finally, have it blessed by a teacher you respect.

You might also want to buy a rosary, or *mala*. There are many kinds, but except for small prostration malas, they should all have 108 beads. The best are bodhi seed beads, which are made from the same species of tree under which Lord Buddha attained enlightenment, or lotus seeds, which generally come from China. Different practices might recommend different types of beads, but one of these two will probably suffice for quite a while. You'll also eventually want to pick up a *vajra* (Tib. *dorje*) and bell. They should be bought together as a matching set. Other ritual objects can wait.

Now that we've discussed the time and place, let's talk about you, especially your body. Try to stay healthy. If you're not, try to get healthy. It's best to rely on more natural methods of healing if possible. Stop taking recreational drugs, especially anything that can be smoked—they're the worst. They block the subtle energy channels in a particularly pernicious manner.

Learn an appropriate posture. It's never easy for anybody and you'll have to put up with a wee bit of pain. But as I mentioned earlier, don't push yourself too much either. If sitting cross-legged on the floor is too difficult for you, use a chair. If possible, it is best not to lean against anything. Mantak Chia, a Taoist teacher in America, recommends sitting on a chair in preference to sitting cross-legged. So don't feel shy or inadequate. Sitting on a chair has become more acceptable as the baby-boomers age; temples and classrooms often have chairs now for those who can't sit cross-legged. Of the cross-legged positions, the full lotus position is preferred and in some advanced practices is mandatory. At least try. Other leg positions are acceptable. The most important factors are: You are able to sit comfortably for the duration of your session, the straightness of your back promotes mental clarity, your chest doesn't feel contracted, and you are able to breathe abdominally without feeling constricted. For the last, one needs loose clothing and a positioning of the legs that can be maintained without abdominal tension. For instance, the normal position Americans use when they sit on the floor, with their legs crossed in front of them and their knees slightly elevated, doesn't work well because it tenses the abdomen. Also, I've found that if people sit toward the front edge of their cushions, this tilts the sacral region forward and nicely aligns the spine and the rest of the body. If these postural factors are met, the energy flow in your body will aid the development of meditational experiences.

Many people seem to like these little kneeling benches. They are gaining in popularity these days, especially among those who have some physical problem prohibiting the cross-legged postures. I like them myself and really appreciate how positively they effect both my posture and my breathing.

Another consideration is whether to practice alone or with other family members. Once again, this is a matter of personal preference. I have almost always practiced alone and am very idiosyncratic, but I feel it would be both supportive and bonding to practice as a family. Practicing with another person can be a very healing experience. If it's someone with whom you already feel close, it will make you feel closer; if it's someone with whom you're having difficulties, it will help to ease those problems. It's hard to remain angry at someone with whom you've just meditated.

Having discussed the outer circumstances or conditions necessary or at least helpful to begin practicing, what then are the inner qualities necessary or useful for the practitioner? First is intelligence. Intelligence doesn't necessarily mean being brilliant or scholarly. In fact, overly intellectual people often have difficulty meditating. Intelligence means listening to the instructions, clarifying doubts and misunderstandings, and applying the instructions correctly. One must investigate one's own state of being and figure out how the teachings apply. Are you using the techniques correctly? Are you noticing your faults?

So many people I know never seem to resolve their doubts about the technique they are using, and so they settle for a very flawed meditation even when conferring with a teacher, even someone like me, could really be of benefit. I have had this experience often since I began teaching— someone will finally reveal a problem with a practice that he thinks is unworkable or is due to some flaw in himself. I will be able to offer a relatively simple and straightforward solution based on my own experience that very easily eliminates the obstacle. It's not that I'm a great or clairvoyant teacher—it's just that the error is so obvious.

A practitioner also needs faith or trust. In this case, I don't mean an emotional feeling toward the teacher or the Buddha. I mean confidence that the instructions will really do what they're supposed to do. It's like the trust a parachutist has in his parachute—he must have no doubt at all that it's going to open. If we don't have the same trust, we also won't be able to jump into the practice—we'll always be hesitating and hedging our bets. To stand too much outside the meditation watching yourself meditating is a big problem. It impedes our progress with our meditation. Too much of our energy is in the watching, which leaves little remaining energy for accomplishing the meditation.

Guru Rinpoche said that we should meditate in the same way that a sparrow enters a nest. A sparrow spends some time investigating whether or not it is safe to enter. Once his examination is over, he then enters unhesitatingly. That's a wonderful metaphor for practice. First clear up all your doubts about your technique, then throw yourself into the technique with no separation or self-consciousness. Of course, it's easy to say, but that is the direction toward which we should be moving.

Another necessary quality is determination. It's easy to gear oneself up for counting mantras or prostrations. For some, physical discipline is also easy. But the determination of the meditator is different. We must will be determined to strive to purify our obscurations until they're completely gone—in other words, until our buddha-nature unobstructedly shines through. When we sit, we decide to do our best not to be swayed by our negativities. We should cultivate this attitude at the beginning of our session. Otherwise, no matter how much we practice, we will daydream a lot and our meditation will always be wishy-washy. I know this from experience—I may do my session of meditation, but it is tepid. Why? I don't have that inner strength to remain unmoved by the arising of the various mental contents.

We also need some renunciation. We may not be able to live in caves or become monks or nuns, but we have to be able to start saying "no" to the distractions of our life. Otherwise, we'll never get any practice done. There'll always be something more interesting to do. We have to understand the impermanence and meaninglessness of most of what takes up our free time. In a later chapter, I'll talk more about the "four thoughts," contemplations to increase renunciation. For now it is enough to understand that some weariness with ordinary life and a willingness to give up a few meaningless things is necessary. Before we began practicing, the day had twenty-four hours and every minute was filled by some activity or another, whether working, sleeping, or watching TV. Lord Buddha does not have the power to add extra hours to the day; the only way to get any practice done is to stop doing something else.

Finally, we need an ability to face pain and hardship, to tolerate a little difficulty in pursuit of the ultimate truth. There will always be difficulties on the path. It's very important to understand that, in general, your progress will be directly proportional to your willingness to endure these hardships. There's the hardship of giving up meaningless but fun activities, the hardship of separating and alienating oneself from family, friends, and community, the hardship of the difficulty of practice, and most importantly, the hardship of actually facing one's pain and negativities and dealing with them directly. Deeper, there is the hardship of giving up the ego. This can often feel like one is dissolving or even dying; experiencing this dissolution can be very threatening at first.

The point here is this: The benefits of practicing the Dharma are innumerable and amazing. But for any one of them to be accomplished, we have to give something up. If we want to be disciplined, we have to give up some other activities. If we want solitude, we have to give up a little of our social life. On a deeper level, if we want calmness, we must abandon discursiveness; if we want to be compassionate, we must abandon aversion toward others. It's not going to happen that first you develop compassion and then that gives you the inspiration to give up your negativity. We must always take the first step, but once that first step is taken there is always some reward, some benefit. And that will encourage us to take that next little step.

A few words on meditation itself. Although there are innumerable techniques, especially within the Tibetan tradition, we can make a few general remarks for beginners. Whatever meditation you are doing, it will always be experienced in the following way: We are focusing on the object, we get distracted, we notice our distraction, and we return to our object. What changes with time is the length and subtlety of these distractions. This process is unavoidable and there are generally no shortcuts for making it easier. If you go to all the highest lamas and learn all the most profound techniques, none of them will tell how to recognize distractions sooner. You simply have to practice until it slowly improves.

That we all have some expectations of what we expect from our meditation makes it more difficult. When we find we are not doing much more than simply churning our thoughts, we can easily become discouraged or self-condemning. Don't. No matter how bad your meditation might seem, it's the effort that counts. Returning to your meditation time and time again will have gradual but very deep benefits that a beginner can hardly imagine. And self-condemnation, feeling that we're the worst meditator on the block and will never get it, is simply indulging in more thoughts.

The experience of cascading thoughts doesn't get the credit it's due—it's actually a fantastic experience that we must acknowledge respect and appreciate. From beginningless time all sentient beings have been completely identified with their thoughts. When they think, "I want a hamburger," for example, they really believe they want a hamburger. When we meditate, we progress from feeling we want a hamburger to knowing we had a thought about wanting a hamburger. Very, very different. I often call it a major step in evolution. The person who is aware of thoughts is a very different being from the one who isn't thus aware. The meditator who is experiencing neverending discursiveness has made a significant breakthrough in development. One is definitely beginning the process of freeing oneself from the power of one's thoughts and their inherent negativity.

Longchenpa summarizes the qualities of the successful student:

...the person who is going to experience for himself life's meaning
Must be one who has confidence, perseverance, and the desire to escape from his present situation and the feeling of disgust with it.
Wearied of Samsara, he must deeply concern himself with liberation,
Dismissing this life from his mind and looking to enlightenment henceforward,
Keeping excitement and distraction far away and having few emotions,
Being contented, leisurely, having visionary experiences, and being full of dedication,
Having a firm mind and a deep sense of reverence,
Such a person will realize most excellent liberation.[10]

Now you're ready to go. Please remember that it isn't possible to get everything right. Don't give up or procrastinate if your room is too noisy or you can't sit in a perfect position just yet. Not practicing is your loss. There is always some difficulty in practicing the Dharma; we'd all be buddhas by now if there weren't. If we put up with difficulties to accomplish the most mundane or trivial of things, how much more important is it to do so to accomplish enlightenment! So, if possible, perfect your conditions, but until then, don't procrastinate.

CHAPTER EIGHT

Getting It Wrong

When I look back on my twenty-three years of practice, I can't but help but feel deeply disappointed by how little progress I've made in my meditation. In a sense, I've done most things right—I've played by the book, so to speak. Why then have the experiences of meditation, so tantalizing, been beyond my reach? Don't get me wrong, it's not as if nothing has happened; it's just that progress has been painfully slow.

So what have I done wrong? Is it my fault? Basically, yes. I've zigged where I should have zagged a number of times. I haven't listened carefully to my teacher or neglected what proved to be a key point of instruction. Sometimes I simply didn't know the right question to ask. Luckily, I've had the leisure to flounder around for a while. Finally, I would right myself and bumble on to the next obvious pothole.

You may, however, not have the leisure to make these kinds of mistakes. In that case, perhaps I can help you by pointing out where some of these potholes lie for beginners. On your part, you have to check yourself carefully. You need to monitor your style of meditation and your attitudes toward your practice. If not, subtle deviations can creep in. They can eventually be noticed and corrected, or they can grow until they are no longer so subtle and can completely derail your growth. So I'll point out a few common errors now and a few more in a later chapter. It will be up to you to check yourself and try to let go of them.

We all have a certain style for doing things—how we drive, how we cook, how we dress. Some of us are shy or cautious, others assertive or flamboyant. We've refined that style over the years based on how successful it is, but it's not usually something of which we're completely aware. As long as it gets the job done, as long as we get the appropriate feedback from others, our style goes unnoticed, and when questioned we'll say, "That's just the way I am." When we begin meditation, it is inevitable that we will meditate with the same style with which we do everything else, because it's who we think we are. Furthermore, this style has proven to be reasonably successful in our other activities. However, in this case, it is not at all appropriate. If there is any style, there is a hidden agenda and an implicit judgment of the various phenomena of meditation. There is not the true detachment or choiceless awareness of real meditation. Our style contains our unacknowledged attitudes toward meditation. Also, a significant amount of energy goes into maintaining our attitude or style, resulting in less energy available for the meditation itself. This is obviously highly limiting to the progress of the practice.

For example, if you are aggressive and ambitious, you will meditate aggressively and ambitiously. This is not correct. It is not the same as being aware in the present moment. I've always been a shy person, so my meditation has had some of that timidity—a very limited approach.

Of course, no one is a perfect meditator. It's not like we have to wait until we have a perfect attitude before we begin. If that were the case, we would never start. This is in itself another obstacle—"I really want to meditate but I can't until my attitude changes." So we try the best we can but we don't want to be stupid either. Don't bash your head against the wall; get up and walk through the door. With time, the purity of your attitude will grow. The Japanese founder of Soto Zen, Dogen Zenji, often taught that practice and enlightenment were the same thing. "Perfect practice is perfect enlightenment." Not so perfect is very little enlightenment. From this we can see that refining one's approach is a lifetime's work and is at the same time the practice itself.

What's the problem in meditating with an attitude? First, a large amount of energy goes into maintaining the attitude. To make this clearer, if we are trying to be aware of our breathing, 100 percent of our attention should be on our breathing. If we're thinking, "I'm a shy person and I'm a little afraid of what's going on here," even if we're not consciously aware of that thought, it will be taking our energy away from the breathing and keeping it tied up in the world of ego. Consequently, this energy is not available for our practice. This also holds true if you're meditating competitively—you're spending most of your energy looking over your shoulder. It's like the old saying of trying to do something with one hand tied behind your back. You're trying so hard to be pure or disciplined or whatever, meditating assertively or cautiously, you have very little energy left actually to be aware.

With these attitudes you'll be heading in the wrong direction. Your evaluation of your practice and progress will be based on your agenda rather than on the Buddha's teaching. You'll be more interested in maintaining your flamboyance, for example, than in true spiritual growth. If your practice starts to undermine your flamboyance, you might feel you're doing it wrong and abandon it.

Last, to meditate incorrectly, with an uptight mind or with a particular style, creates a certain tension between your volition and the natural unfolding of meditation. When done correctly, meditation results in the unfolding of the mind. As it expands, its repressed contents come to the surface. But your attitude might prevent this. So you have this clash— the rising of buried feelings, etc., bumping into the harsh, unrecognized qualities of these various attitudes. These buried feelings are often the same ones that propel your incorrect attitudes to begin with. An aggressive meditator may have a lot of buried rage and pain that needs to be released in order to progress, but the aggressiveness will always be in conflict. I used to think my timidity was a lack of aggression, and I mistook it for true detachment. When my practice started to undermine these patterns by revealing them, I would feel uncomfortable and look for a way out.

You might find this discussion of attitudes threatening or insulting. No one wants to be told they're practicing incorrectly. We don't want to hear that we are uptight or repressed, that we are unskillful in dealing with our pain. We just want to continue doing what we are doing. But there's a Tibetan saying that the highest teaching is the one that reveals our hidden faults. So if you can be made more aware of your faults in practice and any mistake you might be making, it will only result in what you most truly desire—progress in your spiritual development. Remember, I know of these mistakes because I've made them all myself. Practice involves a radical transformation of our being, and we have to learn to face and eventually to dissolve all the attitudes we have about everything, not only meditation. So check yourself out.

This discussion may sound a little depressing, but I can assure you that when you can let go of these strategies, you will really begin to make progress with your practice. There will be a lot more space and energy in your mind with which to meditate and a growing sense of openness as you demand less from your practice.

With that as a lengthy introduction, let's discuss the faults themselves. Some people see meditation as a form of punishment or feel guilty about not meditating. If you come from a very religious upbringing, you might have this attitude. Meditation becomes a burden, a cross to bear. This attitude constricts the mind and prevents any joy from entering it. And guilt is very rarely beneficial—we usually feel guilty as a way to compensate for doing something we shouldn't have. "If I feel really bad about not meditating, perhaps that's almost as good as doing it itself." That's how guilt usually works. If you realize you haven't been as diligent as you should, don't feel guilty. Just practice.

Your meditation session should be a time that you should look forward to. Of course, there will be periods where sitting will be very difficult for you. Nonetheless, even the worst times can be experienced as a challenge, and the best can be a sheer joy. Don't make it into a punishment. If you think of meditation as a kind of punishment, a penance, it will eventually become one. It will become something heavy and depressing, and you'll have no option but to give it up. If you practice with a happy mind, you'll do much better.

My retreat master at Samye Ling, Lama Yeshe Losal, said, "If I were making you build a building, I could push you and, at the end of the day, count how many bricks you had laid. However, meditation isn't like that. Two hours practiced with a happy mind is better than sixteen hours practiced as a burden."

Don't practice to please or seduce your teacher. Although he'll express pleasure with your diligence, don't be coy about it. He's already enlightened; he's not really your proud father. You're not really going to hurt his feelings if you don't practice either. He's beyond all that. What kind of habitual pattern are you acting out with this one? It's almost impossible not to project your father onto the teacher, but it's up to you to be aware of it as it happens. We practice because our buddha-nature demands it; we practice to purify our minds and heal our being; we practice to liberate all motherly sentient beings. We don't practice to please anyone else.

Many people have very strong self-discipline to the point where they always seem to be competing with themselves. With some practices such as the preliminaries, where you have a set number to do, this attitude seems almost unavoidable. "I've done 300 prostrations today. If only I could push myself a little and do 400, I could be finished in March." I've counted how long I could hold my breath, how long I could sit in the full lotus position, how little sleep I could get by on, how often I lost semen in my sleep. So what? Does it really matter? Maybe a little. But the attitude becomes overwhelming. Everything becomes a test; everything becomes measured and quantified. If it can't be quantified, how do we know how we're doing?

The basis of this pattern is a separation of oneself into a good mind and a bad body. The good mind is always monitoring and controlling the bad body. "If only I could control my (fill in the blank), then I'm sure my practice would take off."

Of course, discipline is necessary. It's the attitude that's problematic. There's actually nothing inherently wrong with the body—it's just our temporary guesthouse. Our watching, judging mind is an altogether different matter. That is the real problem. This is exactly what we're trying to *eliminate* in our practice—not to glorify or worship. This kind of discipline trip can only reinforce the ego. Then, as your practice starts to undermine your ego, you are torn in two. Be forewarned—this could become very dangerous if carried to extremes. You might even become schizophrenic.

A very similar pattern is to meditate with a competitive attitude. The person next to you is sitting in full lotus, so you sit in full lotus. Your friend finished his ngondro, so you break your neck trying to finish yours. You might even do a three-year retreat just because others have done one. How silly. You might even try to accumulate as many empower- ments or teachings as your friends. I've noticed this a lot among Western followers of the Nyingma lineage—we're always finding out about new termas. Be the first one on your block...

Or we can compete with historical characters. All Tibetan Buddhists, but especially the Kagyupas, are inspired by the example of the great yogi Milarepa. His biography and songs have been available in English for a long time. When reading them, it's difficult not to measure yourself against him. But how much do we really know about him? What was a sane and successful style of practice for him may not be so for us, who are very different people. Also, did Milarepa practice the way he did to compete with someone else, or was his diligence a natural expression of his own character and understanding? Let our diligence be the same—a sincere expression of our deepest aspirations. Once again, practicing based on competition can only enforce our ego, not undermine it. Don't do it.

Obviously, another fault or wrong attitude would be to meditate chiefly for worldly benefit. You might meditate for the traditional bene- fits of long life, good health, and prosperity. Although these three are very helpful for practitioners, if they become ends in themselves, they become obstacles. Also, you could be practicing to appear more spiritual. Perhaps you'll have better luck finding a partner! You might want to be famous as a meditator. The needs of our ego are vast, and this list can go on and on. It becomes more and more subtle, too. An attitude that's appropriate for newcomers would be an obstacle for older practitioners. To learn more about this, please read that most excellent book, Trungpa Rinpoche's *Cutting Through Spiritual Materialism*.

Many people come to meditation to relieve themselves of stress or anxiety. As a teacher, I have found that students with this motivation usually don't succeed. There's nothing wrong with wanting to be free of stress and anxiety, but if that wish isn't conjoined with a sincere interest in spiritual transformation, it won't carry the student along. There are probably better ways (at least in the short term) of dealing with stress or anxiety, and an anxious practitioner might find that her practice simply throws her right into the center of her anxiety.

If I had to name one fault as the most prevalent and dastardly, both for my friends and myself, it would be using meditation to escape from pain. Let's face it, we all hurt. If not, we wouldn't be contemplating something as weird as getting involved with Tibetan Buddhism. Then we think, "If only I could find a nice peaceful space inside where I could hang-out, free from my depression, my sadness. If I were to meditate, I would feel blissful and would, therefore, have no time or place for the pain." Don't we all think like that? So we use meditation as an escape from pain. It seems we're doing everything right, following the instructions perfectly. We might even become successful in creating an inner sanctuary for ourselves. When we sit down, the pain and stress dissolves and we feel calm. We start thinking about changing our conditions so we can become even calmer and hurt even less.

What's wrong with this? With this attitude, we are never addressing the cause, the source of our pain. We are not purifying it, we are not understanding it, we are not transforming it. We are simply using spiritual techniques to ignore and run away from it. Your pain is still there. It will stay there until you decide to do something about it other than pretend it's not there and hope it will somehow go away. No matter how long you meditate like this, it'll catch up to you.

One way your pain might manifest is in psychosomatic illnesses. Your blocked energy will start to hurt your health. Another is through projection; you'll project your unfinished business onto others by judging them. I was celibate for a long time. Although this can be a wonderful discipline, freeing oneself to practice more, for me it was an escape from all sorts of relationship problems. I would, therefore, judge any noncelibate practitioner as not really serious and then feel myself superior. It was my way of not dealing with my issues. I feel that many of the difficulties at centers and of "Dharma politics" come from projections similar to this. It's especially difficult for people who are trying to be spiritual to acknowledge their anger; and as a result, that anger is frequently projected outward. Everybody projecting everything onto everybody else. What a mess!

Sooner or later something will happen that upsets your calm in such a way that you can no longer ignore your patterns. You start to see yourself for who you really are. It's very insulting. For me, it was doing a group retreat. Try living with seventeen other men in a very claustrophobic environment for four years! It is impossible to pretend to be calm and peaceful for too long. My faults would eventually annoy someone else; others' faults would always be annoying me. There was no place to hide. Also, you can no longer use the Dharma as a weapon against others—they'll throw it right back on you.

So when we practice, we must always practice into the pain. If you are angry, go into the anger. If you're depressed, go into the depression. It's the only way to purify it. Your courage and ability to jump right into your pain will determine how fast you progress, how quickly you heal. Remember, there's nothing really to your pain. What are its characteristics? Where does it live? What can it really do to you? Resisting it, trying to run away from it, gives your pain a certain solidity and a hold over you. A brave friend of mine repeats to herself, "It's only pain," almost like a mantra.

When we turn around and begin to face our pain, we discover there's really nothing to it. It's strange— from one side, it looks so solid and formidable; from the other, it's only a light mist. Your resistance is probably a remnant from an earlier period of your life when you had no resources to deal with it. You had no other viable options other than denying the pain or disassociating from it. So it just sat there in the back of your mind, seemingly out of the way but secretly running your life.

Things have changed. You're older, stronger, and wiser. You don't have to escape pain anymore; it's simply an old habit that you've outgrown. Now you have the best resource possible—the Buddhadharma. Now when we look at our pain, it may hurt for a little while, but so what? It slowly disappears, and we wonder what the big deal was. Each time we do this, we heal a little more. We reclaim a little more of our lost selves. We become more confident in our ability to cope with life. And our deep trust and confidence in Buddhism and the path of meditation will only increase.

At this point, we will be happy when garbage comes up, when situations provoke hidden flaws to come to the surface. We will have gotten into the rhythm of dealing with them, and each time we do so, our mind will open up more.

The reader might be wondering that if what I'm saying is so important, why don't the lamas speak of it more? When I last saw Chökyi Nyima Rinpoche in Nepal, I asked him about this point. He agreed with my analysis and added that lamas assume that when they teach the Dharma, the listeners will apply the teachings correctly to their own minds. It takes a while for the lamas to learn that Westerners are not necessarily able to do this immediately, that the issues of personal problems and woundedness must be addressed distinctly and explicitly.

As I have gained the confidence to practice in this way and as I have gotten to know more people as a teacher and friend, I have learned that we all have a tremendous burden of pain and unresolved issues from the past. It's not just you and I, it's everybody. We're all carrying this big bag of shit around. It's universal—nobody is special or exempt. Of course, we have a hard time meditating. Who wouldn't, carrying this bag? So open the bag up and go through it, turd by smelly turd. As any hiker can tell you, the lighter your pack, the faster and easier will be your walk. So throw away those turds! Why would you want to keep them?

Please check carefully. When any negativity arises in your mind, how do you deal with it? Do you use the Dharma to go toward it or away from it?

Related to attitude is our intention or motivation. Why are we really embarking on this journey? Why are we giving up our precious sleep to get up a little earlier to do our practice?

In theory, if we're Hinayanists, we are practicing to escape the suffering of samsara, and as Mahayanists, we are practicing to bring all motherly sentient beings to buddhahood. However, to develop even a sincere Hinayana motivation is actually very difficult.

The essence of the Hinayana view is egolessness. In other words, the Hinayanist meditates to unravel his or her mind in the same way that we might unravel a blanket until it is nothing more than a pile of yarn. Everything we think we are dissolves in that process. How can we, as beginners, possibly aspire to do something so utterly radical and seemingly suicidal?

For now, we must always check our motivation. For most of us, it is likely that our motivation is still quite worldly. Let's examine a few of these possibilities.

We may want to have magnificent experiences. If we took LSD when we were younger, we might imagine that the purpose meditation is to reproduce those kinds of experiences. Similarly, we may want to sedate ourselves. In the first example, meditation was a substitute for LSD; here it takes the place of alcohol, marijuana, or tranquilizers. We might want ecstatic experiences, cures for illnesses, or feelings of being loved by a higher being, or we may simply want to have a more relaxed, simple, mellow life.

Who doesn't want experiences like that? I sure do. Unfortunately, none of this has anything to do with unraveling the mind. It is simply creating entertainments for the ego.

Also, we could meditate to become a certain type of person or to fit a certain kind of role. We could meditate to gain respect, admiration, or power. We see this in the worst spiritual scandals all the time. People always ask, if so-and-so has been practicing for so long, how could he act this way? The answer is that so-and-so was practicing with the wrong motivation; he didn't check up, and he got the wrong results.

Here is where we need to think about the Mahayana motivation: compassion. We're not practicing to become rich, powerful, or respected. We are practicing to become the perfect servant of all motherly sentient beings. So the dissolution of the ego must be even more complete than in the Hinayana—we can't just sit back and watch ourselves dissolve. Toward the end of this book, I will discuss in greater detail the dissolution process and how it relates to our Western ideas of self. Here I want to emphasize that although we, as ordinary, flawed human beings, may have very real needs that we feel meditation can address, we can't separate our practice from the view. As we hear teachings and read books and contemplate them, our understanding of the spiritual path will deepen. We must take that understanding and work to bring our meditation in line with it. It's a slow, gradual process. A good motivation is a sign of practice; a truly compassionate or egoless being is already highly accomplished.

A more subtle or, one could say, somewhat more advanced mistake deals with mindfulness. Mindfulness is the basis of any meditation, tantric or not. If we're not attentive, how can we possibly meditate correctly? However, we can also make mistakes while being mindful.

If, when you were young, your strategy for dealing with pain was to disassociate, separating from your experience to diminish its intensity, then you may have developed a personality that observes your life rather than living it. In this state of observation, one does not feel one's pain. When a person with this tendency meditates, he will appear to be doing quite well and will always seem mindful, calm, and meditative. The fault here is subtle but very important as it applies to many of us. In a sense, we are too distant, too detached. Our detachment is based on fear. We feel that if we were to really experience what is happening, it would be unbearable in some way or other—too intense, too painful. So our detachment is not real detachment or mindfulness; it's a kind of habitual frozen fear or paranoia. We think we are being mindful and meditating in the present when in actuality we're fearfully disassociating and living in the past. We can go on like this for quite some time and in the meantime feel drawn to the Buddhist tradition with its emphasis on detachment.

Many of us Westerners are this way. I certainly am, although I'm trying very hard to break this pattern. People who are very cerebral or intellectual can be like this. We feel Buddhism gives us permission to be disassociated. Other people will see us as meditative and will compliment us. We'll feel we've finally found what we've been looking for—Buddhism will seem so right to us. And why? Because finally our negative patterns are supposedly supported. And meditation can serve to enforce this pattern almost indefinitely.

A good test to see if this applies to you is to check if you're capable of true feeling. Do you ever cry? How do you feel about your teacher? How do you react to the suffering of others? Can you love, be passionate? If you don't think your feelings are very strong, you might be this kind of person. You need to have a capacity for true, deep feeling and its attendant responsiveness as well as an ability for real detachment. Remember, true detachment happens in the present and is born of choice—you choose to observe, to be mindful. Detachment should be free of judgments, free of condemnation, and free of fear. Fear is something from which to detach yourself; fear is something to purify, not to indulge in as a kind of meditation. But you must be able to feel. Without an ability to feel you will never be able to generate compassion, and your development will always be stunted.

This is a mistake that takes more than noticing to correct. You actually have to try to be emotional! Whatever makes you feel, try to cultivate it. Notice how it feels to feel! Get a puppy, fall in love.

I will tell you the story of how I overcame or at least began to overcome this problem. It's rather long; I hope you don't mind.

I had been a fairly diligent and consistent practitioner for about twenty years before I began teaching. Also, I seriously believed in the value of living a celibate, solitary lifestyle. Underneath, however, I was quite disassociated, although I was hardly aware of it.

Almost as soon as I began teaching, I was approached by a very lovely woman who was seriously interested in my guidance. Her physical beauty was matched only by the beauty of her heart—I had never met such a loving being. I, of course, fell immediately in love despite every effort not to do so. I kept my feelings to myself but saw her quite frequently as we were living in the same small spiritual community.

How did I feel? Believe it or not, the unrequited love was wonderful. Although at times the longing was very painful and it was excruciating to see her with another man, it was the most transforming experience of my life. I was able to feel, able to love. The joy of opening up was far greater than the pain of longing. I was able to see all the negativity I held behind my veneer as a detached meditator. And I was able to let go of these negativities. I became a very different person—the change was also quite obvious to my friends.

Circumstances changed, and we started contemplating becoming partners. We consulted Gyatrul Rinpoche, who said to me, "You've lived in a shell all your life. You haven't hurt anybody, but you haven't been of any benefit, either. Now you have the chance to take care of someone." This was his commentary on my twenty years of serious practice!

Since we've been together, the shell continues to break. I continue to grow, and my meditation is also much stronger. I'm not putting down retreats or celibacy, but sometimes I feel that you truly have to love samsara before you can renounce it; otherwise, your renunciation is simply fear or aversion. So if you feel drawn toward celibacy or solitude, I'm just warning you of some possible hidden attitudes behind that attraction that could undermine your practice the way they undermined mine.

The opposite of being too detached is to be too merged, another common mistake made by Western practitioners. Some people identify or seem to become one with whatever they place their minds on. They are very empathetic with others. When this identification focuses on our inner world of thoughts and emotions, it can become problematic. Being too merged means becoming absorbed in one's inner landscape, the thoughts and emotions. The merged meditator becomes fascinated with the thoughts and feelings that arise through practice and prefers the fascination to true meditation experience. Wonderful insights keep arising! The time flies, and we feel we could practice all day. Or else we become intoxicated with our feelings. We wish we could stop sitting so we could write a poem about the weather, or the back of the head of the person in front. We could rush to our therapist and spend hours sharing our experience. Trungpa Rinpoche said the two groups of people who had the most difficulty meditating were poets and therapists—the two groups most identified and merged with their thoughts and feelings.

Another aspect of this fascination is what I call "emotional enthrallment." When we look at our mind, it is often in one of two states: a strong defiled state such as anger or anxiety or a prolonged heavy state such as depression, grief, or sadness. We become aware of this state (let's take depression as an example), and as a result, we feel that we are being mindful. But somehow the depression persists. With time, not only does it persist, but through our attention, we notice more and more about it and eventually start analyzing the various causes of this condition. We might spend a great deal of time discussing our depression with our friends, and we might even write about it. Many years of valuable time and practice can pass and be wasted in this manner.

The purpose of Buddhist meditation is to purify the mind of suffering (depression, etc.) and the causes of suffering (anger, etc.), but our practice doesn't seem to be working. We feel we are being mindful, yet the depression persists rather than dissipates. What are we doing wrong?

Our fault lies in confusing attachment with mindfulness. Of course, we are aware of our depression; if we weren't, we wouldn't know that we were depressed. We are not, however, aware of how "sucked in" or enthralled we are by the depression. We are similar to zoned-out TV viewers who are barely above the drooling state. Although we are aware, all of our power, life force, clarity, etc., has been surrendered to our emotion. Our depression has taken all our energy, leaving none for us, the supposedly mindful practitioner. No wonder the state persists and we are unable to do anything about it. We have been weakened and drained through our fascination.

Obviously, this is not the correct practice of mindfulness. What can we do? Based on my own experience, I can make several suggestions. Other practitioners can try any combination that they feel might help:

- First and most essentially, notice that you are in a state of enthrallment rather than mindfulness. Otherwise, nothing else will work.
- Rather than being aware of the emotion, be aware of the attachment to it. This will lead to a clear detachment.
- Be aware of the situation energetically. Breaking enthrallment involves pulling energy from the emotion back toward the aware practitioner.
- Try to create a spacious, clear state of awareness. Notice your emotion from that perspective.
- Try to visualize something—for example, a clear light or a letter in your heart. Notice your emotion from that perspective.
- Pray. Once again, notice your emotion.

With any of these techniques, the more correctly they are done, the more one will find the strength of the emotion decreasing. It will start to be purified. In the beginning, it will take tremendous effort to have even a momentary experience. But with that momentary experience one sees the contrast between the enthralled state, originally believed to be a form of mindfulness, and a more correct and pure state of mind. With time, it will take less effort, the positive state will persist longer, and the habit of enthrallment will slowly be broken.

Many times I've heard lamas asked why it seems Westerners make so little progress with their practice. Rather than talking about laziness, differences in upbringing, lack of faith, etc., lamas almost always say that Westerners are using their practice time for self-psychoanalysis rather than for correct meditation. As I've become more aware of the enthrallment in my own mind, I see how easy it is to become stuck for long periods of time and have come to agree more and more with their assessment.

Both the detached and merged attitudes have their positive aspects. The detached meditator has a sharp, nonjudging awareness. The merged practitioner has a greater capacity for opening ego boundaries and developing a sense of oneness and compassion. Both of these qualities are needed on the path.

As we practice, we'll notice more and more of these hidden agendas. They're all based on using meditation to prop the ego up rather than to undermine it. Each time you notice one of these mechanisms, you'll feel shocked and a little embarrassed that you have been fooling yourself. But once released, your meditation will deepen.

CHAPTER NINE

Systems and Stages of Practice

W y this time, we should have at least the beginnings of a relationship with a genuine teacher. We should have received some instruction and should be applying ourselves to establishing a daily routine. All that is general. Now I'd like to get more specific about Tibetan Buddhist practice, the Vajrayana or tantric path.

The teachings of Tibetan Buddhism are unbelievably vast. There are so many categories and lineages of teachings and instructions; it can be quite daunting for a beginner to try to sort it all out. But it's also quite essential—knowing the context of a teaching will make it much more meaningful for you. You might sometimes come across contradictions between the teaching you're receiving now and others that you have previously heard or read; such apparent contradictions can only be resolved by understanding the differences between the various systems represented. The three different methods to introduce the student to the mind's nature presented in chapter 6 can be seen as examples of this. In some sense, these three presentations can seem contradictory and it would be confusing to try to study a little of each approach. Similarly, different kinds of behavior such as drinking or sexual activity are evaluated differently in different teachings.

When you study them all, it starts to make sense. Teacher A prohibits drinking of alcohol. Perhaps he's speaking from a Hinayana point of view. Teacher B allows his students to drink a little because he feels it relaxes them in social situations and permits them to open up and bond with each other—he could be teaching from a Mahayana perspective. When you understand the "big picture" of Tibetan Buddhism, you realize how truly amazing it is and how incredibly realized the lamas must be to have grasped it all. Also, how kind they are to provide you with a teaching that's just right for you. Instead of feeling confused and overwhelmed by the vastness and complexity of the Tibetan system, we are actually incredibly fortunate to find a path that can be adapted to our exact needs.

Let's begin by looking at the basic divisions and subdivisions of Tibetan Buddhism. I'm not going to explain what everything means here; I'm only presenting the outline to give an overview. More traditional teachings and books will very clearly fill in the details. Some of the ideas I'll discuss in later chapters. You might find all the different names and lists boring or confusing; however, with time you may refer to this outline for clarification. Throughout the rest of this book, I will use many of the more commonly used Sanskrit or Tibetan terms of Buddhism; if both the Sanskrit and Tibetan terms are used often in common conversation among Buddhist practitioners, I'll use both. Please be flexible; even the broad divisions are not rigid, and the same terms may be used in different contexts.

First, the three *yanas* or "vehicles"—Hinayana, Mahayana, and Vajrayana. Hinayana translates as the "lesser vehicle," Mahayana, the "greater vehicle", and Vajrayana, the "adamantine vehicle." The *vajra* is an indestructible weapon of the gods; here, it refers to the indestructible buddha-nature. The word "vehicle" is intended to convey the meaning "spiritual path."

Hinayana can be subdivided into Shravakayana, the path of the listeners, and Praytekabuddhayana, the path of the solitary realizers. Together, Hinayana and Mahayana can be called the Dharma of the sutras; Vajrayana is the Dharma of the tantras. Vajrayana is regarded both as a subdivision of Mahayana or as a separate vehicle.

"Sutra" and "tantra" are often used to refer both to the spiritual approach and to the texts or teachings of the Buddha that discuss these approaches. If you wanted to learn more about Mahayana meditation, you would read a sutra; if you wanted to know about Vajrayana, you would study a tantra. We believe that both the sutras and the tantras are the actual words of the Buddha.

A chart of the various vehicles looks like this:

Hinayana	Shravakayana	Sutra
	Praytekabuddhayana	Sutra
Mahayana		Sutra
Vajrayana		Tantra

Chart 1. The Divisions of the Vehicles of Tibetan Buddhism

Paramitayana, the path of the six perfections and Bodhisattvayana are synonyms of Mahayana. Tantra and secret mantra are synonyms for Vajrayana.

People usually fall into one of the yanas depending on their approach to practice. The yana system of Tibetan Buddhism does not travel well to other Buddhist traditions. We might say that Theravada is basically Hinayana while Zen is mostly Mahayana. However, the point of our discussion is not to compare different forms of Buddhism but specifically to understand Tibetan Buddhism as a whole. The three-yana approach is taught within Tibetan Buddhism; the lesser yanas to serve as a foundation to the Vajrayana. It is not meant as a put-down of other Buddhist traditions by the Tibetans. Here in America, Trungpa Rinpoche especially emphasized the three-yana approach and felt that his students had work their way up through each vehicle. Some experience and understanding of a lower vehicle was considered necessary before a higher one would be introduced.

Many lamas encourage their students to practice all three yanas simultaneously—Hinayana with body, Mahayana with speech, Vajrayana with mind. In this approach, the yanas are not seen as mutually exclusive or contradictory; rather, they are interpreted as governing different aspects of one's spiritual life. Another chart:

Hinayana	Body	Moral discipline
Mahayana	Speech	Helping others through one's words
Vajrayana	Mind	Maintaining rigpa or pure perception

Chart 2. The Vehicles as Related to Different Aspects of Practice

To continue this explication, we have to mention the lineages, since their subdivisions differ.

As I mentioned earlier, there are four main lineages, or orders, of Tibetan Buddhism. The Nyingma is the oldest; it can be called the "Old Translation School." The other three can be grouped into the "New Translation School" or, in Tibetan, Sarma. Originally monks wore red hats; when the Gelug, the youngest order, was founded, they switched to yellow hats. You'll see this in the older Western books about Tibetan Buddhism—they talk about the Red Hat Lamas and the Yellow Hat Lamas. This division is hardly ever used anymore. Again:

Red Hat	Nyingma	Nyingma
Red Hat	Kagyu	Sarma
Red Hat	Sakya	Sarma
Yellow Hat	Gelug	Sarma

Chart 3. The Lineages of Tibetan Buddhism

Don't forget, many lamas will know more than one lineage and will teach from these differing perspectives as they feel appropriate. Kagyupas especially are equally well versed in the Nyingma teachings. As I mentioned earlier, my training has been in the Nyingma and Kagyu, and this book reflects my attempt to present a framework for their wisdom. A technical note: the *pa* at the end of many of these words means "one who" or "practitioner of." Thus, a Nyingmapa is one who follows the Nyingma teachings. The suffix *pa* is generally masculine; *ma* is the feminine.

The Nyingmapas divide all the Buddha's teachings into nine yanas or vehicles. There are also corresponding terms used by the Sarma traditions:

Nyingmapa			Sarmapa
Sutra	Shravakayana		Shravakayana
	Praytekabuddhayana		Praytekabuddhayana
	Bodhisattvayana		Bodhisattvayana
Outer Tantra	Kriya Tantra		Kriya Tantra
	Upa Tantra		Carya Tantra
	Yoga Tantra		Yoga Tantra
Inner Tantra	Maha Yoga Tantra	Father Tantra	Maha-anuttara-yoga-tantra
	Anu Yoga Tantra	Mother Tantra	
	Ati Yoga Tantra	Nondual Tantra	

Chart 4. The Divisions of the Nyingma and Sarma Lineages

Once again, this is not the place to explain the nine yanas in detail. I'm just trying to show you how all the pieces fit together.

In general, the Outer Tantras refer to the practice of the peaceful deities, who are usually without consorts, such as Tara, Manjushri, or Chenrezig. The Inner Tantras contain the wrathful deities and the deities in union such as Chakrasamvara and Vajrakilaya. A particular deity might have an Inner Tantra and an Outer Tantra representation; For example, the white, four-armed form of Chenrezig is an Outer Tantra practice; when Chenrezig appears as red with a consort, he's called Gyalwa Gyamtso, whose practice is from among the Father Tantras (in the Kagyu system). The most profound methods of Tibetan Buddhism, such as the *tsalung* (the meditations on the winds and channels of the body) and *thogal* (a very advanced Dzogchen practice) are contained within the Inner Tantras.

Not many of the tantras have been translated. The *sadhana*, or liturgy, for a particular practice may be available, but there are many other parts to the tantra. There will be numerous rituals to accomplish various activities such as long life or an increase of wealth, an overview of the practice with more general teachings, and the more advanced practices. So when you have a particular *yidam*, or meditational deity, you aspire to work your way through all its associated practices, not only the mantra recitation. It's a lifetime's work. Commentaries have been written by accomplished masters that give many of the most valuable details, such as what to visualize while reciting the mantra, how to begin and end retreat, what are the signs of success, etc. Unfortunately, most of these texts have not been translated into English.

The practices for a particular deity are divided into two stages. The practices for visualizing a deity while reciting its mantra are called *kyerim*. Kyerim has been variously translated as "creation stage," "development stage," or "arising yoga." Kyerim is the topic of chapter 15. When one has stabilized the practice, one moves on to *dzogrim*, the stage of completion or perfection where the advanced yogic techniques are practiced, which I will also discuss later. Different tantras emphasize different dzogrim practices; Hevajra emphasizes *tummo*, or heat yoga, while Guhyasamaja practice stresses a breathing practice called the *vajra recitation*. The term *dzogrim* can be applied to elaborate yogic practices or to simply resting the mind in buddha-nature after a period of mantra recitation. This dual use of the term *dzogrim* can be a little confusing.

Remember the four empowerments? They are derived from the Inner Tantras; they cover the different subdivisions in practice. The vase empowerment permits you to practice kyerim, the secret and wisdom empowerments permit you to practice dzogrim, and the fourth, or word, empowerment permits the practice of dzogchen, or mahamudra. Also, among the Inner Tantras, the different levels of tantras emphasize different practices: The Father Tantras, or Maha Yoga, emphasize kyerim; the Mother Tantras, or Anu Yoga, emphasize dzogrim; and the Nondual Tantras, or Ati Yoga, stress the mahamudra and dzogchen. In a chart:

Empowerment	Stage	Meditation	Emphasized by
Vase	Kyerim	Kyerim	Maha Yoga and Father Tantras
Secret	Dzogrim	Tsalung	Anu Yoga and
Wisdom		Union	Mother Tantras
Word or fourth		Mahamudra and Dzogchen	Ati Yoga and Nondual Tantras

Chart 5. *The Tantras and Their Correspondence with the Four Empowerments*

So, if you aspire to practice tsalung meditations, such as inner heat, you will seek instruction on a Mother Tantra deity; if you aspire to the Great Perfection, or dzogchen, an Ati Yoga Tantra will be best for you. You'll certainly find this overview more useful as you learn more about what the different entries mean.

Another very useful subdivision that you should learn is between the *path of skillful means* and the *path of liberation*. This is a division also within the inner tantras. The path of skillful means contains the more elaborate deity practices, tsalung, etc., while the path of liberation contains the simpler practices of *shinay* and *lhagtong*, calming the mind and gaining insight. These practices will be explained further in later chapters. Many Westerners don't feel comfortable with the complexity of the path of skillful means; they are drawn to the simplicity of the path of liberation. Both paths start with the preliminaries and end with mahamudra and dzogchen; they diverge, however, in the middle:

Path of Liberation	Path of Skillful Means
Preliminaries	Preliminaries
Shinay	Kyerim
Lhagtong	Tsalung and union
Mahamudra and dzogchen	Mahamudra and dzogchen

Chart 6. *The Path of Liberation and the Path of Skillful Means*

In reality, serious practitioners will practice a combination of both.

What is the normal sequence of practice for your typical practitioner? In the Kagyu, Sakya, and Nyingma systems, first comes the *ngondro*, the preliminary or foundational practices. The ordinary or common preliminaries are the contemplations of the four thoughts that turn the mind (see chapter 11), which give the practitioner the motivation and energy to throw him or herself into the practice. Next come the uncommon or extraordinary preliminaries that consist of refuge and bodhichitta (chapter 12), Vajrasattva practice and mandala offerings (chapter 13), and guru yoga (chapter 14). These purify obscurations, accumulate merit, and gather the blessings of the lama and his lineage. These four extraordinary preliminary practices are common to all four schools in Tibetan Buddhism. In the Gelug tradition, however, the practitioner can engage in as many as nine preliminaries, the abovementioned four, plus another five, which include Dorje Khadro fire puja, the purification practice of Samayavajra, and several others. Upon completion of the ngondro, one is given a deity practice to do (chapters 15 and 16). After that are the yogas associated with the energy systems (chapter 17). Meanwhile, the practitioner studies and applies the teachings directly related to buddha-nature, i.e., mahamudra and dzogchen (chapter 18). That is a typical progression in the Vajrayana. It is important to accomplish each step before moving on to the next. In the the Gelug, the largest of the traditions, practitioners often engage in the ngondro and deity practices during the time of their academic career; it's generally not considered necessary to complete the ngondro before engaging in deity practices. After that, the sequence is the same as the other lineages.

Vajrayana is vast. It's an incredible system containing an amazing collection of techniques for rapid transformation. In this chapter I've presented the bare outline of how those teachings fit together and correlate; in the remainder of this book, I will flesh out these charts. As you receive empowerments and teachings and begin your practice, this framework will help you integrate all this material and, with time, help reveal the underlining simplicity beneath all the subdivisions. *Vajra* refers to buddha-nature, and the Vajrayana is the path that constantly points to our buddha-nature and helps us realize it. All these different techniques serve only that purpose.

CHAPTER TEN

The Four Noble Truths

The life story of the Buddha always has something to teach me. It's amazing. Although I'm quite familiar with it, different parts will suddenly take on a new and deeper meaning. There's something universal in the story of the prince who abandoned his kingdom and luxuries to search for the meaning of life.

A few weeks ago I was preparing for a class, and I stopped to consider the part of Lord Buddha's life where he studied meditation with several renowned Hindu teachers without feeling satisfied. They felt that he had completely mastered the teachings and had become their equal. But he felt that their teachings did not lead to the cessation of suffering, so he eventually sought his own truth under the bodhi tree. The rest is, as we say, history.

The question that comes to mind is this: Did Lord Buddha discover a further, deeper state of meditation, or did he discover something fundamentally different? I had always simply assumed the former—that the Hindu teachers had only gone part way and had, therefore, failed to eradicate suffering completely. When they eventually arose from their samadhi, the seeds of misery would once again ripen, and the process of dissatisfaction would return. Buddha had, however, taken another step, one that rooted out all those seeds and from which no backsliding was possible.

As I made my lesson plans, I saw the story in a new light. Maybe it wasn't a question of one-upmanship, of going one step further. Maybe what Lord Buddha discovered was the nature of all states, that the state of the Hindu yogi and that of the ordinary person were fundamentally equal on some level. Perhaps the basic problem was the search for states itself. So instead of finding the ultimate state, the last state one could possibly attain, Lord Buddha saw the nature of all states and the basic futility of striving for one state while being averse to the state we're in.

This gave me a whole new way to look at desire. The problem isn't whether our desire is sexual or material, psychological or social. The problem is the basic dissatisfaction we have toward our state of mind and our desire to replace it with something different. From that point of view, those Hindu yogis had as much grasping as the greediest American, only they were subtler in their approach. Of course, I also saw my own grasping at meditational states, my own desire to "bliss out," to escape the mundane trivia of my own mind. I realized that the path could be one of completely accepting and relaxing into the present moment, even when that moment was a highly poisonous state of mind.

After attaining enlightenment, Lord Buddha began teaching. His first teaching was that of the *Four Noble Truths*. Most readers are probably familiar with these already. It's easy to understand the Four Noble Truths on a basic level. I've taught them to American high school students without a problem. On the other hand, thorough insight into these truths is tantamount to a high degree of realization. Thus, if we're really going to understand the intricacies of tantric Buddhism, we should start here, at the beginning.

The Four Noble Truths are: the truth of suffering, the truth of its cause, the truth of its cessation, and the truth of the path. I read somewhere that the Four Noble Truths follow the same formula that Ayurvedic doctors use when talking with their patients: the disease, its cause, its cessation, and the treatment. That's how Lord Buddha saw himself—as a doctor for the suffering of humanity.

We all have bad times. It's amazing how miserable we can be. Even when most things are okay, just a small thing can ruin our day. Lama Tsering said we are like someone with a beautiful cup who only notices the small chip in it. We're just waiting for the next bad thing to happen.

Suffering can be gross, such as when we're really sick or in pain, or it can be a very subtle mental pain. Whatever it is, we're not operating optimally, and the focus of our attention is not on the positive. We're like the princess with the single pea under seventeen mattresses!

Some people say that Buddhism is wrong for concentrating on this unhappiness. Chökyi Nyima Rinpoche replies, "If people were happy and the Buddha said they were suffering, that would be an error. But we should examine closely our real condition. Did the Buddha make it up, or was he simply describing the way things really are?"

What is the cause of suffering? Traditionally, the Buddha taught that desire is the cause, but there are many slightly different variations. Sometimes it's taught that the disturbing emotions in general are the cause; sometimes karma is also included. Chökyi Nyima Rinpoche often explains the cause of suffering in terms of the yanas: Hinayanists consider desire to be the cause of suffering, Mahayanists, aversion, and Vajrayanists, ignorance.

Perhaps these poisons are different aspects of the same experience. When we're experiencing some negativity, the awkwardness it causes is aversion, the yearning for another experience is desire, and the lack of insight into the situation is ignorance. Hence, all three poisons are present. For example, if I'm feeling shy, that feeling will be causing me distress. Why? Because I don't understand its true empty nature. That's ignorance. I will want that experience to go away—I hate feeling shy. That's aversion. I will long to be a confident, assertive individual. That's desire.

Nonetheless, whatever poison you are more aware of will color your approach to the path. If you are more aware of desire, you will feel more drawn to a renunciate's life. You will see ordinary life as an indulgence in desire and attachment, and you will always be trying to simplify your life, to find contentment in whatever situation you find yourself.

On the other hand, if you perceive aversion as the cause of suffering, your approach will be the opposite. Renunciation will seem like *avoidance*, indulging in aversion. You will try to lead a normal life and use the experience of work and family as a way of overcoming aversion and generating compassion. Retreat might tempt you, and it is always beneficial, but you will find normal life challenging, rewarding, and rich.

The Vajrayanist tries to overcome ignorance, the lack of recognizing one's buddha-nature in all mind states. This practitioner may lean toward a life of either renunciation or involvement and may occasionally become wild or nihilistic in an attempt to eradicate conceptual mind. These people, no matter how lofty their view, must also eventually settle down and apply themselves to the disciplines of the lower vehicles.

I think there's a little of all three in all of us. We don't really have to make any rigid classifications or barriers in our lives. In fact, we must always work on all three poisons, and we must always deal with any situation in which we find ourselves. There's no question that a simple life provides greater opportunity for formal practice and the cultivation of deeper experiences in our practice; however, daily life, especially its conflicts, gives us an opportunity to discover our blind spots, unconscious attitudes to which we are holding on that can block our meditation. Chökyi Nyima Rinpoche has always advocated for me a lifestyle that alternates between practice and being with others. With time, I have come to appreciate his wisdom. Each facet touches a different aspect of our being. So we can see that all three poisons are always present; all three poisons cause us to feel this constant dissatisfaction.

To repeat, the third truth says that the cessation of the causes is the cessation of suffering. Easy to understand, right? But when we practice, aren't we trying to create experiences (desire) or escape from our annoying present mental state (aversion)? It seems like we're doing it right, but aren't we really indulging in the three poisons? If we are, can we ever hope to attain freedom from suffering?

Milarepa said that the first main deviation for a practitioner is to drift into Hinayana quietism. I did it for years. I wanted a peaceful environment so that I could cultivate blissful experiences; I was lucky (or unlucky!) enough to find them in the mountains of India or living near my teacher in the Kathmandu Valley. When there was some disturbance,

I longed for an even quieter, more peaceful and removed environment. Rather than dealing with the disturbance, I blamed everything on the conditions—never myself. If only I could find a place free from mosquitoes, traffic noise, or whatever, *then* I could really meditate! Disturbances were to be endured with a sense of self-righteous patience, hoping to get back to the bliss as soon as possible. When some experience or conflict with a person intimated that I was still holding on to a truckload of neuroses, I avoided dealing with it and dismissed the problem as "only" psychology. I was above all that. I reasoned that if only I could stay in retreat and continue to bliss out, the problem would automatically disappear, that meditation in itself would uproot it. After all, great yogis who attained high levels of realization were hardly neurotic people.

There is both truth and value in that approach. It will work for some of the people some of the time. I certainly benefited from those years. But it took more active involvement with others, in a group retreat, as a teacher, and as a husband and stepfather, for me to start to confront my deeper layers of defilements. For me, these take the form of strong aversion, resistance, or negativity toward most people, activities, and situations. This aversion has hidden behind my yearning for solitude and retreat. By dealing with this negativity, much growth has resulted. And I'm not talking about a purely psychological or therapeutic growth; by dealing with aversion as it manifests in ordinary life, my meditation has deepened in a way it never did in a more idyllic retreat. Why? Because I'm working on the defilements that create suffering, and as they slowly abate, I'm experiencing a more wholesome and less samsaric life. From the outside it might seem that I've given up my practice and become more worldly, but internally I know I'm practicing more sincerely than before, that my practice is in harmony with the Noble Truths and not some sort of hippie fantasy.

I'm not putting down retreats themselves. Twenty-five hundred years of Buddhist history speaks for itself. If you have the opportunity to do a retreat, great. In fact, I would suggest even going so far as to take on some hardship so that your retreat can take place; that would be wonderful. I would, however, like to emphasize this: Make your practice harmonize with Lord Buddha's teaching, not with some idealized dream you have. In retreat or in the world, we always have to deal with our minds and with who we are. When in retreat, we are always longing for the pleasures of the outside world in the same way that many people who are seemingly trapped in endless busy-ness long for the serenity of retreat.

How do we eradicate the defilements that cause suffering? For that, of course, we need to follow a path; this is the fourth and last of the Noble Truths. The path can be subdivided into eight parts, which are called the noble eightfold path, or into three parts, which are called the three higher trainings. I will discuss the latter since it is briefer and I'm more familiar with it.

The three higher trainings are: morality (Skt. *sila*; Tib. *tsultrim*), meditation (Skt. *samadhi*; Tib. *ting nge dzin*), and wisdom, alternately called knowledge, understanding, or intelligence (Skt. *prajna*; Tib. *sherab*).

One can say a lot about morality. Western philosophers certainly have, and one of the main collections of the Buddhist teachings, the Vinaya, is a compilation of ethical *dos* and *don'ts*. Briefly, morality means ceasing to harm others and engaging in helping them. Negative acts are usually subsumed under the *ten nonvirtues*. The ten nonvirtues are divided into three of body, four of speech, and three of mind. The three of body are killing, stealing, and sexual misconduct; the four of speech are lying, harsh words, slander, and idle gossip; and the three of mind are covetousness, ill will, and wrong views. Greater detail can be found in many available sources; The *Jewel Ornament of Liberation*, mentioned in the introduction, is a good place to start. Also, we may decide to take the five precepts for laypersons: refraining from killing, stealing, adultery, lying, and the use of intoxicants. Again, more details about these can be found in *Jewel Ornament* or elsewhere.

Besides the obvious merit of not harming but instead aiding others, I think we can look upon morality as the first step in eradicating the poisons. If we can't bring our gross behavior under control, how can we hope to settle and purify our minds? Can we meditate well while stealing or cheating on our partner? Many nonvirtues require considerable work. Imagine committing a crime and keeping all your stories and alibis straight; when meditating, you would find yourself having to review them in your mind. So first we have to act in an outward way that conforms to our aspirations. We do so as much as possible, and as we progress in our practice, we will become aware of subtler and subtler aberrations as well as develop increasing strength to remedy them.

So we should check our lifestyle. Is it sane? Are we holding down a job, maintaining a stable relationship, staying healthy? If not, we are probably blocked somewhere. Many people practice with the naive idea that others will take care of them. Some people are lucky that way (I have been), but for most it is not going to happen. Don't regard those you meet who are wealthy and prosperous with greed.

We have already become somewhat familiar with the second training, meditation. Meditation consists of calming, settling, relaxing the mind into a state of serene clarity.

But that serenity is not enough. We need wisdom, prajna. We need to understand, contemplate, investigate. We need to know if our behavior is appropriate and that we are meditating correctly. We need to listen to and read teachings and clearly discern what the point is. It's not enough to receive teachings from a high teacher as if it were some foreign ritual where mere attendance assured benefit. We must listen carefully, remember as much as we can, check up with ourselves what the teaching implies, and integrate the knowledge with the other teachings and books we have assimilated.

I'm always surprised by how little most Westerners understand of the teachings they've just listened to. I'll leave a teaching and ask a friend for clarification only to find he doesn't remember the part I'm talking about or didn't get it and just shrugged it off. Perhaps people assume that the teachings are supposed to be over their heads and impossible to comprehend. Perhaps they see the teachings as a social event, a place to be seen and a credential to accumulate. Or perhaps they feel that the connection or blessing is sufficient and that clear understanding is not the purpose.

But I'm afraid that a clear understanding is, in fact, the purpose. All these teachings that are given by high lamas are for one purpose only, to benefit your mind, and they will only do that if you listen carefully and contemplate the meaning deeply. Many teachings begin with instructions on how to listen, explaining the faults in terms of the three pots. The student who is completely distracted during the discourse is likened to an upside-down pot; the student who doesn't remember to a pot with a hole in the bottom; and the student who mixes what he's heard with his own ideas to a pot filled with poison.

When you leave the teaching, discuss it with your friends. How does their understanding differ from yours? What did they hear differently than you? Be clear about how the teaching fits into the bigger picture. Was it a Hinayana or Mahayana teaching, one on relative truth or absolute truth, a traditional teaching or one specifically for Westerners? This is why I presented all the classifications in chapter 7; one must know how all the pieces fit together or they remain just that—pieces. If you have done all this, you should still have questions or doubts; if you haven't examined the teaching in this way, you probably wasted your time by attending the teaching or reading the book. With your questions, search out someone who knows more than you: a high lama, a local teacher, or perhaps a senior student whom you trust. Check those books sitting on your shelf. This process of understanding is endless but rewarding and enriching. Your insight will deepen and deepen, and you will begin to understand the underlying simplicity and logic of the Buddha's teachings. By going through this process, you will eventually be able to share your insights with others in a way that can really benefit them.

The most important function of prajna is in refining your meditation. Is your meditation going as well as it should? Do you really understand the instructions, the technique, or are you meditating with a sense of blind faith, believing that although nothing much is happening, you are receiving some sort of blessing that will ripen for you at some time in the uncertain future?

As I mentioned before with the teachings, I'm repeatedly surprised by how easily many of us will settle for second-rate practice. As a teacher, I've seen this often: While engaged in the practice of a meditation technique, a person will simply accept a mediocre experience of meditation, without questioning whether that practice could be improved. We would never do this with our other pursuits—if our car couldn't go over 20 mph, we would certainly get it fixed. Perhaps questioning would open too many doors: our own unwillingness to delve deeper into the practice, the lack of real communication between us and our teacher, our real aspirations and self-image as a practitioner, etc.

Never settle for second best. It's your meditation and it should be as good as it can be. You should understand what you're doing and why you're doing it. If you don't ask, you might stay stuck for a long time. That lack of knowledge could be what's keeping you from the very growth you yearn for.

Meditation is always a progression from stuckness to stuckness. We make effortless progress for a while, but we get stuck again. The more quickly one identifies the problem, of course, the more quickly it will be remedied. Generally, it is stepping back and asking, "At this moment, where am I stuck?" that will provide the clues you need to make the next step. All this is the functioning of prajna.

At its deepest level, prajna is what discerns *rigpa*—self-cognizing awareness of buddha-nature—from its opposite, *marigpa*—ignorance or, more precisely, the lack of recognition of buddha-nature. Through insight and the application of all that you have read and heard, you evaluates your experience to determine whether genuine realization has arisen. Without a sufficient effort in study, you will not be able to recognize buddha-nature without hesitation nor will you be able to communicate your understanding or lack of it to your teacher.

All of these examples show the use of wisdom, which is perhaps the single most important cause of enlightenment. It should be clear by now that neither morality nor meditation on their own are sufficient to progress very far on the path. However, with these three—morality, meditation, and wisdom—the path can be traversed, the causes of suffering eradicated, and the cessation of suffering approached.

CHAPTER ELEVEN

The Four Thoughts

Kalu Rinpoche was considered by many, including His Holiness Karmapa, to be a fully enlightened buddha. He was often compared to Tibet's greatest and most famous yogi Milarepa, having spent twenty-seven years in retreat, both in solitude and later leading group retreats at Palpung Monastery.

I met him at his monastery in Sonada, near Darjeeling in northeast India. At an altitude of 7,000 feet, the almost constant thick fog obscured any of the available views. The spiritual atmosphere was similar; one could feel Kalu Rinpoche's power as a constant strong presence like being in a magnetic field.

Almost every day he would teach whatever Westerners were gathered there. One day, he began his talk, "Just up the hill is our monastery's retreat center, and there are a group of monks diligently engaged in a three-year retreat. Right now, they are practicing dream yoga, which means they are training to be consciously aware in their dreams so that they can manipulate and even develop the ability to go to the pure lands and see the buddhas and receive teachings from them."

"Oh boy!" I thought. "This is going to be great! From Tibet's greatest living yogi, I'm going to receive some really juicy teachings!" I was completely awake and attentive.

He continued: "Their ability to practice dream yoga is based on their practice of *tummo*, inner heat. That practice is based on their deity practice, and that is based on having completed the preliminaries, the ngondro. That, again, is based on only one thing: their understanding of the four thoughts that turn the mind. So today that is what I will talk about: the four thoughts that turn the mind!"

Actually, that is what he talked about every day, and I was getting bored. I wanted the deep and esoteric stuff. Nobody wants to hear about the different hells over and over again.

But hear about them we must. Kalu Rinpoche knew what he was doing, and he was exactly right in his talk; all subsequent progress is based on one thing and one thing only: your realization of the four thoughts that turn the mind.

You might already be familiar with these contemplations. If not, there are many excellent books that contain extensive discussions of them. Both *Jewel Ornament* and Paltrul Rinpoche's *Words of My Perfect Teacher* contain excellent material on them. I won't do that here; I just want to highlight some points and perhaps point out some areas where Westerners get stuck.

First, what are the four thoughts? They are: precious human rebirth, death and impermanence, karma and its result, and the suffering of samsara. The basic logic of these thoughts is that we now have a wonderful opportunity to practice the Dharma, but it won't last very long. Death will come soon, and unless we've practiced a lot, it will most likely propel us into a rebirth a lot more miserable and longer lasting than what we experience now (which isn't all that great anyway) due to all the negative karma we've accumulated in both this life and others. Therefore, we must be extremely diligent in our practice if we don't want this to befall us.

This argument is very persuasive if one is raised in an Asian culture with the appropriate belief system. Otherwise, it's not so convincing. So when I teach the four thoughts, I always introduce the hidden assumptions first. If we can accept these assumptions, the subsequent presentation of the four thoughts themselves will have much more power.

I feel there are three main assumptions: rebirth or reincarnation, the law of karma or cause and effect, and the existence of realms invisible to us. None of these three can be logically, rigorously proved, but if we allow ourselves to examine them, I'm sure they will seem sensible.

Also, there is one main belief that many intelligent people in our culture hold that limits their ability to accept these arguments: That belief is that the mind is something like a biochemical computer, that we are really our brains and all mental experience can simply be reduced to physical or chemical activities. Thus, when the body dies, so do we. This view has great appeal, especially as more and more is learned about the brain. However, we are dealing with reductionist reasoning here. This is not the place to try to refute this view. Let me just advise adherents that reductionism itself is a belief, not something provable, and that clinging to it will be a great detriment to delving deeper into spiritual topics. Remember our discussion of buddha-nature in the first chapter? To what can buddha-nature be reduced? Neurotransmitters? Quarks? If you happen to be someone who holds strongly to this materialist view, please at least be willing to question it or suspend it for a while.

It's been almost thirty years since I received my degree in science, but I like to keep up by reading popular books by leading physicists. None of them seem to adhere to a reductionist perspective. For a physicist, this perspective would translate into something like, if we could understand all the quarks in your brain, we would know everything about your personality (very simply put). Most of the recent discoveries and theories in physics seem to contradict reductionism. The reductionist point of view is more an unexamined common view of our culture rather than a correct interpretation of modern physics. I hear it more from my kids' middle school teachers than from leading physicists. So it might be a good idea to consider dropping it if you find yourself thinking strongly along those lines.

I'm sure we all know what rebirth means. It seems pretty weird at first, the idea that we go from life to life, body to body. It's hard to imagine being reborn as a fish or that the dog keeping you awake at night with its incessant barking could be the rebirth of your Uncle Irving. But weirdness isn't refutation, and neither is the lack of remembrance, which is often cited as an argument against reincarnation. We are also unable to remember deep sleep or being in the womb, yet no one would dispute that these events occur.

What are the reasons to accept this belief in rebirth? First, highly realized beings assure us that it is so. This is not a proof, of course, but neither have most of us personally proven that the speed of light is 186,000 miles per second. We believe it because we trust the intelligence, integrity, and expertise of the scientific community. The Buddhist community has the same qualities within their field of expertise, which is the mind. In my opinion Buddhist scholars and teachers have repeatedly demonstrated their trustworthiness. Nothing is accepted by lamas on faith; many of them just love to debate. It's quite embarrassing to consider yourself reasonably intelligent, as I do, and then to be defeated in a simple debate by someone who hardly speaks English. With this kind of refinement of their discriminating, critical faculties, any major flaws in their doctrine would have been discovered ages ago. I think we can believe what they say about such a basic principle.

Second, many people remember their past lives. Although most don't, that's hardly a rebuttal against those who do.

Who remembers past lives? We probably all know some very open person, perhaps someone who is generally psychic, who speaks of his or her past lives. That might not be very convincing. People have remembered their past lives through hypnosis and have even described buildings that were at that time buried but upon excavation corresponded exactly to the descriptions. Many children remember their past lifetimes, and this has also been carefully tested and documented. Professor Ian Stevenson, in his books such as *Cases of the Reincarnation Type*, has devoted considerable research to investigating claims of young children regarding memories of past lives. And, of course, practitioners and realized beings remember theirs relatively routinely. We all know the story of how the Dalai Lama's recognition is confirmed by his recognizing his possessions from the past. Some tertons remember whole teachings from previous lifetimes. The opposite is also true: Some lamas predict exactly where they will be reborn, and it always results in the discovery of a remarkable child.

There is also a subtle argument that I once read that was presented by the Dalai Lama. It is convincing to me, but somehow it rarely seems to touch others with whom I share it. (Could it be that I'm not His Holiness?) But anyway, here it goes. If we examine the mind, does it have shape or color? Does it have any discernible physical qualities? Some reflection reveals that no, the mind has no physical qualities and, in fact, resembles space. This argument relates very much to the above discussion of the brain. If you firmly grasp the belief that the mind is simply the brain, this argument will seem very obtuse to you. If you directly ascertain that the mind is indeed formless like space, the remainder of the argument will make sense. So one must look directly at the mind rather than just repeating beliefs.

If the mind is like space, what could cause it to come into existence? Can the union of our mother and father bring something like space into existence? If you answer "yes," then there is no relationship between a cause and its effect. If parents can cause something like space to be created, then anything could cause anything else to arise. There would be no rhyme or reason to our world or our experience. A little reflection reveals that there must be some similarity between a cause and its effect. Sheep always give birth to sheep, rabbits to rabbits. What can give birth to something space-like?

The answer is nothing. There is nothing material in our world that could possibly be the cause of our space-like mind coming into existence. Therefore, our mind has always existed (it's the only other option) and will always exist. Even more precisely, we can say that not even this mind is permanent but is a momentary phenomenon caused by the previous momentary mind. Of course, that mind was caused by the mind one moment before it, and so on, since beginningless time. I've found that if one believes in either one permanent mind from beginningless time or a succession of momentary minds from beginningless time one will be able to grasp further arguments although the latter view if most likely closer to the truth. Once we accept the logic of this, it's easy to see how the mind merely identifies with each life's body from birth to birth, endlessly, until it realizes its own true nature.

Of course, on a gross level there is some connection between the mind and the body it inhabits. We're not happy when we're sick. In addition, I don't experience your body's pain in the same way that I experience mine, for example. But again, if we didn't have some sense that there was something deeper to our nature, something more basic and profound than the body-mind connection, we probably wouldn't have developed an interest in Tibetan Buddhism. We should consider whether the relationship between our mind and body is immutable, or whether it is something based on habit and open to change.

What propels this mind, and what gives it its unending display of myriad experiences? Karma. Karma means activity; when we do something either with body, speech, or mind, it creates causes that we will later experience as effects. This law cannot be proved. Although the word *karma* is used quite often now in everyday English, it's really the most difficult concept in Buddhism to comprehend. Lord Buddha himself said that karma was more difficult to understand than emptiness; emptiness can be logically demonstrated, karma cannot. A total understanding of karma exists only in the mind of a fully enlightened being. But simply put, all we need to trust here is this: Virtuous actions of body, speech, and mind will yield positive results; nonvirtuous actions will yield negative ones. That's it.

Once again, we can accept this through trusting our teachers and because it seems sensible. How else can we give some meaning or value to the countless types of experience people have? How else can we view the patterns that flow through our lives and gain some acceptance and understanding as well as perhaps some meaning and direction? To develop more faith in karma, one can examine the way life experiences unfold for people. Is it coincidence, or is there a deeper underlying cause? Consider, for example, identical twins. They have the same upbringing and the same genes. However, their lives can often be quite different from each other. Another example: Someone quite close to me was once accused of a very serious crime, simply because of being "in the wrong place at the wrong time." If he hadn't stopped to urinate, the police would never even have known he existed. We all know of many cases like this. They can never prove karma, but at least to me, they make it seem very sensible.

The third assumption that may cause us trouble is the belief in realms or kinds of beings that are at present invisible to us. As we gain more and more scientific knowledge of the universe, none of these realms have been discovered. Also, many of them seem quite fanciful to us; for instance, we talk about beings who live in the clouds and live off odors. The variety of beings like this is almost endless. They are generally invisible to us, but some have the ability to interfere with our lives in one way or another. When I lived in Britain, I was amazed at the number of stories people told: fairie circles, haunted houses, unhappy spirits in the woods, and so on. The storytellers were all convinced of the veracity of their stories, and the tellers themselves were always credible. One teller was an Olympian wrestler turned plumber, a man of incredible strength and gentleness whose down-to-earth manner made his experiences completely believable.

In Buddhism, especially Tibetan Buddhism, we are presented with a vast array of nonhuman beings—gods, ghosts, water-spirits, smell-eaters, etc. At the end of most Mahayana sutras, some of these types of beings in Lord Buddha's audience voice their approval of the teaching and vow their willingness to embrace it and protect others who also practice it. In tantra, nonhuman beings are referred to even more frequently. Various tormas are offered to a wide variety of spirits and gods. And in both sutra and tantra, pure lands or buddha-fields are frequently mentioned.

Once again, we might find this difficult to believe. Where are these beings? If they can influence our lives, why can't we see them? Where are the hells and pure lands? Are the hells in the hot core of the earth; are the pure lands somewhere in outer space?

None of this can be easily understood if we grasp solidly to this world as being real and concrete. If for a moment we can accept the primacy of mind, we might be able to understand how the mind could create any of an infinite variety of worlds, beings, and types of experience. Could you dream of being in hell? In a pure land? That's not so difficult to accept. The next question is the obvious one—what's the difference then between waking and sleeping? If you can demonstrate some real fundamental difference, the other realms of being might seem implausible, but if waking and dream are basically similar in nature, then it's easy to understand how other realms can exist: We simply dream them.

I tend to think of these various realms like different TV channels. None of the channels is more real than the others. The events on one channel have no spatial relationship to the events on another; the characters in the soap opera cannot influence the basketball games I'm fond of watching. This makes it easier for me to imagine that there are different realms filled with many kinds of beings, each realm existing with its own space and time.

Therefore, if we can resolve our doubts about rebirth, karma, and other realms, contemplating the four thoughts will have real power. With these assumptions cleared up, we can talk more about the thoughts themselves.

As I mentioned before, the first of the four thoughts is the contemplation of the precious human birth. That does not necessarily imply that being human is in itself precious; rather, there's a subset of human beings that is called precious. Why? Because these lucky few, including you and me, have the opportunity to follow the Buddhist path and reach a state free from suffering. That's precious!

We take so much for granted. You go to a bookstore and buy a book of profound teachings; you drive into town and receive an empowerment from a very special lama. It seems to happen with so little effort. How can this be special? Perhaps your seat wasn't so good during the empowerment, or your mind drifted due to a fight you had earlier at work. It can seem like no big deal.

But it is. How many beings have the opportunity to participate in something like an empowerment? How many different causes and conditions must come together for this to happen? If you had simply been born one generation earlier, the chances of your receiving a tantric empowerment would have been very slim indeed. Do any of your friends or family have any interest, even though it's just a short drive and a few dollars? "But Mom, if you take this empowerment you'll never have to be reborn in lower realms again!" Does she believe you? Does she care?

So you have to be at the right place at the right time with all the right internal qualities. If the place is wrong, it won't happen. No matter how ripe you are, you're not getting any empowerment in Iran. You also wouldn't have been able to receive any empowerment in the West only a short time ago. Fifty years ago Tibet was perfect; a hundred years ago so was China. Now in both places it's very difficult. Due to politics, circumstances have changed. Who knows when or where it will change next?

And you must have the interest, the leisure, and the intelligence to benefit from your external circumstances. If you don't care, are too busy, or are not bright enough to understand, it also won't happen. Traditionally, there are eighteen circumstances and qualities like those I've mentioned; if just one is missing, forget it. No path, no practice, no chance to escape from the terrible sufferings of cyclic existence. An incredible, mind-boggling confluence of conditions must come together to produce the very life we have right now. It is indeed rare and precious.

No matter how wretched our life seems, we have that chance. I remember being in my cloistered group retreat feeling very sick and very sorry for myself. I kept comparing myself to all the other men who seemed healthy and strong enough to glide through the physical demands of such a strict retreat. But after contemplating the precious human birth, I was quite humbled. Compared to the most glorious, exalted worldly life, mine was much better. I had a chance to reach permanent happiness and do something completely meaningful for both others and myself. What did it matter if I was sick?

How often do we whine, if not to others, at least within our own thoughts? But we have the precious jewel of this life, a chance to progress on the spiritual path. We may feel our conditions aren't perfect, but were they ever? They're good enough. Who doesn't have the opportunity to be mindful during the day, to silently intone OM MANI PADME HUM as we go through our activities?

Being as plugged into the world as we are gives us manifold opportunities to consider our lives. Whenever I watch a movie or read the news, I become acutely aware of how different life can be. I could be a refugee in Rwanda, moving in a human wave of a million destitute persons, with no real place to go. Am I really better or different than those poor folks? I just feel very lucky.

Or watching movies...I recently saw the film *Braveheart* for the first time. Imagine living in a place where your wife gets raped by the local ruler. Could I maintain my mindfulness? Could I control my anger and refrain from nonvirtue? If someone approached me and told me to watch my mind or to pray to Guru Rinpoche, would I have the reason to listen?

Needless to say, there are countless opportunities to reflect like this. Be happy to be alive, to be able to think, to be aware, and to love. It's an amazing situation. Life can be hard, and I'm no stranger to self-pity either. But waking up is worth it all.

Unfortunately, this amazing opportunity will not last long. We will die.

Traditionally, death contemplation has three parts: the certainty of death, the uncertainty of the time of death, and that only Dharma will be of help when one dies. The first two seem obvious enough. None of us knows anyone who is approaching immortality, and we all know of people who have died young, suddenly and unexpectedly. But do we live our lives in harmony with that understanding? If you examine what you've done today, what would you have done differently if you knew you were going to die in a year, a month, a week, a day? Many of us have friends who, when they found out they had a fatal illness, became diligent practitioners.

We had someone like that in retreat. Al had been a long-time student of Akong Rinpoche in Scotland, but he had never practiced much. However, when he was diagnosed as having colon cancer with only a few months to live, he was admitted to our retreat even though it was already in progress. He practiced very diligently and was extremely grateful for every day he had. When he died, he left us cheerfully and with love. Both Akong Rinpoche and H. E. Tai Situ Rinpoche were there with him with prayers and blessings. He was a true inspiration to us all.

But it's always "not me." It's always the other guy who gets cancer, isn't it? Recently, someone at our center came down with a very vicious cancer, and that's exactly what he said: "I always thought these things happened to someone else."

As my mom got older, she moved to a senior citizen's apartment in Sacramento, California. It was run by a Jewish agency under HUD, and most of the residents were Jewish ladies. Being a good Jewish son and feeling more than a little guilty for all the time spent abroad away from my mother, I visited her often.

It was a pleasant and well-managed place with many caring people on the staff. Most of the residents were still healthy although I'm sure they all had their aches and pains. But the sense of meaninglessness and depression was palpable. People seemed to be just sitting around, waiting to die. Very little seemed to interest anyone. They had no Dharma, something that could give both their lives and their deaths meaning. Although they had every reasonable comfort Western society can provide, they were lacking in this one thing. I vowed that this would never happen to me, that I would never abandon the one thing that gives my life meaning and value, while also preparing me for death.

On the other hand, in the East I've been acquainted with older Tibetans, both lay and ordained, who, although they were both ill and destitute, faced death joyfully because they had their practice and an unwavering faith in the power of the Three Jewels. When I was living in Kathmandu in the eighties, my cook told me about her mother. Her mother lived in her attic, eating one meal a day and reciting *mani* eighteen hours a day! Who do you think was more prepared for death, that woman or my mother and her friends in Sacramento?

It's especially difficult to take death seriously in this country. I just heard of a luxurious senior condominium where those needing care are placed in the basement where the others can't see them. Prospective buyers are not shown that part! Television shows and movies are filled with young, beautiful people. We're always trying to look younger. As Albert says in the movie *The Birdcage*, "When you say I look good, what you really mean is that I look young. When you say I look tired and need a rest, what you mean is that I look old and am no longer attractive."

Inwardly, we defend against death by the very structure of our ego. Our ego claims to have the ability to provide us with happiness based on its belief in its own permanent existence. On the one hand, to believe in ego results in denying death. On the other, to accept death is to question the very nature of ego as a permanent, on-going structure and to confront very strong defense mechanisms. As a result, we have strong resistance to contemplating death. This resistance is also the same resistance that comes up when we meditate. Please recognize it for what it is and move on.

What happens when we die? We are no longer grounded by being in a body; we are blown along by the winds of karma. If we have acted virtuously, we will have positive results; nonvirtuous behavior will result in negative results. So we need to check up: What actions have predominated in this life? Have our actions been motivated by positive mental states, or have most our actions been propelled by desire, anger, and ignorance? I don't know about you, but I very rarely have a good thought;

it's all garbage. Every one of these thoughts, verbalizations, and actions will bring a result. I haven't liked it very much in this life when my negative actions from the past have resulted in unhappiness; I'm pretty sure I also won't like it in the future when the negative actions I've done in this life ripen.

Even relatively virtuous, kindly people have done things worth regretting. Who hasn't killed ants or mosquitoes? Who hasn't hurt a relative or a dear friend with an unkind or thoughtless word? If your actions are not purified by your practice, their result will be experienced later.

Contemplation of the four thoughts can be our best friend on the path. When we begin our practice, we must find the time. Unfortunately, nobody is going to add an extra hour or two to the day just so you can practice; even the Buddha doesn't have that ability. That leaves two alternatives: sleep less or do less. In the long run, sleep is hard to do without. So, understanding the four thoughts gives us the impetus to examine our daily activities to see which ones are really essential and which ones aren't, to learn the difference between "want" and "need." We should always be asking ourselves, "Would I being doing this if I knew I were going to die next week?" I'm afraid you probably won't find much time for practice without at least some restructuring and reprioritizing of your life.

I'm always amazed by how busy Americans are! I read recently that the average American works two months a year more than the average German or Frenchman and one month a year more than he did thirty years ago. This seems insane to me. We're the world's most prosperous country; it shouldn't be that difficult to restructure our lives to trade some hectic activity and the accumulation of goods for time to practice something that would bring true, permanent happiness.

For example, the citizens of the U.K. have a per capita income that is 60 percent of the average income in the U.S. This means that if we worked an average of 40 percent less, we could still live as well as they do in Britain; it certainly wouldn't be like India or Tanzania. I know this is easier said than done, and some of you are truly quite busy with no flexibility in your schedule; but I think my point is still valid and clear. If we can't work less, at least we should be saving money for a time when we can.

I feel very strongly that our understanding of the four thoughts manifests in how we spend our money. Do we buy more or better stuff, or do we put some money aside so that we can work less now or possibly enter retreat in the future? The problem I see is that many people take a certain standard of living for granted and often confuse yuppie values with spirituality. Consequently, our time and wealth go toward maintaining that standard, and practice time always seems far away.

In Buddha's time, monks begged for food and ate whatever was placed in their bowls. One day, a leper's finger fell into a bowl, and the monk ate it. Contrast that with our lives today: How many of us are satisfied with ordinary Western fare, Western clothes, or Western housing? Spiritual people seem to be even fussier than ordinary folk. For example, when I was young, my father was quite successful, and we were quite prosperous. That prosperity was reflected in their purchase of Yuban coffee. I would never do that now—I always purchase the much more expensive whole bean coffee.

Even once we have found time and have established a regular practice, temptations and distractions will arise. Even Milarepa was tempted to leave retreat to go to a nearby village for some entertainment and companionship. If Milarepa was distracted by a simple Tibetan village, how can we resist the countless distractions of modern Western life? Your best friend, your most trustworthy advisor, will be the four thoughts. Always examine your actions in their light; always remember death.

Beyond that, there will come a time when practice is just too hard or painful. It's not that we're distracted or that we desire something else, it's that merely doing the practice is painful. You begin to see things about yourself that you've always ignored. You experience mysterious kinds of physical pains while sitting that make every moment unbearable. At times like these, the four thoughts may be the only thing that pulls you through. You understand you are ripening previous negative karma and saving yourself from possible rebirth in the lower realms. And if you don't have any previous meditative experience with these four thoughts, you will have no allies to cope with these difficulties.

As I discussed before, these winds of karma can blow us to places beyond our imagination. Unfortunately, most of these places aren't much fun. Remember all those gruesome hells we've either heard or read about? Why do these miserable states predominate? Because most of us are driven by the three poisonous minds (sorry—I think I prefer three poisons) most of the time. It's like trying to play a computer game at a higher skill level than we have yet to reach: Those little black stones keep accumulating faster than we are able to eliminate them or able to accumulate the white ones. There doesn't seem to be much we can do about it on our own; we need some help.

CHAPTER TWELVE

Ngondro: Refuge and Bodhichitta

Ngondro is Tibetan for the preliminary practices that begin one's career as a tantric practitioner. They are divided into two sections: the common, or ordinary, and the uncommon, or extraordinary. The common preliminaries are the contemplation of the four thoughts that we discussed in the last chapter. The extraordinary practices are taking refuge and generating bodhichitta, which are generally done in conjunction with prostrations, the purification practice of Vajrasattva, offering the mandala, and guru yoga. These four preliminaries are always done; sometimes the practices of *chod*, offering one's body, and *phowa*, the transference of consciousness, are also added.

For every lineage of practice, there is a set of preliminaries. For instance, within the Karma Kagyu tradition, there is a ngondro for mahamudra and a different one for the six doctrines of Naropa. Other Kagyu schools will have their own systems of ngondro. Although they are very similar, it is preferable to do the ngondro that corresponds to the lineage, root lama, and practice you will most likely be following. If you change lineages, you may be asked to do a new ngondro in order to make a connection with your new school. You generally don't need an empowerment to do ngondro, but having the Vajrasattva empowerment certainly can't hurt. However, you definitely need the *lung*, or reading transmission, as well as the oral commentary for the ngondro practices. In addition, there are many fine books on the preliminaries.

The manner of doing the ngondro varies among the different lineages of Tibetan Buddhism. I'm most familiar with the Kagyu and Nyingma approach. There, the preliminaries are done in one block from beginning to end. Completion of at least one set of the preliminaries is often necessary in order to begin a deity practice, attend more esoteric teachings, or even to participate in some empowerments. I've heard that the Sakya approach is quite similar—one completes the preliminaries in one big bundle. However, the Gelugpas, who were the largest tradition in Tibet, have a different manner of working with the ngondro. Completion of the ngondro sets are not a prerequisite to tantric practice for Gelugpas; instead, the ngondro practices can be done alongside tantric practice throughout the practitioner's life. However, Gelugpas often will complete the full set of ngondro practices at the beginning of a three-year retreat, just as the practitioners of the other Tibetan Buddhist traditions do.

The ngondro begins with taking refuge. Refuge has three levels: outer refuge in the Buddha, Dharma, and Sangha; inner refuge in the lama, yidams, and dakinis and protectors; and secret refuge in the dharmakaya, sambhogakaya, and nirmanakaya.

What does taking refuge mean? The image that always comes to my mind is that of a shelter in a storm. It's raining heavily, you are getting soaked, and you look for something to protect you. Recalling the discussion on the four thoughts, we are being buffeted by the winds of our own karma, which are threatening to blow us into the miserable realms of existence. We need help!

Who can help? Obviously, someone who isn't being blown about by karma. Such a being is called a buddha. Only he or she can help. For anyone else to try is dangerous—a drowning man cannot save another drowning man. The help itself is called the Dharma. Dharma refers to both the teachings and the truth they represent. The Sangha are those who help and support you while you are practicing the Dharma.

Entrusting yourself to these three is taking refuge. Let's face it, we haven't done so well on our own. Sometimes we can keep our heads above water; sometimes we cannot. When things are going well, we might feel we're doing fine; but a little difficulty, a small reversal, and suddenly we seem completely unable to cope. If that happens now, what will happen as we die? What will happen in the *bardo*, the treacherous and dangerous period between death and our next birth?

Some people have an aversion to the idea of taking refuge. It seems too religious or too weak. Only a wimp needs someone else's help. I don't buy it. We are always taking refuge. The main differences are that our present ways of taking refuge are poorly thought out and that our objects of refuge are not very useful.

Ask yourself: In who or what do I take refuge now? To whom do I turn when things are rough? What will I do when I die? If you believe in another spiritual path and take refuge in that, that's fine. If you think you're strong enough to handle death and the transition process by yourself, you are probably fooling yourself. If you prefer not to think about your death, you are simply taking refuge in your own ignorance.

We take refuge in many things, such as our intelligence, our beauty, our aggressiveness, or our wit. A friend of mine once said, "When I have a problem, I just throw money at it." These methods can all be called "taking refuge in the ego." By now you should be convinced that this is probably not a good idea. Our ego is not doing a great job right now; it will only do worse when we die.

So the point is this: We all take refuge all the time. Now it's time to do so intelligently.

I think we have to admit to ourselves that the ego can be a good general manager, but he makes a lousy king. Taking refuge is the first step in ego's descent from that throne. And there is probably no better way to embody that understanding and demonstrate a willingness to restructure one's inner landscape than by prostrating. Prostrations become the physical expression of the willingness to de-throne the ego and enthrone a king who is wise and compassionate. Each prostration should be accompanied by the sincere feeling of taking refuge and giving up a little of ego's domain.

You must learn how to practice prostrations and refuge from a teacher. How to recite the liturgy and what to visualize will vary from practice to practice. I will try to make a few general observations.

Since you will be doing 100,000 of them, you will need a method of keeping count. A small rosary of twenty-seven (one-forth of 108) that fits over the palm works fine. Then you need to count the groups of twenty-sevens, and so on.

You will need a place to do prostrations as well as some gear. (We're Americans, aren't we?) But please remember, prostrations are supposed to be difficult and painful. Each one becomes a test of your commitment, and the more difficult they are, the more committed to your own unfolding you will be when you complete them. Also, prostrations are said to purify physical karma, the karma created by violence, stealing, and sexual misconduct. So it's better to have sore knees than to be reborn in hell. Of course, a little common sense is necessary. We don't want to wind up in a wheelchair or abandon our practice because it was too gruesome.

Lama Thubten was the lama who sealed us into retreat in Scotland. When he was young, he did the three-year retreat at his monastery, Palpung, the seat of H. E. Tai Situ Rinpoche. Lama Thubten was very diligent and truly believed he was purifying his bad karma with his exertion. Therefore, he prostrated until his knees became bloody pulps. Situ Rinpoche (the previous one) spied on him and discovered his condition. He called all the monks in retreat together and told them that Lama Thubten was the only one doing it correctly; by taking care of themselves too much, the other monks weren't purifying their karma. What did he do? He had them all hung from hooks like slabs of meat and whipped them!

Now when we prostrate, we like to have special pads for our knees, something for our hands, and a very smooth board! I recommend very firm foam for the knees, myself. On the other hand, I have prostrated many, many times until I was so weak I couldn't lift myself off the board anymore. I prostrated until blood ran down my legs, and I prostrated (and did other demanding practices) until I had arthritis in my knees and had to walk awhile with a cane (I'm better now, thank you). It's up to you how diligent you are, how much suffering you're willing to take on to complete the practice. I understand that after a grueling day at work, whiny kids at home, and a fight with your spouse, the last thing you might feel you need is an hour of pain. It's not exactly why you got involved in the first place.

Also, with all the ngondro practices, you have a quality versus quantity payoff. You can try to do them perfectly, or you can try to do them quickly. The implications are obvious; if you sacrifice speed for quality, you might never finish, but if you really exert yourself to complete them as fast as possible, you might find yourself unprepared for the next practice without having changed or having had any real experience.

I did my first ngondro when I was twenty-five. I practiced very diligently. My roommate, Jeffrey, was an extremely gung-ho practitioner (he's now in retreat in the woods somewhere in Canada), and my competitive nature forced me to try to keep up with him. He would slap himself in the face in the late evenings to keep from falling asleep! I think I learned a lot from him about discipline and the value of pushing, just doing it no matter how difficult. I was almost continually sick with mysterious ailments that no doctor could treat, but I never quit. I would prostrate and do the other practices until I simply couldn't do them any more.

I think it's good to push yourself like that sometimes. You discover what your limits are and what you can really do. At other times, you can balance that kind of fanaticism with greater quality. But you start to know where the lines are within your being. Also, you will please your teacher.

Pushing like that gave me an unshakable desire to practice. Before then, I was somewhat wishy-washy; afterward, I was much more consistent with my discipline. So I owe whatever subsequent benefits I've derived from my practice to that year of militant pushing and the example of my good buddy Jeffrey.

I did my second ngondro in my cloistered retreat at the age of thirty-eight. It was a whole retreat full of Jeffreys, all very militantly disciplined practitioners. One is great, but a whole building full of them...! Anyway, because the retreat was already so structured so that there was no real way to lose one's practice, I tried to do the ngondro as best as I could from the quality perspective. That is, I tried to do each practice to the best of my ability without worrying about the numbers. I found that this could be further broke down into two techniques.

First, I could try to perfect the visualization. I could make that my main focus and judge my success by the clarity of the various images I was producing.

The other technique was to emphasize the emotive, devotional aspect. That is, to take the open-hearted feelings that come with devotional practice, focus on them, and try to maximize their power, using whatever techniques, images, or associations that evoked them. Personally, I feel the latter has more power and benefit than the former. Visualization can become a dry exercise without the devotion. Devotion without the connection to the visualization can really open your heart but can also lead to becoming overly emotional. For a while, I felt like a rhythm-and-blues singer singing emotionally about something completely silly and trivial. It was close to cultivating feeling for its own sake, divorced from any kind of meaning. Visualization grounds the feeling in context and value; the devotion elevates the visualization into something real and meaningful. Once again, we have things here that we must learn to balance.

It would be nice if we could easily integrate those two—visualization and devotion—into one practice, but I have found that they are two different mental functions. Hence, I start by alternating between the two, until they begin reinforcing each other. Having some sense of presence through the visualization can increase one's sense of devotion. And devotion can convince you of the reality of the visualization, making it clearer.

To return to the discussion about quality versus quantity with the ngondro: The point is that both approaches work, and like other aspects of practice, some balance is necessary. It is also necessary to try it yourself. What happens to you if you push yourself? Does it raise you to a higher level of commitment, or does it burn you out? Does it open you up, or does it make you more uptight? Does an allegiance to quality become an excuse for not practicing, or do you monitor yourself to do the very best you can?

With prostrations, expect a real drama to unfold. All the issues of commitment to the Buddhist path and to commitment in general will well up completely and intensely; the inner voices, "Push harder!" and "Stop!" will be screaming inside your head. I hope you listen to the right one at the right time.

Usually accompanying the refuge and prostration practice is the generation of bodhichitta. *Bodhi* means "enlightenment," *chitta* means "heart," "thought," or "mind." *Bodhichitta* means "the thought for enlightenment" or "the enlightened mind." It's hard to define the term precisely as it has several related meanings. *Ultimate bodhichitta* is the enlightened mind itself; *relative bodhichitta* is the desire to attain that enlightenment. The idea here is that we aspire to attain enlightenment to benefit all sentient beings. We are no longer practicing for the sake of our own liberation from suffering; our motivation encompasses all that lives. Thus, generating bodhichitta means to train oneself away from a selfish motivation and toward a completely altruistic one.

That's easier said than done. Luckily, in Tibetan Buddhism there are very simple, direct, and effective techniques to make that transformation. I will speak of them at length now.

These teachings are called *lo-jong*, which can be translated as "thought transformation" or "mind training." These teachings change the mind from self-centeredness to the altruistic motivation of bodhichitta. They were introduced into Tibet in the eleventh century by the highly revered Indian pandit and saint Atisha. The teachings became incorporated into all the lineages in Tibet and have proved to be quite popular in the West. I've taught classes on lo-jong several times, and I feel these classes have been the most beneficial I have taught. I'm always deeply touched by the real and meaningful changes and breakthroughs my students make in this class.

Most techniques in Tibetan Buddhism are very deep and profound. Unfortunately, they are also very difficult to practice in terms of both the spiritual acumen of the student and having the proper conditions in which to practice. Lo-jong excels in being very down –to earth and completely suited to our times and to the lifestyle of a layperson—hence, its great effectiveness. However chaotic and miserable your life, the lo-jong teachings have a technique that will enable you to use that very experience for growth. No more whining about not being able to go off to retreat; here is a teaching perfect for your busy and stressful lifestyle!

The original lo-jong teachings are lists of slogans—for instance "Be grateful to everyone." Various lamas have written commentaries over the years; so have a few Westerners. Without going through all the slogans, I'd like to say something about what I feel is the main point and then mention the main formal practice from lo-jong: *tong-len*, or taking and sending.

The slogans of lo-jong reveal a profound psychological insight into how the ego develops, maintains its territory, and refuses to consider others. The slogans demonstrate how we have a strong tendency to accumulate positive experiences, to push away negative ones, and to get angry with anyone who interferes with this process. This would be fine if it worked; for a variety of reasons, it doesn't. Among the reasons are, of course, that experiences are only temporary and that the ego doesn't really exist. The ego is playing a losing game here. It may occasionally seem to be winning, like someone who wins a jackpot at a slot machine. But over time it's inevitable that, like at the slots, the ego will come out a loser.

Hence, with lo-jong we take those three processes—hoarding the good, pushing away the bad, and blaming others—identify them, and exert ourselves in reversing them. How can we do that? Because the ego doesn't really exist! The lo-jong teachings start with a short explanation of absolute bodhichitta, which, if you remember, is the ultimate nature of the mind; by having a little familiarity with that, the mind develops both the courage and the flexibility to undertake reversing its bad habits.

To use the abovementioned slogan, "Be grateful to everyone," as an example: When you find yourself thinking, "If so-and-so weren't getting in my way all the time, I could really...," you first recognize the thought and its attendant aggression. You then cultivate a sense of gratitude, "If so-and-so hadn't been obstructing me, I never would have seen what an aggressive and obsessive jerk I am. Thanks to him, I have this new self-knowledge and am able to change."

Each slogan is really saying that we are its opposite; they are actually a list of our flaws. When we hear, "Drive all blames into one (our ego)," we know we have the tendency to blame others for our trouble; if we don't, we can ignore this particular bit of advice.

What does this have to do with compassion and bodhichitta? Our selfishness and aversion cover up our own intrinsic compassion. It is natural for us to feel loving and compassionate toward others, but as we grew up, we learned to defend ourselves more and more. Defending means pushing away or denying pain. Because we are always pushing away pain, we push away others who feel pain. Therefore, we must first break the habit of pushing pain away; only then can we acknowledge others' pain. When we remove the defense, we automatically begin to feel the compassion. Once we feel the compassion, it's easy to take the next step, generating bodhichitta.

Once you let go of blaming others and getting angry with them, you will naturally feel some love toward them as you experience gratitude. Once you experience that love, consider that others are also suffering; you will feel the wish that they be free of it. Then resolve, "The only way to completely eradicate suffering is by becoming enlightened. If I want to remove the misery of others, who have helped me learn about myself, I must become a buddha." That thought is bodhichitta.

In the beginning, it all seems very contrived and artificial. After a while, it becomes more natural, and eventually, applying the slogans is almost automatic; they start to replace all the usual voices in your head. You can develop a lo-jong superego.

This whole process can be greatly accelerated by doing the meditation of tong-len. Briefly, the practice of tong-len, or taking and giving, means to breathe in others' pain while you breathe out and give your happiness and virtue to them. Having practiced tong-len as a one-month retreat during my longer group retreat, and having taught it many times since then, I have developed a certain style or technique for teaching and practicing it that seems to work.

It's very easy to sit back and have compassionate and loving thoughts toward the world, all humans, nature, or something like that. This does-n't really threaten us; in fact, we feel good and a little high from that kind of thinking. But I don't feel that this kind of thinking actually changes anything. You can check for yourself: Do those expansive feelings really change how you relate to others in your everyday life, or do old patterns return? If you're like me, the old thought patterns return.

The reason is, those feelings are not really connected to the structure of the ego, which, as I mentioned earlier, is about pushing away pain while accumulating happiness. You must be very precise in your observation of that process before it can truly be changed. Because of that, the lo-jong teachings recommend that you begin the exchange with yourself.

Many students who are somewhat familiar with the teachings have ignored this advice, but I feel it is the real key. We must learn to see our strategy of denying pain before we can truly generate the strong wish for beings to be free of it. By pain, I primarily mean mental pain, even the mental pain of having physical discomfort. If you try to do tong-len for others while denying your own pain, your practice becomes a technique for perpetuating avoidance and will never yield any meaningful results. So first, simply be aware of your pain at the moment. Notice your awkwardness, your wish to squirm away from it somehow. Allow yourself merely to feel it.

Now you are ready to begin tong-len. You might want to imagine an unhappy version of yourself standing in front of you; this can make the visualization flow better. Take in your suffering; give yourself healing, white light. It is advised to link these with the breath: Breathe in the suffering as black gunk; breathe out the goodness as healing white light.

Do it until it works! You should "get it," have some definite sense of healing, acceptance, and transformation. You should develop the insight that blocking out or denying pain is actually what keeps you in a place of pain, that it is entirely within your power and ability to do something very simple and effective to change this. Your ego mechanisms developed when you were younger and had no other defenses for dealing with difficulties; now you're older and have had the great good fortune to meet the Dharma. Thus, although it is everyone's habit to push away discomfort, there's no practical or logical reason to continue to do so.

At this point, the teachings say that we should focus on the suffering we will experience in the future. I prefer to deal with the past. As Westerners who have been raised, educated, and immersed in the psychoanalytic tradition, we are accustomed to think of our present discomfort as being caused by events in our past. So here is a chance to do something about it! Many people will find with this method the kind of healing they would expect from a long and costly program with a therapist.

Let your mind drift backward in time. Remember the pain of being younger. When the feeling is there, do tong-len practice conjoined with the breath(why did you add that? Many people find linking the tonglen visualization with the breath a little rushed and I advise them to delink them.). Spend as much time as you can remembering different incidents.

You can definitely heal yourself of the wounds of your earlier life by doing this practice.

I once asked my teacher what practice wounded Westerners should do. He advised either the practice of tong-len or meditating on the nature of the mind. The latter is difficult and requires the close supervision of a high lama; the former, tong-len, is relatively straightforward and easy to do.

I had one student who had been raped as a child. Through this practice she was able to forgive her rapist. It was an incredibly moving moment in class when she recounted her experience and really convinced me of the power of Lord Buddha's teachings not only to help people attain the highest levels of awareness possible but also to heal the deepest wounds and sufferings that ordinary people experience right now. I gained a certainty that for all but the most deeply disturbed, Buddhism is the perfect medicine; we needn't think of combining or mixing it with anything else. It works just great on its own.

After you've opened up to yourself in this way, you are ready to move on to the sufferings of others. Start with the one person to whom you feel closest. Traditionally, this would be your mother, but as many Westerners have problems with their mother, it can be anyone—a parent, a spouse, a friend, or a child. Feel their pain and do the tong-len practice, taking it on. Do you feel yourself shutting down? Can you open up through the experience?

When I did the practice in retreat, I spent a lot of time doing tong-len for my mother. I was only partially successful. I felt a lot of resistance to feeling her pain, probably because I felt like I had abandoned her to go to Asia and into retreat in Scotland. However, I felt it was necessary to do. Wherever we are shut down, there we must work to open up. It's not simply a question of becoming compassionate; any place where we are blocked will limit our meditation and our overall growth. It's not possible to develop strong meditation while maintaining a coldness toward others. I think one of the main lessons of Buddhism is that it is in our own best interests to be compassionate. We won't become boundaryless slobs, we will become open and loving.

After our loved ones, whom I recommend taking on one-by-one, we can move to all those toward whom we feel neutral, those people we pass every day who we hardly notice and about whom don't care. They are suffering as well. We cannot remain insensitive to their pain.

The most difficult and potentially the most powerful objects are, of course, our enemies, the people toward whom we harbor ill will. Is it in our own best interests to hate these people? Are we happier hating them and obsessing about them or forgiving and loving them? Your ego will scream that it's not fair to forgive these people and to give away your goodness to them, but by now I hope you're becoming a little suspicious of listening to your ego. It has been wrong before! So because this is where the greatest resistance is, this will be where the greatest change will be. Once again, I recommend taking your enemies one-by-one so that you can completely unblock your mind from the aversion that's constricting it.

Once you've done that, it's easy to move on to animals and to the beings of other realms. We have no real unresolved issues with any of them. We can then conclude with all sentient beings in the universe. Having worked through at least some of our blockages, it's now appropriate to cultivate those expansive, loving feelings.

Some people are afraid that when they do tong-len, they will literally develop the symptoms of their object. For instance, if you do tong-len for Aunt Betty who has cancer, you might develop cancer or at least get a little sick. This is a very common worry.

What I've been told is this: Although it's theoretically possible literally to transfer another's suffering onto oneself, it seems to happen with only the most spiritually gifted practitioners. And those who are actually able to do this don't resent it at all—they are really quite delighted to suffer for others and to purify themselves by doing so. For the rest of us, the practice is mainly about generating compassion and bodhichitta; rather than being about taking on beings' actual suffering when you practice. If you are able to remove others' suffering through the power of your practice, that is a wonderful bonus, but we should be content with the inner transformation that will result in our attaining buddhahood, with its ability to remove *all* beings' pain.

CHAPTER THIRTEEN

Ngondro: Vajrasattva Practice and Mandala Offerings

THE PRACTICE OF VAJRASATTVA

The next two ngondro practices are the Vajrasattva purification practice and offering the mandala. As I mentioned before, it's not necessary to have the Vajrasattva empowerment to do the practice, although it would be beneficial.

To summarize the practice briefly: You imagine Buddha Vajrasattva above your head. In some practices he's alone, in some he has a consort. You invoke the wisdom beings, imagining that they merge into the visualization. You then pray for purification. Nectar flows from Vajrasattva's body and enters yours, pushing your defilements, obscurations, and transgressions out of your body in the form of various gross things. As you recite first the long hundred-syllable mantra and then the short six-syllable mantra, you continue to meditate on this nectar flowing through you. At the conclusion of the mantra recitation, which occupies the bulk of the session, you recite a confession prayer. Then Vajrasattva dissolves into you, and you rest in a state of being merged with him.

This practice is based on applying what are called the four opponent powers. These are four techniques taught in the sutras for purifying non-virtuous activity. Visualizing Vajrasattva above us is the power of reliance. Recollecting one's nonvirtue and repenting is the power of remorse. Resolving never to repeat these nonvirtues is the power of the vow. Visualizing the nectar while reciting the mantra is the power of the remedy. When these four are complete, the purification is effected.

Some people really like this practice; others never connect. I've listened carefully to what other Western practitioners have said about this practice, and I've discerned a clear pattern. Those who, while reciting the mantra, consider all their nonvirtue item –by item or who even do some sort of life review eventually find the practice tedious. Those who focus instead on the flow of nectar and get into that experience enjoy the practice and find it beneficial.

I'm fortunately among the latter. I can't say it's the superior method; I just know that most of us prefer it. I've done Vajrasattva as my main practice for many years. I've been satisfied with the results, and I feel it's an excellent beginning practice for Western Vajrayanists.

By focusing on the flow of nectar, one brings one's awareness into one's body and also into one's energetic system, the inner body of channels and energy. As many of us know from Western concepts of body armoring and bioenergetics, we hold unexpressed emotions in our musculature. This is experienced in practice as a sort of tension and solidity in the body. Letting the nectar flow through the body slowly releases this chronic tension. It's an important process; so much is held in the body. As one perfects the practice, the flow of nectar becomes stronger, and one can direct it into more and more blockages. More negativities are released and one develops one of the main signs of progress: a lightness of body, or what in English we would call suppleness.

Also many of us aren't even in our bodies. We are either dissociated, lost in fantasy, or "in our head." We might even feel that spiritual practice should serve to enhance that kind of separation. I'll talk more about the body in a later chapter, but for now let me say that this is not exactly the correct attitude. Doing Vajrasattva and visualizing the flow will help you greatly integrate your mind and body.

If you feel true remorse for previously committed nonvirtues, of course, don't ignore that feeling. Hold that feeling as the nectar washes away any remaining trace of your actions. This will help you to let go at an even deeper level and will aid you in abandoning yourself to the nectar's flow. Then you don't have to hold onto that feeling anymore.

What I'm emphasizing here is this: Make the practice experiential rather conceptual. Your stains exist at a level deeper than the chatter of your thinking mind; to remove them your practice must go deeper as well.

There are many ways to visualize the flow. One lama told me to imagine it like a waterfall flowing through me. That kind of visualization develops a lot of power and brings awareness to the area associated with the central channel.

Chökyi Nyima Rinpoche told one student to go very slowly and carefully. The student was instructed to take about half an hour imagining one downward movement and very carefully to feel the nectar in every part of his body, for example, imagining the nectar moving into each and every finger.

I've done a combination of both. I'll usually start with the waterfall. When I feel it getting stuck or blocked, I'll work very carefully, imagining the nectar permeating the blocked area.

Some teachers recommend visualizing the nectar filling the various channels and chakras; you must learn this directly from them.

Whatever way you do it, it's up to you to make it effective. Not only should you feel physical benefits, such as a lessening of chronic tension and a lightening of the body, but you should feel that whatever you are mentally holding on to is washed away, just as sticks are dislodged in a strong current. Therefore, the stronger the current, the more and larger are the sticks that are washed away. Thus, feel free to throw everything into the stream: your previous nonvirtue, your present defilements and ego clinging, even your sicknesses and physical pain. It's an amazing practice—simple and easy to do but very effective.

After you have completed your mantra recitations for your session, you recite confessional prayers. We don't have to remember everything; since we're not enlightened yet, we must have done a lot in the past to obscure us even if we can't remember every act. Even if we don't remember specific acts, all our suffering, limitations, and slowness in spiritual progress is due to previous nonvirtue. When we contemplate their very real and present effects, we can feel strong remorse even without knowing exactly what we did. Of course, when you do remember those acts that you truly regret, this is the time for sincere confession.

Vajrasattva is especially effective and is generally considered to be mandatory for purifying transgressions of tantric samaya, the vows that accompany Vajrayana practice. It's up to you to find out what they are, but be assured that you're breaking them all the time. It's quite daunting to consider, but we are taught that doing twenty-one of the long Vajrasattva mantra daily protects us from experiencing the results of these numerous infractions.

Lord Atisha said of himself, "I never violated the smallest of the monastic vows, not even in a dream. I occasionally considered something that would be a violation of the bodhisattva vows. But my violations of the tantric samayas were like rain." If that were true of Atisha, how much more true is it for us? Samaya can be broken merely by thought. If you for a moment consider someone with whom you have taken an empowerment to be a jerk, you have broken your vow. Therefore, once you've have entered the gate of the Vajrayana, even if you don't do any other formal practice, please try to do a little Vajrasattva daily without fail.

At the end of the practice, Vajrasattva melts into light and dissolves into you. Your mind and his mind merge. You enter a state that is completely free of the stains of defilements, transgressions, and nonvirtue: the mind of Vajrasattva.

MANDALA OFFERINGS

The next practice is that of offering the mandala. It takes an enormous amount of merit to become enlightened; it even takes a huge amount simply to have the appropriate conditions to practice. We make these offerings to accumulate this merit so that we can progress along the path in a smooth, obstacle-free manner.

The practice is as follows: Using an ordinary or specially constructed plate, one offers the whole universe, filled with all that is positive and precious, to one's guru and the other objects of refuge. This is done by placing piles of rice and other substances on the plate to represent the various components of the universe while reciting an appropriate verse. The verses are recited 100,000 times. There are concluding verses that mention deeper levels of offering followed by the usual dissolution and dedications.

In this practice, we use the ancient Indian concept of the universe as made up of certain similar units. The basic unit has a central mountain with continents, islands, and seas symmetrically arranged around it. The central mountain is called Mount Meru and is the home of the gods. Other god realms are located above Mount Meru. A billion of these units make up the universe.

As modern, scientific Westerners, what are we to make of all this? It's definitely the teaching of Lord Buddha that the universe is constructed this way; do we have hesitation in accepting it? Of course, we can think of it as an Indian legend that Lord Buddha didn't want to challenge, so he just played along. That's the simplest explanation.

What I've come to believe is this: The universe appears differently according to whether one investigates it physically or mentally. That is, if you get into a spaceship and probe far into space, you will never see any Mount Merus or discover any pure lands. However, if you expand your mind in meditation, the realms that become apparent conform to Buddhist cosmology. These two universes exist on different planes, and an attempt to reconcile them or to reduce one to another as is frequently done these days will never be successful.

Another point of view would be to consider the actual construction and structure of the physical universe as completely irrelevant; the purpose of the meditation is to generate the merit of giving away everything wonderful and imaginable. There is no particular need to make the representation resemble the physical universe as we perceive it scientifically; as well, doing the practice in its traditional form brings with it blessings of the practice.

When I do this practice, the issue of clarity of visualization versus feeling becomes very clear for me. The last time I did mandala offerings, during my group retreat, I was able, at least for a while, to generate a clear and detailed image by keeping the visualizations growing. That is, I would imagine something I wanted to offer as part of the wealth of the universe, and when my mind would start drifting, I would use that mental energy to add more details to my visualization. For instance, I would imagine a beautiful lapis lazuli stupa. When my mind couldn't hold the image and wanted to move on to something new, I would add butter lamps on the stupa with sweet yellow light. Next, I would add gardens with pools reflecting this most beautiful of stupas; next, I would fill the paths in the gardens with people who were very devotedly offering it or circumambulating. And on and on...

But this can become a mental exercise devoid of feeling. So I would try to conjure up images that were the most touching to me and then offer them to my precious teacher.

Before the retreat, I had an extremely difficult time helping to construct the retreat facility. It was hell for me. Finally, I had a day off and was able to go to the nearby city of Dumfries to go shopping. I was completely burned out and exhausted from building and experiencing a lot of apprehension about the retreat and my ability to do it. Dumfries, however, is like many Scottish cities, very gray and damp. Through it flows a river, and on the river several swans floated, trying to find food. The sight of these swans deeply moved me. Something about finding such beauty and grace in the midst of both this internal and external grayness left a deep impression on me.

So when doing the mandala offerings, I would remember the image of those beautiful swans on the river and would devotedly offer it to my lama. It would always have an opening effect on my heart. Another method that had this effect was to offer a chorus a sweet-faced youths singing praises to him. During the breaktimes, the monks in retreat would compare the various offerings we were making; it was fun hearing about all the marvelous things that my friends were imagining in their offerings.

It's also nice to get pretty little things to add to your rice. Since I've spent so much time in Nepal, I always use the plastic beads that Nepalese women love to wear. It makes my rice colorful and sparkling. I also try to use a few semi-precious stones. Some people like to add things that have special significance for them.

However you do it, it can be very wonderful to spend one's time making offerings to one's teacher. What he has given us is priceless! What Gyatrul Rinpoche emphasizes is cultivating the ability to offer without any holding back. One offers one's possessions, body, and merit without any hesitation. It is a practice that can truly open your heart and prepare you for the next stage of ngondro, guru yoga.

CHAPTER FOURTEEN

Ngondro: Guru Yoga and Devotion

Guru yoga is the final and the most important part of the preliminaries. It might also be the most important practice you ever do. It is the key or the hub of the Vajrayana, around which everything else is oriented. I've repeatedly referred to the importance of the teacher-student relationship. Here, we are consciously endeavoring to open and broaden the channel for greater blessing and transmission.

Let me describe the practice. As usual it varies from lineage to lineage, liturgy to liturgy. In the Nyingma, the guru is visualized as either Guru Rinpoche or Samantabhadra (Kuntuzangpo); in the Kagyu, as Vajradhara (Tib. Dorje Chang), either with or without consort. The practitioner visualizes himself or herself as a deity, usually as Vajrayogini. By visualizing ourselves in a divine form, it's easier to make a connection between the guru's enlightened qualities and our own incipient ones. The guru can be imagined in the space in front of you, on the crown of your head, or more rarely, in your heart.

Subsequently, a series of prayers follows, invoking both the guru and the lineage from which he descends. A mantra, such as the vajra guru mantra, might also be repeated. The prayers and/or the mantra are what are counted and accumulated.

At the conclusion of the session, you imagine the guru bestowing on you the four empowerments. In chapter 4, we talked about receiving these empowerments in person. That is the empowerment of the ground. Here, the principle and visualization are similar, but you engage in the process as you practice on your own. This is the empowerment of the path. The actual attainment of enlightenment is the empowerment of the fruit. Here, the actual procedure will vary slightly from liturgy to liturgy but is basically as follows:

White light flows from an OM at the lama's forehead to your forehead. This bestows the vase empowerment, purifying your body and enabling you to practice kyerim, the development stage. This will result in the attainment of the nirmanakaya.

Red light flows from an AH at the lama's throat to your throat, bestowing the secret empowerment, purifying your speech, and enabling you to practice *tsalung*, the meditation on the channels and energies. This will result in the attainment of the sambhogakaya.

Blue light flows from a HUM at the lama's heart to your heart, bestowing the wisdom empowerment, purifying your mind, and enabling you to practice the meditation of union. This will result in the attainment of the dharmakaya.

White, red, and blue (or sometimes a fourth color from a fourth center) lights flow together to our three centers. We receive the fourth empowerment, purifying our body, speech, and mind, and enabling us to practice mahamudra and dzogchen, resulting in the svabhavikakaya.

At the conclusion of the empowerments, the lama dissolves into light and merges into us. Our body, speech, and mind become the lama's body, speech, and mind. We then rest in that state.

Everything I've heard, read, or studied in the past twenty-five years have emphasized the extreme importance of this practice. Let me quote Jamgon Kongtrul at length:

> In general, in order to follow the Mantrayana or Vajrayana, especially to receive instructions in the meditation of the Fulfillment

Stage, you must first receive the guru's blessing. Until you have received it, you will not be on the true path.

It is said that a disciple who is intensely devoted and reverent toward a fully qualified Vajrayana master with whom he has formed a sacred bond will achieve supreme and worldly siddhi without doing anything else. But a person who lacks devotion and reverence for the guru, even if he performs a great [number of mantra recitations] for the yidams of the four tantras, will obtain no supreme siddhi whatsoever.

As for worldly siddhi, he will not achieve long life, wealth, power, etc., no matter how hard he may strive. Anything he does achieve will have been won through great hardship. This is the "non-profound path."

On the other hand, if he develops true devotion and reverence, all obstacles will be cleared, uprooted, and expelled from his path, and he will obtain supreme and worldly siddhi by this method alone. Therefore, we call it the "profound path of the Guru Yoga."[11]

The practice of guru yoga goes hand in hand with the path of devotion. I've mentioned devotion often in the earlier chapters, but I want to treat the subject more extensively now, especially warning the reader of many of the pitfalls that can easily befall the average Western devotee.

What is devotion? It is a complete opening up to the state of enlightenment as embodied by one's teacher. All our longing for liberation merges with all our love, appreciation, and gratitude toward our teacher to produce a tremendously powerful force. This force can truly cut through our conceptual mind. In that moment of openness, we are receptive to the lama's blessings, and our own buddha-nature is very near.

All of our samsaric mind, our ego, is an inward contraction, a fascination and identification with some particular contents of our minds. Devotion provides the strength to fight against that contraction, to locate the focal point of awareness outside the usual restricted confines of one's own small mind. So true devotion is very expansive and thought free.

Devotion has often been compared to falling in love. When we fall in love, our mind also opens up and focuses outwardly. The experience feels blissful and liberating. With ordinary love, however, expectation, desire, and attachment soon creep in. We see our beloved, and we feel this tremendous wave of openness, bliss, and love. But in the next moment, more ordinary thoughts fill us: I want to snuggle, she doesn't seem so happy to see me today, etc. This kind of love leads only to more ordinary states of mind. I sincerely believe that romantic love can be used to produce many of the benefits of devotion if the lovers conscientiously will it; however, the main emotional difference between romantic love and devotion is that our lover seems to have the potential to satisfy our desires. Because they can be satisfied, it is easy for us to let them go unexamined.

The guru won't do that. Of course, not only won't the guru make love to you or marry you, he won't give you the adoration we come to expect from our partners. The guru may be very kind and affectionate, or he may be distant and wrathful, but we will never feel completely satisfied or consummated. Trungpa Rinpoche said, "Devotion is unrequited love for the guru."

It's that unrequitedness that provides the path. We open up to him, feel the surge of love, but then immediately stumble upon our desires. "I hope he acknowledges how good my meditation has been," "Will he smile at me?" etc. We all go through this. Letting go of these ordinary desires and attachments and deepening the love is the path. One must always remember that the guru is a buddha who has impartial love toward all. If he smiles at you today, it's his skillful means; if he's wrathful toward you but affectionate toward someone else, that's also his skillful means. This play allows us to see and subsequently deal with deeply conditioned parts of our minds as we persevere in our attempt to open.

As our openness becomes more free of our emotional needs, it becomes purer and approaches a state of true devotion. In that state of true devotion, it is very easy for the lama to transmit buddha-nature to you. It is much better than a pat on the back. And of course, this intensifies your devotion and encourages you to persevere further on the devotional path.

The real key, I believe, is to have the intelligence and wisdom not to get stuck in emotional states, not to confuse them for true devotion. They are not. They are simply needy, unconscious states that we have never properly dealt with before. If we get trapped there, our devotion will always be off, and we'll simply be indulging in old habits rather than receiving a transmission of buddha-nature. Many of the problems we've seen in the West over the past two or three decades related to the issues of gurus, cults, and devotion have been because of this very theme—the confusion of unconscious emotion with very conscious devotion.

I want to take some time and expand on some of the emotional states that may arise for you as you deepen your devotion for your teacher. Because they represent some of our deepest conditioning, they are often very difficult to recognize. I know this, because I've been trapped in all of these states many times.

The key concept here is the one of transference. We learned our habits of love from our parents when we were infants so that when we fall in love again, either with a teacher or a lover, we unconsciously reproduce those habits and patterns. In psychological terms, we are unconsciously projecting our feelings toward our parents onto our new loved one; I prefer not to think of it so much as projection as simply the repetition of our habits of love. If it always rains where we live, we will habitually reach for our umbrella whether it is rainy or sunny; if our parents expected us to act a certain way to receive their love, we will habitually act that way when we want to be loved.

You can see here one of the differences between the devotional and the romantic relationship—your teacher has no emotional needs of his own and is quite aware of the process you must go through to get beyond your emotional needs and habits. He will act in a way that will enable you to do so. Your lover, on the other hand, is just as confused and needy as you and will most likely keep you reinforcing your old patterns.

Whether you see it as transference or as habit, when we become devotees, we are in a sense regressing to infancy. What are some of the emotional patterns that might arise?

We might want to be taken care of, either spiritually or materially. We may feel that we don't have to do anything, that the guru will provide. We might feel we no longer have to take responsibility for our behavior since we're under the guru's umbrella. I even met one fellow who wouldn't ask his teacher any questions. He expected his teacher to provide the answers automatically from his omniscience.

We will either fear losing our autonomy, our sense of being a distinct, strong individual, or we will fear autonomy itself because we sense it will anger the guru or lead to separation from him. The latter goes back to our

original separation from our mother, and colors many of our relationships. Actually, our teacher wants us to develop into strong, self-sufficient
individuals. It is the habit of our infancy that we can't be autonomous
and simultaneously merged with another being. As we practice devotion,
we learn that these two are not in opposition at all. The stronger we
become, the cleaner is our opening into a state of pure love. We are now
strong enough to surrender because we have confidence in our ability to
cope with the dissolution of our boundaries. Our inner autonomous
strength actually enables us to merge more deeply; the blessings of our
union with our teacher gives us more self-confidence. At this stage, these
tendencies positively reinforce each other.

We must always remember that although our parents weren't buddhas and our lovers aren't buddhas, our teacher is. He doesn't fear your
growth; it isn't threatening to him in any way.

When I first started teaching, the very first thing I taught, at Gyatrul
Rinpoche's request, was the ancient text *Fifty Stanzas of Guru Devotion* by the
Indian saint Ashvaghosha. We spent a long time discussing it, and my
friends asked many questions. Much later, well after the end of the discussion, I realized what the key, unspoken issue was this: All of us students were afraid of being rejected by our teacher. If we didn't prostrate
right, if we were too serious, not serious enough, whatever the issue was
for each particular student, it always boiled down to one thing: the fear
that if we made a serious mistake, the guru would take us out of his heart.

It was an interesting insight; I'm sure I had many of the same fears.
But how can a buddha possibly reject you? You might have felt rejected
by your mother or your childhood sweetheart, but your lama will never
reject you. It's quite a relief to realize that. It's okay to make mistakes, to
experiment a little, to learn from experience. Sometimes you can try
being very formal, like a Tibetan attendant; at other times, be friendly
and playful. Your lama will understand what you are trying to do internally and, if you are sincere, will support your efforts and guide you with
appropriate feedback. Feeling confident that your teacher is truly committed to you provides a lot of space. Your fear of rejection is simply one
more of the habitual emotions we must learn to relinquish. Beyond that
fear is a very open state.

Some people use devotion to surrender common sense. Either they
think the guru has all the answers and they don't have to think for them-

selves anymore, or they feel that if they think or question, it will incur the guru's wrath. But as I said before, gurus won't reject us easily. If we are habitually thinking too much and not getting on with our practice, our teacher may, of course, comment on this. On the other hand, a clear intellect is part of the independence he is trying to cultivate in you. So if you find yourself becoming an unquestioning follower, be careful. I don't think you will be able to penetrate the depths of the teachings without a keen mind. If the lama asks you to do something that doesn't make any sense or seem appropriate, there is no rule prohibiting simply inquiring as to the reason behind his request.

Another mistake is to exaggerate the lama out of all proportion in your mind. He's already a buddha, but if you start to consider him the greatest yogi or the greatest scholar or whatever, you have a secret agenda there somewhere. Either you're identifying with him and feeling proud of yourself ("My lama is the greatest and I'm his favorite student."), or you're using his greatness to diminish yourself.

The latter is especially disturbing. If we have low self-esteem (and most of us seem to), the exalted nature of our teacher may reinforce that. The higher he seems, the lower we seem; the lower we seem, the higher he seems; and on and on. It feels like devotion, but is it? It is simply reinforcing our wretchedness.

Some students idealize their teacher to such a great extent that they become quite disillusioned when they perceive what they consider to be a fault. For instance, you might feel a high lama should be celibate and after a while discover that your teacher has a consort that he kept secret. This can be very upsetting to many.

First, before you make a firm commitment to a teacher, consider what are your non-negotiable demands regarding the behavior you consider to be appropriate or inappropriate. Check him out thoroughly. Once you've made that commitment, if you then discover things about your teacher that you don't like, be willing to work with them. They could be an indication of some attitude you are clinging to.

A teacher to whom I feel very close appeared as a monk. After many years, when I discovered he wasn't, I was a little upset. Now, looking back, I can see it was my own unresolved issues around sexual activity that made me uncomfortable. I felt safer with a celibate teacher as a role model; it didn't threaten my own repressions. When this discovery became painful for me, I reasoned, "I know this teacher has been very skillful and very kind to me. Why shouldn't I feel he will be the same to the women in his life?" Later I thought, "When I was immature and needed a celibate teacher, he manifested as one. Now my mind is more flexible and his manifestation has changed—how amazing!"

So when you find faults with your teacher's behavior, try to see what this says about you, and try to have pure perception. If that doesn't work, admit to yourself you aren't really qualified to judge the behavior of an enlightened being. If that still doesn't work, and you have very sincere doubts about his behavior, remember that the teachings of the Buddha are pure and can be transmitted through less than perfectly pure vessels. Try to learn what you can from him and don't make a big deal about his faults.

Akong Rinpoche addressed this issue when he said, "The difference between a good and a bad student is this: When a good student sees a pile of gold and a pile of rocks, he takes the gold. When the bad student sees the piles, he takes the rocks and complains."

By now I hope that you, the reader, have understood my point and are not too deeply offended. To reiterate: Our teacher is not a parent or lover. He will not reject you; he is not afraid of your growing up. On the other hand, he will not be seduced by your offerings, your praise, your groveling, or your flirtatiousness. Always check: With whom am I relating? The key here is to remember one of the main points of the devotional path—always consider your teacher to be a buddha.

There's a famous Kagyu saying:

If you see your guru as a buddha, you will receive a buddha's blessing. If you see him as a bodhisattva, you will receive a bodhisattva's blessing. If you see him as a siddha, you will receive a siddha's blessing. If you see him as an ordinary person—a good spiritual friend—such is the blessing you will receive. If you feel no devotion or reverence for him, you will receive absolutely no blessing.[12]

If we act in a flirtatious or infantile manner, are we really regarding our teacher as a buddha?

One thing that has helped me greatly with my relationship with my teacher is falling in love and marrying. Many of the needs I once unconsciously expected my lama to fill are now being met by my wife. I don't expect my lama to say I'm wonderful—that's my wife's job. This has made my relationship with my teacher purer and even more wonderful. By having fewer expectations and needs, I can remain more open. Every moment with him is special and blessed.

As you purify these many unconscious needs through the path of devotion, you will heal some of the deepest and most difficult conditioning. You will grow stronger and more independent while developing a greater capacity to love, and your mind will open to the true blessings and transmission of your lama, the transmission of rigpa.

CHAPTER FIFTEEN

Kyerim

Perhaps the most obvious aspect of Vajrayana practice is the meditations associated with the various deities, called *yidam*s in Tibetan. Even the most casual observer of Tibetan Buddhism has noticed these striking iconographic representations—flawless statues and minutely detailed scrolled paintings called *thankha*s that show all manner of yidams. Some are beatifically peaceful with loving, serene smiles and gazes; others are incredibly malevolent, surrounded by flames and brandishing a wide variety of weapons from a multitude of arms. Then, of course, there are the deities in sexual union—what are we to make of that?

Practices associated with visualizing these deities and reciting their mantras are called *kyerim* in Tibetan. *Kyerim* has been variously translated as "arising yoga," "generation stage," or "development stage." It is contrasted with the completion stage, which will be discussed later. Briefly, in kyerim, you use a liturgical text called a *sadhana* that is related to the specific yidam you are practicing. You recite the text, visualizing as you go along. At the mantra section, you pause and recite the mantra, and then you conclude the practice. There are many stages within a sadhana, and not every sadhana will have every possible section; nevertheless, all sadhanas follow a fairly typical format, and this allows us to discuss them in a generic way.

When do we do kyerim? In other words, at what stage of our practice is it appropriate? As I mentioned before, in the Kagyu, Sakya, and Nyingma systems, we begin a serious yidam practice only after we have completed the preliminaries (Gelugpas alternate some deity practices with their ngondro practice). The ngondro is very important before commencing the practices of kyerim, especially if we aspire to practice a wrathful deity or a deity in union, or if we are interested in the completion stage practices of tsalung. Ngondro prepares the mind in a number of essential ways, as we previously discussed, that enable subsequent practices to be efficacious.

Some lamas in the West prefer that their students do some simple sitting practice for a while before beginning Vajrayana practice. The flexibility and insight that arise from sitting will also enable the kyerim practice to be more effective. I agree wholeheartedly. With its visualizations and rituals, there is the danger that kyerim practice can become a kind of dissociative fantasy unless the student has a strong background in working with the mind. I will talk more about this later when we consider the dangers of kyerim.

A few teachers give their students kyerim practice—almost always in the form of a peaceful deity's practice—right from the start. For instance, Kalu Rinpoche had all his students practice Chenrezig, the buddha of love and compassion; Chagdud Rinpoche instructed all his students to meditate on Red Tara. It's nice when all the students of a lama know the same practice; whenever they get together, there is a practice they can do together. In general, it is necessary to have the appropriate empowerment; these days, however, that requirement is being loosened for some of the peaceful deities.

Many of us Westerners have great difficulty with the deities and their attendant rituals. We are usually attracted by the depth and profundity of Buddhist philosophy and the charisma of the great teachers; the existence of these deities and their practice does not seem to fit in our scheme of things. "I thought Buddhism didn't have any gods and believed in egolessness. If there is no ego, no creator, and everything is empty, what are all these deities anyway? This must be some kind of Bonpo or Hindu perversion!" I imagine we've all thought like that at times, especially while trying to navigate an especially long and confusing sadhana.

When we try to understand what these yidams are, we usually formulate two categories or answers which we then assume are mutually exclusive. The first is that the deities are basically symbolic, representing our own latent qualities and buddha-nature. If we're familiar with Jungian psychology, we may regard them as archetypes. This approach is more satisfying to the more intellectual, nontheistic practitioner. It's very safe and appealing. We're not actually worshipping an external deity as the folks down the street are doing when they go to church; it's really much more esoteric and profound than that. In other words, it doesn't threaten us, our autonomy, or our conceptions.

The other approach is to consider the deities external to oneself, powerful enlightened beings with the ability to manifest and bless us at our invocation. For the more devotional this is also quite comforting, knowing someone's out there watching over us. Even if it seems that nothing is happening in our practice, we know they will reward us later. This is similar to the lay Asian view but seems difficult to reconcile with Buddhism's nontheism.

You wouldn't believe how often I've heard this point debated (often within my own mind). From one viewpoint, some rituals just don't make sense whereas other rituals or different parts of the same one will flow just fine. I will be doing some long ritual or puja and thinking that the deity is just a symbol of my buddha-nature; it will all make sense, and I will even feel inspired and somewhat pleased with my high view and for having figured it out. Just then, I will have to imagine the deity within some strange Hindu god or something, and the whole edifice I'd been constructing and congratulating myself about will come crumbling down!

The answer, I believe, is that both approaches are partially true; their union, that the deities are both symbolic of inner states to be developed and are tangible external beings who can intercede and help the practitioner, is the real solution. I would like to quote the great modern meditation master, Bokar Rinpoche. Although he is speaking of one deity in particular, Chenrezig, his words can be applied to any of the other myriad yidams. Here he is at length:

> Who really is Chenrezig, deity with a white body and four, sometimes one thousand, arms? ...Is it a luminous god, soft and compassionate, who from the far heavens keeps watch over the fate of beings as most of Tibetan people believe? Is it a simple symbolic image as Westerners sometimes think? Is it still another reality, deeper and richer?
>
> First, we need to know that Chenrezig is both an appearance, the divine manifestation, as well as an essence, the inner reality, with one not excluding or contradicting the other. The appearance of Chenrezig is the symbol of his essence made manifest. Through this appearance we can approach the essence of Chenrezig. The appearance does not exhaust the essence anymore than the essence negates the appearance. To pretend that Chenrezig only has an existence outside ourselves would be a mistake. But it would also be a mistake to see him only as an abstraction. Grasping the link between the two aspects (appearance and essence) is necessary in order to understand both his nature and meditation.
>
> Chenrezig is the mode of being of the mind that is the union of emptiness and compassion. From the viewpoint of the definitive meaning Chenrezig is the ultimate nature of the mind. In other words, one may say that Chenrezig is bodhichitta in its two aspects:
>
> • Absolute bodhichitta corresponding to emptiness,
> • Relative bodhichitta corresponding to compassion.
>
> Chenrezig is within us because love and compassion are not qualities added to the mind. These qualities are part of the awakened state even if, for the moment, this state exists only as a potential for us.
>
> Saying that Chenrezig is the ultimate nature of the mind does not negate his form manifestation. The essence expresses itself through an appearance. Chenrezig exists on the level of definitive

meaning and also on the level of literal meaning where he appears in the form of the deity by which he is usually known. He is the visible expression taken by all the buddhas to help us activate the love and compassion that are presently only a potential in us and to reveal the ultimate Chenrezig in ourselves.

The relationship between Chenrezig as the potential of compassion in our mind and Chenrezig appearing as a divine form is the real foundation of the practice:

- On one hand, Chenrezig as a manifested deity is charged with and transmits the power of the grace and compassion of the mind of all buddhas;
- On the other hand, our mind is endowed with the potentiality of love and compassion;

- Thirdly, the ineluctable interconnection that links everything causes the first factor to necessarily act on the second one and reveal it.[13]

There are three key points while practicing kyerim: the clarity of the visualization, the pride of the deity, and the recollection of the meaning. In theory, visualizations are supposed to be clearer than real life. In extended commentaries, the minutiae of visualization are taught with amazing detail. In one practice I've done, I had to visualize myself as a deity. Inside that deity were the subtle energy channels. Inside the channels were more deities. Inside the deities were Tibetan letters. Light circulated from letter to letter. In retreat it is possible to spend a lot of time building up a visualization like this, and in the process I've discovered a trick or two that helps.

In general, visualization can be extremely difficult if not impossible for most people. On the other hand, some people are natural visualizers. Without effort or training, they can visualize clearly. A friend of mine can visualize so clearly that he can mentally walk around the visualization, viewing it from all angles. According to research about one in ten people are natural visualizers, and of these three out of four are women.

Here are some of the tricks I've stumbled across while trying to master this skill. First, believe that the visualization is really there. If you're trying to visualize a deity in front of you, develop the conviction that the deity is really there and that you're just trying to see it, rather than trying to create it from scratch. It's as if you are tuning into a radio station that you know is already broadcasting.

Second, emotion helps. If you feel devotion toward the deity in front of you, that will also help make it clearer. Yearning will bring it closer.

Third, try to keep the visualization moving. Scan the visualization. Move from top to bottom, adding details as the visualization fades. If you're visualizing the Buddha in front of you, start with his hair. When that starts to fade, add the eyes, the ears, etc. Work down to the lotus seat and then scan upward. Most people find this easier than trying to hold and stabilize a static image. This also makes use of our tendency to indulge continually in discursiveness. When you feel the beginning of a thought welling up, use that energy and momentum to add another feature to the visualization. With the Buddha, for instance, if you feel a thought coming, add some folds to his robes. If you really like to think, you can add the wheels to the soles of his feet or decorate his robes with brocade-like patterns. This can be a lot of fun. You can really get lost in this, and the time can just fly by. Lamas feel that very complicated visualizations are completely appropriate for Westerners because we are so very discursive. We may long for simple practices, but simple practices require that we block the tendency to be discursive. In these practices, we are using that tremendous momentum of the mind to progress instead of squashing it.

The fourth trick is similar to the previous technique: Intensify the visualization. If I visualize a Tibetan letter, I try to make it three-dimensional and glistening as if it were made out of ice. It's actually clearer that way than if I try to visualize a flatter, more lifeless letter. Hence, an important point is that the more complicated and difficult the visualization, the easier you might find it and the clearer the resultant image will be.

Fifth, remember the emptiness aspect. We may not be completely clear what that means at this point, but there are a few things we can keep in mind that can enhance our ability to visualize. We've already dissolved our ordinary body at the beginning of the practice; therefore, we shouldn't allow ourselves to refocus on our physical sensations. Also, we've dissolved our ordinary mind; therefore, our visualization should exist without a strong sense of a watching, judging, manipulating mind.

The visualization just hangs by itself in space. I'll talk a little bit more about this idea in a while.

Perhaps none of these suggestions will help. Your visualization might still be exceptionally hazy, almost completely nonexistent. Don't despair. There are lots of us out there who are having the same problem as you. Luckily, these practices are so rich that even if visualization doesn't work for you, another aspect will give the practice meaning and value and will provide a technique for your growth and development.

One technique I have found to be amazingly successful is the deity's pride. The general instruction is to consider oneself as the deity rather than as your usual Bob or Jane. For many years I had great resistance—who was I fooling? I knew what a hopeless jerk I was. What was the use of pretending?

Then, while in retreat, I read a quote from Je Tsongkhapa, the great founder of the Gelug school. Tsongkhapa said that in the beginning one's pride is very conceptual; it is simply the thought, "I am this deity!" But one should check one's mind and notice the ordinary or nondeity aspects of it. These are to be abandoned as one returns to the deity's pride.

This quote in a very obscure book really opened a gate for me. Instead of thinking "How could I possibly be a deity?" I saw that I could use this technique as a method to abandon those very self-images that were keeping me from feeling like a deity in the first place.

Like most Westerners, I have been plagued by many intense and well-entrenched negative self-images. "I'm unlovable," "I'm not attractive," "I'm weak," etc. Sound familiar? Well, these self-images are nothing more than clusters of thoughts, albeit with a tremendous amount of energy invested in them. We spend our life crippled by these images, and we view all our experiences through these very distorted lenses. I know from my own experience that these images make us completely miserable.

But these images have power only if we identify with them. And the buddhas have been insightful and compassionate enough to give us a very easy technique to overcome this tyranny. We simply acknowledge how we are identifying with a self-image and then recollect the pride of the deity. When we disidentify with the self-image, its power completely evaporates. And the thought, "I am the deity," gives us something to hang onto. It's like jumping out of a sinking ship into a shiny cruiser.

Once you get the hang of it, it's an easy and effective method for dealing with a variety of problems and negativities. It requires no skill in visualization, simply the intelligence to identify where you're stuck and a willingness to change. Believe me, it is a most effective technique.

When you're not crippled by negative self-images, your invocation of divine pride can be subtler. Tsoknyi Rinpoche explains deity pride as that which holds the disparate parts of the visualization together. Without that pride, you have only parts. Tulku Urgyen has said that invoking divine pride has more merit than having a clear visualization; from my own experience I completely concur. My teacher, Chökyi Nyima Rinpoche, told me that during rituals, divine pride is more effective than visualization in realizing the ritual. For instance, if you are doing a ritual for long life, believing that you are really Amitayus, the buddha of long life, even without clear visualization, is more effective than visualizing clearly but still harboring some doubts about pride.

Traditionally, clear visualization precedes pride. In fact, visualization when done properly elicits pride. The imagery gives you a sense of being the deity. We all know how good we feel about ourselves when we're nicely dressed—it definitely affects our minds. Here we are allowing the visualization to work in the same way. Having the various forms and attributes gives rise to the appropriate sense of being the possessor or inhabitant of those forms. Instead, I often teach divine pride first so that my students get some sense of it before struggling with the visualization, especially since so many of us can take ages before we feel really comfortable with this process. In that case, the visualization can flow out of the pride. "Since I'm this deity, I must have this body!"

The third aspect of kyerim that one must embrace is recollection of the meaning. Remember, the first is clear visualization, and the second is divine pride. First, all deities are made of rainbow light. They're not flesh and blood like you and me nor are they clay or brass like statues. They are completely pure. Also, they don't have ordinary insides, such as livers or small intestines. They're either completely hollow, or they contain subtle energy channels, moon disks, mantra circles, and so on. There's a deep and pure symbolic meaning to their attributes, weapons, and ornaments. It is not that they are in union because they're horny; they're not brandishing swords because they feel angry and they want to get even. Their union represents the union of skillful means and emptiness, the swords cut through duality or ego clinging, and so on. If you think they're just like us, that's a big mistake.

Understanding the discriminating wisdom that cuts through dualistic conceptions is difficult; visualizing a sword is much easier. But because of the blessing of the practice and the power of symbols to act deeply on the mind, visualizing brings the symbolized reality closer. You really start to feel that you are cutting through ignorance, and you can start to feel that this is truly happening rather than being imaged. Other deities are depicted trampling on representations of the ego or one's negativities; visualizing oneself like this can be quite empowering and a great aid in overcoming one's limitations. When one has experiences like these, one can genuinely appreciate the profundity of these techniques.

Although it may be difficult to remember or to practice perfectly, one should never forget the connection with emptiness. We can easily comprehend that the deity is no different than our mind; it has no separate existence from it in any way. Can we truly distinguish between a mind that is doing the visualizing and the visualization itself? Where does one end and the other begin? The visualization should be merged with one's experience or understanding of rigpa. If that is too difficult, remember the advice of Jamgon Kongtrul:

> Though a beginner has difficulty in realizing [the correct view], he or she can, however, understand that the mind appearing as the deity is the generation phase, that knowing the deity to be one's own mind is the completion phase, that realizing these two to be inseparable is the yoga of union.[14]

If one's visualization and pride are both stable, but there is no recollection, there is the danger of taking the whole set-up too literally. "I am the Great Wrathful One crushing all enemies." Remember that what you're really crushing is your ego. If not, you can become demonic, taking the whole thing very literally and using the images to fortify your ego and project it out against others. You might become like the yogi who couldn't leave his cave because he believed he had grown all these extra arms and horns.

When one begins a deity practice, it is good to receive as much commentary on the practice as possible. For any kyerim practice, there will be instruction manuals explaining the shrine set-up, the appropriate visualizations for each stage, especially what's to be visualized while reciting the mantra, which can become very elaborate and sometimes quite juicy, and how to do retreat on the practice. There will be notes on subsidiary practices, signs of progress, both in your sitting and in dreams or visions, and how to deal with various obstacles. The above quote, for instance, comes from Jamgon Kongtrul's commentary on a Guru Rinpoche practice called *Konchog Chidu*. Although many of these commentaries are not yet translated, they're worth seeking out. Some of the most useful information on Vajrayana practice is contained within them.

There are also some good general commentaries on kyerim such as Gyatrul Rinpoche's *Generating the Deity*. Also, a manual of teachings for one deity may contain good general advice for any practice. The earlier long quote by Bokar Rinpoche came from *Chenrezig: Lord of Love*, but obviously, his words can be applied to any deity. Be somewhat discriminating, however, in mixing advice; visualization details cannot be transposed from one sadhana to another, even for the same deity. These books and other teachings you receive will not only teach you the visualizations but also clarify the meaning of the practice as a whole and of each individual stage, such as refuge and bodhichitta, throwing a torma to the obstructers, etc.

The main concept of kyerim is *dagnang*, which is usually translated as "pure perception" or "sacred outlook." Dagnang means to regard all beings as deities, all sounds as mantra, all thoughts as the play of the deity's awareness. What does this mean? Does this mean that the objects of perception change form? Your friends are really walking around with consorts in their laps and swords in their hands? And when they ask you how you're doing, they're really saying OM MANI PADME HUM? How would you reply?

The exact meaning and method of practice of pure perception is quite elusive and subtle. It is true that advanced practitioners actually do have experiences of the world as a mandala. Devoted students would see Je Tsongkhapa as Manjushri, for example. On the other hand, it's difficult to fake. How can we twist what we're actually perceiving?

We can start by being willing to concede that our judgments are merely that—judgments. They don't necessarily correspond to the outer world. Let go of them and then see how the world appears. When appearances are not being judged quite so heavily, you might notice a change in their quality; your perception will shift somewhat. It will give you a clue on how to proceed. Keep trying to see through your rigid judgments. The world will be much more open.

One problem that always arises is how to deal with difficult people in that state. Are we breaking our samaya by having a clear understanding of what they're doing? Chökyi Nyima Rinpoche answered me as follows: "No matter how much people seem to be careening off the road, they always have a good heart." Later, he added: "The negative things that they do are due to their *not* having pure perception."

Rinpoche has further explained to me that there are two aspects to pure perception—contrived and absolute. The former is the fabricated visualization of deities and the recitation of their mantras. The second is how the world actually appears to someone experiencing absolute reality. The former is valuable because with time and cultivation it leads to the latter.

Some of the difficulties we have with deity practice and pure perception can be clarified by examining a little bit of Tibetan Buddhist philosophy. If we believe emptiness means reducing everything to a kind of neutral grayness, it's hard to understand where deities come from. But the philosophy of emptiness, especially the presentation of the Kagyupas and Nyingmapas, emphasizes that when one overcomes conceptual designations generally associated with the explication of emptiness, what remains is the inconceivable qualities, the wisdoms and embodiments. In deity practice and in the cultivation of pure perception, one is connecting with these inconceivable qualities.

What are some of the dangers of kyerim practice for Westerners? First, kyerim can be an indulgence in dissociation or fantasy. If you have problems that you're not dealing with, it can be pleasant to escape into this world of deities and magic. Of course, this merely enforces the underlying problem by giving it a reality from which it is necessary to escape. By trying always to be "pure," you repress anything that you perceive in yourself or in the outer world that would appear as impure. This can feed what the Jungians call the "shadow," the dark, repressed side of our mind. I feel it takes a considerable amount of practice and spiritual sophistication to be able to use kyerim to deal directly with our negativities. If we try to have pure perception of our worst faults, we can open up to their twisted energy and free ourselves from their grasp in a very quick and powerful manner. This is quite different from trying to be "pure" in too literal a way. Detailed instructions for this kind of transformation are not usually included in the commentaries, and we're usually left on our own.

Chökyi Nyima Rinpoche told me that lamas assume that practitioners will use the techniques to benefit their minds. When the lamas discover the instructions have been poorly applied, it can possibly be too late. That's why I feel that a period of sitting meditation before beginning Vajrayana practice can be extremely beneficial. When we do simple practices, we develop the habit of dealing directly with our stuff. We get the point, and as a result, our subsequent Vajrayana practice can be very effective—it is an even more direct technique! The techniques I mentioned earlier of using the pride of the deity for confronting negative self-image is an example of that directness.

It's easy to forget the association with rigpa or buddha-nature while doing kyerim. Our visualizations or experiences can be very solid and can cause one to forget the connection. Or we can get lost in detail, trying so hard to perfect the endless details of the visualization that we forget we are actually trying to benefit our mind and realize our buddha-nature. We can also become absorbed in the broader details of the tradition of kyerim and tantra, the different tertons and terma, different lineages, outer aspects of rituals, etc. so that tantra becomes more of a hobby than a spiritual path.

We can also be naive about pure perception. A friend of mine bought a real lemon of a car and drove it coast to coast because he happened to have pure perception of the man selling it. Somehow we have to balance our yearning to perceive others purely with the need to function effectively.

We can confuse ordinary purity or beauty with pure perception. We might consider organic food to be more spiritual than non-organic food, the woods to be purer than the city. While there may be some truth in these views, they are not the correct meaning of pure perception. Pure perception is always pointing to the absolute.

By developing these skills of deity practice, incredible transformation can take place. We can leave all those painful negative self-images behind. We can begin to connect with the reality embodied by the deity. Kyerim practice is sometimes mystifying and confusing, but our effort to penetrate the truth that the deity manifests will be extremely rewarding.

CHAPTER SIXTEEN

Rituals

The life of a typical Vajrayana monastery revolves around its cycles of rituals. At Ka-Nying Shedrup Ling, the monastery where I lived and studied in Nepal, an extensive purification ritual is done toward the end of the Tibetan year. It lasts nine days and includes *tsog*, the offering of food, powerful music, and lama dancing. There are different shifts of people practicing all night so that the mantra is being recited continuously. Many great lamas will "drop in," and I've been fortunate enough to see H. H. Dilgo Khyentse Rinpoche, H. E. Kalu Rinpoche, and other great masters at this puja.

This is followed by a several-day protector ritual that ends right before Losar, or Tibetan New Year. Most Kagyupas practice Mahakala before Losar, while Nyingmapas usually perform Vajrakilaya rituals. During these rituals, all negativities and obstacles will be repeatedly driven into a huge torma, which is fashioned into a humanlike form, that will be burned on the last day. The highest lama present, wearing full ritual regalia, will start the fire by shooting a flaming arrow at the human effigy. It is quite powerful, and one can certainly identify with what is going on—everything negative and unpleasant being burned, going up in smoke ...

Then comes Losar, the biggest holiday for Tibetans, consisting of three days of constant partying. Even the monasteries get into the spirit of things. Everyone puts on their finery, including jewelry that looks as though it should be used for weight training rather than ornamentation, and visits the lamas to offer them huge trays of (for us Westerners) almost completely inedible food.

This is followed at Ka-Nying Shedrup Ling by a nine-day ritual for long life. It is also quite extensive, including lama dancing, etc. And on it goes.

Sometimes I go; often I don't. It's nice to sit with my teacher, even in a room with hundreds of others. There's an undeniable power—it is obvious that something is going on. But in the end, especially because it's all in Tibetan, I feel a little confused and alienated. I know something is happening, but I don't know how to connect.

During our retreat in Scotland, we spent approximately one quarter of our time in pujas. Some of us liked them; many like me were overwhelmed, bored, or alienated. Our rituals were almost as elaborate as in Nepal. Back here in Oregon, Tashi Chöling has a yearly schedule of three long pujas. Since I've moved into town, I rarely attend.

Like many Westerners, my main tool for dealing with life is my intellect. Especially when confronted by a situation I do not understand, I try my best to analyze and examine it until I have a tool for coping, a gateway for entering. Unfortunately, it is difficult at this time to receive sufficient instruction in the theory behind rituals to the degree that an intellectual person like myself actually feels comfortable with what is going on. Although there is a power and profundity to Tibetan rituals that can speak to us in a language much deeper and more basic than logic, the rituals themselves have clearly delineated meanings that have been clearly explicated in traditional Tibetan sources.

Because so much of what really happens at Dharma centers is ritual, it's a subject we really can't ignore. So although I'm not the best person to speak up for this tradition, I have given it a lot of thought. Also, rituals have, at times, been very moving and powerful for me. I'll be discussing my interpretation of rituals here; much of it I've gleaned from my teachers, some from other Buddhist readings, some from more general Western sources, and a little from my own struggles. If you're a person with the same difficulties or resistance, I hope this will help.

First, let's discuss the ritual itself. Although of course each one is different they follow a similar format. Different rituals will emphasize different sections.

Rituals or pujas are all centered around a major deity. For example, the three major pujas at Tashi Chöling are focused on the three deities of Vajrakilaya, Vajrasattva, and Tronma Ngagmo, a wrathful dakini. Two are from the termas of Dudjom Rinpoche, and the last from his predecessor, Dudjom Lingpa. Other centers will do other pujas.

Each ritual will have a main text associated with it. Different sections of the text will be chanted in each session. In addition, commonly known prayers will be occasionally inserted, such as the lamas' long life prayers. The chanting will be punctuated by the playing of music. The chant leader or *umdze* will play the cymbals; someone else will play the drums. The high lamas, here called the *dorje loppons*, play the small hand drum, the *damaru*. If your center is more established, or if there are Tibetan monks in the community, they can be additional instruments: the *radong*, the longhorn, an oboe-like reed instrument called the *jaling*, and a trumpet-like horn called the *kanling*.

Every ritual has a shrine master or *choppon*. It is his or her job to prepare the shrine and make sure all the tormas are made. The choppon must also prepare the tsog so that it's ready to be shared during the puja itself. During the puja, the choppon is usually hectically running around acting out what is being chanted—lighting incense, making offerings, taking tormas outside. That person will have to make prostrations at certain times and will probably get very little sleep.

During the ritual, all participants without other jobs are expected to chant, play their bells occasionally while holding the vajra, do the visualizations, make the beautiful hand gestures called *mudras*, and recollect the meaning while the chanting and the rest are going on. It is, however, especially the job of the dorje loppon to maintain the visualization. Therefore, the dorje loppon will be the highest lama present. If there are many high lamas, they will all be loppons; playing damarus, they will sit higher than the other practitioners on the shrine side of the umdze. If there are no high lamas present, the job can be done on a rotational basis along with the other jobs. It is also obviously everyone's responsibility to help with the preparation and the cleaning up.

Learning the various jobs is a great way to learn the puja itself. As the umdze, you learn the chanting and the order of the ritual. As the choppon, you actually act out the visualization, which makes it more real and deepens your understanding. And, of course, as the dorje loppon, you learn the visualization, the main part of the practice.

The more familiar you are with the ritual before it begins, the more you will get out of it. At least try to read the English translation before it begins so you have some idea what is going on. In retreat, we did different practices on our own. At their conclusion, we would meet and do more extensive rituals together, but by then we were already quite familiar with the visualizations and most of the liturgy, greatly enhancing their power.

Most pujas follow a fairly standard format. They'll begin as in an empowerment, with offering a gektor, reciting the lineage prayers, taking refuge and engendering the enlightened attitude of bodhichitta. There will be a section on purifying obscurations and accumulating merit. This usually takes the form of a seven-branch prayer, but it may involve a short ngondro. Next, a wheel of protection or a vajra tent will be erected. Within that vajra tent, the environment, practitioners, and offerings will all be blessed. These sections are very similar to those we discussed that take place at the beginning of an empowerment; these are the preparation.

The next section is called the "main part" and is similar to the deity practices one would do on one's own. It entails developing the visualization of the deity, inviting the wisdom deity, making offerings and praises, and reciting the mantra. These stages as well as the preparatory ones are extremely important, and the student should learn the meaning and appropriate visualizations.

Next come the stages that are unique to each specific puja. Associated with the offering of food will be the consecration of the tsog, the invitation of those to whom it will be offered, and the actual offering, which might have several subdivisions. There will be confessions and fulfillment (*kangwa*), which help to restore broken samaya. If it is a Nyingma puja, a *phurba* (a ritual dagger) will be used to liberate obstructers. While standard prayers, especially long life prayers for the lamas, are recited, the participants will also partake of the tsog offerings. Leftover food offerings are offered to the worldly protectors, and the *siddhis*, or spiritual accomplishments, are received.

The concluding stages will be more familiar. The deity and its mandala surroundings will dissolve and re-emerge, and there will be the dedication of merit.

More elaborate pujas will contain additional sections such as self-empowerment and fire offerings. This briefly introduces the main structure, but you must learn the details and meaning from a qualified lama after receiving empowerment.

No discussion of ritual would be complete without mentioning protectors. Most rituals have a section for protectors, which is usually recited between the mantra recitation and the tsog. Also, there are many pujas specifically for the protectors —I've already mentioned the yearly Vajrakilaya ritual that is performed at my monastery in Nepal. In our retreat in Scotland, we did a daily protector practice for our main protector, the two-armed Mahakala, Dorje Bernag Chen, as well as a four-hour monthly practice and a one-week yearly practice.

There are two kinds of protectors—wisdom and worldly. Worldly protectors are powerful, unenlightened beings who have promised to aid practitioners. If you read the Buddhist sutras, you will notice that most sutra texts end with a chorus of many nonhumans who vow to protect the practitioners of that particular teaching. Also, in the life stories of great yogis such as Guru Rinpoche and Milarepa, we can read how they subjugated powerful spirits who came to disrupt their meditation and made them become servants of the doctrine.

Wisdom protectors are like yidams; they are emanations of the buddhas. In fact, some deities are regarded as both yidams and protectors. Vajrakilaya serves this dual function for the Nyingmapas; Yamantaka is both for the Gelugpas. They are generally but not always extremely wrathful and often in union. The majority are female. As is the case with the yidams, different people connect with different protectors; hence, the variety.

What is the function of these protectors and the rituals in their name? Their job is to clear away obstacles for practitioners.

When we practice, we experience many kinds of obstacles. In general, these can be divided into the usual classifications of *outer*, *inner*, and *secret*. Outer obstacles are sickness, poor conditions, lack of leisure, etc. Inner obstacles are difficulties with the tsa, lung, and tigle—the channels, winds, and essences of our "vajra body." (I'll be saying more about these in the next chapter). Secret obstacles are subtle conceptualizations that obscure our buddha-nature.

When we practice, we are purifying eons of negative karma. Its ripening effect would be overwhelming if we were without any outside help. Luckily for us, every instant in the universe someone attains complete enlightenment, and these countless buddhas have nothing but the best wishes for us. Although not completely omnipotent in the way that some people imagine their god, the buddhas are not without power. One way that power manifests is in the form of these protectors.

It is up to us to connect with that power. That is the purpose of the rituals. Generally, protector rituals are straightforward: We visualize them, make offerings and recite their mantra, and imagine them somehow destroying or removing obstacles. Of course, even with these rituals, practitioners will still have difficulties; these practices should, however, help lighten the load.

It's not always obvious what our obstacles are. We can think that being sick or poor is slowing our practice, but we may have some subtle attitude that is even worse. When in retreat, I was dreading a particular practice and becoming very negative about it. Right before our monthly Mahakala puja, I dreamt of a basketball team in white uniforms miraculously defeating the team dressed in black. During the subsequent ritual, I felt my negativity toward that practice dissolving, and I did it with an open mind. I was later pleased with the results.

In the beginning of our puja are the following lines:

> *Daypa dang ni damtsig gi*
> *Palden gonpo chendren na*

These words mean something like: "With faith and commitment, the holy protectors are invited." This simple line said so much to me. There are all these enlightened beings out there who have vowed to aid me. I also yearn for their assistance. What do I need to invoke their help? Faith and commitment. Commitment here means keeping the vows of Vajrayana. When the vows are kept and there is the openness of faith, we can receive the blessing and assistance of these protectors.

We usually need an empowerment to do protector practice, and there is generally a daily commitment to make offerings, usually the offering of a *serkyem*. *Serkyem* means "golden cup" and is an offering of some grain, usually prepared with black tea or sometimes with wine or beer. The offerings are accompanied by a short liturgy. Please exert yourself in keeping this commitment. I've been told the worldly protectors can get upset if you break it.

Also, please never use these kinds of practices for your own power or to harm others. You may think other people are an obstacle, but don't use Buddhist ritual to harm them. In the first place, it probably won't work (you would be lacking the abovementioned commitment because of your attitude), and second, you would be creating very bad karma and breaking many vows.

To return to the main discussion: What is the purpose of all these rituals? I've discerned five main reasons for doing group pujas: social relationships, accumulation of merit, reparation of broken samaya, symbolic or mythic meaning, and magic. The first three are easier to understand than the latter two. The social and mythic explanations tend to be Western attempts to understand something foreign; the other three are the standard replies you might receive from your teacher.

When I complained about having to do so many pujas in retreat, rather than justifying them on their own terms, Lama Yeshe spoke of the social benefits: learning to get along, working together, etc. At the time, I thought it sounded trivial, but with time I learned that group activities give me a chance to step out of my rigidity and to harmonize with others. It can be a powerful practice, and it is far from trivial.

I think we all have something to learn in this way. Even the various jobs during the ritual can be a teaching. One week we can be the loppon sitting majestically on throne maintaining the visualization; next time, we are the lowly drummer. There are always people in the community with whom we don't get along; in this way we can try to work it out rather than avoiding them or being negative. Meditating with others can be very healing in this way. Even the chanting itself, learning to harmonize your voice with the others, has a healing, symbolic effect. We are neither overwhelming others with our shouting nor retreating into a withdrawn silence. The proper chant becomes the proper stance and, as usual in Buddhism, another opportunity to follow the middle way.

Pujas are also intended as a means to accumulate merit. In Buddhism, there are two accumulations—the accumulation of merit and the accumulation of wisdom. When we're on our own we can have better conditions for meditation, especially meditation on the nature of the mind. These practices mainly accumulate wisdom. To balance this, group practice mainly accumulates merit. Extensive offerings are made repeatedly, and it is believed that the merit is additive for the group. That is, ten people each accumulate ten times the merit by being in a group than if they were to do the puja on their own. The merit is shared equally, so if you are the choppon running around and not focusing on the visualization at all, the benefit for you is the same as that quiet, meditative person in the back. The converse is unfortunately also true. If there is negativity it too is shared.

Pujas repair broken samaya. As I've mentioned before, we take a whole collection of vows when we receive empowerment. Even when we try our best, we are still breaking them all the time. What can we do to restore the vows, avoid vajra hell, and keep the stream of blessings flowing? Although there are innumerable vows that one can break, they can all be reduced to losing pure perception, the view that all beings are deities, that the environment is a mandala, that all sounds are mantra, and so on. We lose pure perception of our teacher, our vajra brothers and sisters, our environment. The ritual is a way of reconstructing that purity. Of key importance is the tsog, where the main food offering is the meat and alcohol, foods that were considered completely impure in ancient Brahmanic India. If we see them with Western eyes we miss the point. We take something that we regard as impure, and with our minds we transmute it into something pure. We then offer it to those in front of whom we made the original vow to maintain pure perception.

Almost all pujas have a section called the *kangwa* that takes place after the tsog has been offered to the invited holy guests. Lines are often chanted that end with *thug dam kang*. *Thug* means "enlightened mind," *dam* means "samaya" or "commitment," and *kang* means "fulfilled." So the general meaning would be something like, "I have broken my samayas and hence my connection with your enlightened energy. Please accept these transformed offerings as my attempt to rectify and restore this transgression, and may your enlightened mind be satisfied with my effort." The kangwa is a very important part of a puja; it's where the reparation of samaya is accomplished.

When we as Westerners get together and try to make sense of this vast Tibetan system of ritual, our own feeble attempts to grasp their deep meaning usually focus on the symbolic meaning. I'm hardly on expert on symbolism, and if you want to learn more about this way of viewing rituals, you can start with the works of Carl Jung or Joseph Campbell, but I'll try to say a little.

We use symbols and rituals all the time. Many gestures, such as shaking hands, are rituals. Forms of polite address ("Hello, how are you?") are ritualized. Moreover, symbols are everywhere—for instance, in the omnipresent Nike logo. Words are symbols, too; in actuality they're just black lines on white paper.

In a sense, symbols are keys to as well as representations of certain states of mind. Symbols are evocative, and what they invoke becomes identified with the symbol. This is true with Nike, and it is also true of religious symbolism. Consider Chenrezig, the buddha of compassion. He is white, with four arms, two outstretched, the other two placed at his heart. If you visualize yourself in this form, the actual imagery invokes compassion. One cannot help but get a glimpse or an intuition of what it would mean to have the love and compassion of a buddha. Or consider Manjushri's sword. Contemplating its sharpness and activity can also aid you to understand and connect with the cutting-through quality of discriminating wisdom that it represents.

Just as a melody is a succession of notes, a puja is a succession of symbols. Strung together, they become a story. We can view this story as a myth or as like a dream.

Myths are stories with which cultures express their deepest truths and most profound wisdom. They are usually transmitted to their children before logical, representational thinking is fully developed so that the children are able to let the wisdom inherent in the myth permeate their being.

Kyerim in general and pujas especially have a story line. In kyerim it can be as simple as the birth and death of a deity. In pujas, the story is more complex with the vanquishing of opponents, the feast, the achievement of spiritual accomplishment, etc. If we were as open to this mythic process as are children sitting around the fire at night listening to the village elders, it would be very powerful indeed.

One day in retreat, feeling bored and alienated while sitting through another long puja, I thought, "What if I were dreaming this? What would it mean to dream that I was this wrathful deity vanquishing opponents?" I tried to place myself in a state similar to just waking up after a dream, where the barriers to symbolic meaning have yet to be rigidly erected. I had a powerful reaction. Instead of being wimpy or timid, I could feel myself with the actual courage, confidence, and strength to overcome the difficulties in my life. It was a moment of real insight into the ritual process.

The last main function of a ritual I would call magical. You won't find Tibetans using this term because of its association with black magic, which is practiced throughout Asia. If you inquire how rituals work, why waving an arrow with five-colored silk streamers helps to increase life, the answer will be *tendrel*. *Tendrel* is a word borrowed from the sutra tradition. There, it means "interdependent origination" and explains how everything arises due to various causes and conditions. The main teachings on tendrel are the teachings on the twelve links of interdependent origination.

When used in tantra in the context of ritual, this terms(term) can still be translated as interdependent origination. However, the meaning is clearly the same as our word *magic*. Magic is the manipulation of appearances. Wherever magic is found, an integral part is always the use of a simulacrum, an image or representation of the object to be manipulated. One can recognize the use of simulacra in all tantric rituals. Tormas themselves are representatives of various offerings, perhaps even flesh. Effigies are, of course, images of various beings. If one asks why manipulating these objects influences the object represented, the answer is tendrel. There is an interconnectedness between the image and the object that is more than symbolic. How things are interconnected in this way is a revelation of the omniscience of a buddha; there may not be an obvious connection.

When we dispel obstructing forces (*gek*) with mustard seed and gugal, there is no obvious link between the mustard seed and the gek. We can't say why mustard seeds function in such a way. We can't say that there's something symbolically evocative about mustard seeds that touches a part of us, making us feel strong enough to overcome any difficulty. All we can say is "magic."

One universal quality of magic is that it must be performed perfectly. That is, if one is making a magic potion, everything must be exact. The right ingredients must be gathered, prepared exactly, and the right magic words must be said. Only then will it work.

This principle also applies to our rituals. The tormas must have just the right shape; so must their butter ornaments. Mantras must be recited accurately. The music is not a creative expression; every note is prescribed by the lamas. Many of the jaling (an oboe-like Indian horn) melodies in our retreat were written by either the Dalai Lamas or the Karmapas. And of course the mudras, the hand gestures, must be correctly done. Most important are the visualization and the activation of the pride of the deity. Only when everything is done accurately can one expect to receive the benefits of the ritual, such as long life, wealth, or the vanquishing of obstacles.

Another aspect of tendrel is that in ritual we are imitating the behavior of a deity, an enlightened being. Traditionally, we would even dress up like one. Now we simply speak, gesture, eat, etc. like the deity and imagine ourselves doing the other activities a deity does. Practice makes perfect!

These five, the social, meritorious, and so on, functions of pujas and rituals are all interrelated. If you are having difficulties with the ritual, find the purpose that means the most to you and use it as a bridge to reach the others. Eventually with time, it's perhaps best to leave the more Western interpretations behind and try to understand the ritual in its own terms.

Even with these five good reasons for participating, many of us still have difficulties with these rituals. These difficulties should be acknowledged and discussed.

The first reason for difficulty is the most obvious: Rituals are almost always performed in Tibetan. In a previous chapter I discussed the merits of learning Tibetan, but for the vast majority of us, we'll never have the opportunity to learn it, so spending hours chanting a language we don't understand can be wearying. Also, the language barrier makes it very difficult to actualize the benefits of many of the purposes of the ritual that I just discussed. It's hard to struggle with the transliteration, sneak glimpses at the English translation, and try to remember the meaning and visualization. The rationale for doing it in Tibetan refers to the fifth function mentioned above: magic. The ritual just isn't complete if it isn't correctly chanted, and that includes doing it in Tibetan. As the rituals are all composed by enlightened beings, the words are charged with power; one cannot say the same of the translation. It's as if the whole puja were one long mantra. The Tibetan is also written in meter, so it's more fun and powerful to chant; it's possible to chant it with the beat of the cymbals and drum.

Another main problem with ritual is cultural. We have very little in our culture that is similar to a puja, and many of us have lost our connection with our own rituals. We have also lost our connection with our great myths. Symbols don't speak to us easily.

Many of us, myself included, have difficulty relating to anything that isn't logically or linearly presented. The practices associated with rituals have generally been given to us without detailed explanations; as a result, we often assume that those explanations don't exist and that the ritual is more a reflection of Tibetan culture than of Buddhist practice. Sometimes Westerners even say that the rituals are a reflection of the pre-Buddhist Bonpo culture and have been kept to appease ordinary Tibetans. Even if we would like to accustom ourselves to these practices, it can prove very difficult to deprogram our modern perspectives. It's hard for us to enter a sweatlodge with the same openness as our forebears; our cynicism seems always to get in the way. The openness of faith and trust is what aids the effectiveness of rituals; if the trust is lacking, the practice seems to not work, further inhibiting trust.

Tibetans are raised in a world of ritual and symbolism. It was one of the things I experienced strongly when I saw the movie *Kundun*. The magic and ritual were always there; they were a part of their daily life the way technology is a part of ours. It's not something they have to learn or think themselves into. Tibetans don't have to talk themselves into ceremony any more than we have to talk ourselves into using a cell phone.

Sometimes the opposite situation will be true. Some people come from a Catholic background that is full of ritual, some of it hauntingly similar to the rituals of Tibetan Buddhism. But for some people, something about their early experiences may have left a bad taste, and when they encounter something in Tibetan Buddhism that seems similar, they feel turned off. When encountering Buddhist ritual, many people may not be able to let go of their previous negative associations.

One problem we all have as Westerners encountering Tibetan Buddhism is trying to discern what is *Tibetan* from what is *Buddhism*, especially since much of what appears in Tibetan Buddhism doesn't appear in the other countries where Buddhism spread. Because of the isolation of Tibet, its form of Buddhism was the last to reach the Western world, and by that time there was already an agreed-upon view of what Buddhism was. Are these rituals really the teaching of the Buddha, or are they a manifestation of Tibetan culture? We may find ourselves with the following attitude: I regard as true, essential Buddhism those aspects of Tibetan Buddhism with which I feel comfortable. Those parts that make me nervous I regard as cultural. I can then dismiss everything toward which I feel resistance or do not understand. This argument is now being applied to more than just ritual; some people are questioning the principle of reincarnation and the importance of the lama in a similar way. Very neat.

It's really not so simple. Tibetan culture has been permeated by Buddhist insight and practice for more than a thousand years. Many of the things Tibetans do, right down to how they pour a cup of tea for you, are thoroughly grounded in Buddhist insight and compassion. We can understand these things if we take the time and make the effort. What we dismiss today might very well be discovered tomorrow to be a manifestation of considerable wisdom. As I have mentioned, Buddhist ritual is completely grounded in Buddhist philosophy, especially in the teachings on emptiness. We can even say that they are a natural expression of that understanding. So we should be very cautious about what we discount without having made the effort to investigate deeper. That especially includes the world of ritual.

Other areas of resistance may be related to how Tibetan Buddhism is taught in this country. When lamas teach here, they talk about ngondro or other topics that are related to the theory and practice of ultimate truth. They will only rarely talk about kyerim, and they never, to my knowledge, discuss ritual. I've never seen anything like a weekend seminar entitled "Theory and Practice of Tibetan Magic" advertised in any of the Buddhist journals. With time, I am sure that the more extensive, profound commentaries on ritual practice will be available to sincere Western practitioners, and we will be able to understand what we are doing. Until then they will remain a mystery.

Hence, we are not really prepared for the pujas when we encounter them. If we were attracted to ritual in the first place, we would have sought out a spiritual path that openly promoted a ritualistic approach to life. We were probably drawn to something else in Buddhism—perhaps the effortless simplicity of the most advanced practices. It can be disappointing to find that what we're expected to practice, especially in groups, is not what we have heard or read about.

Also, we haven't been instructed in the rituals themselves. The talk we went to hear was on relaxed awareness, not magic for life extension. When we come to do the magic part, we haven't been properly trained. After all these years, I still don't feel properly trained, and I find that I've picked up much of my understanding in pieces—some from lamas, some from outside sources, some from my own cogitation.

One lament I always hear, sometimes even within my own mind, is, "Can't we skip all this ritual stuff? I just want to sit." This is a question we should think about very carefully, since we'll all ask it at one time or another.

Let's consider the common basis of all forms of Buddhism: the teachings on egolessness and the practice of meditation. That's where our interest is. But Vajrayana is supposed to be the esoteric, speedy path. If we neglect ritual, we are neglecting one of the components that make Vajrayana distinct and quick. It is taught that the Buddha said that in the future there will come a time when people will no longer be able to gain realization through the sutra techniques. For these people, the Buddha provided a technique that would be more rapid based on three aspects: mudra, mantra, and samadhi. Aren't we those people? Can we really progress by merely relying on simple techniques? If we could, that would be best. For those of us who cannot, it behooves us to create some kind of working relationship with this vast system of Buddhist magic.

CHAPTER SEVENTEEN

Dzogrim and the Body

As the reader can probably tell by now, I'm a fairly intellectual person, the kind others would speak of as "being in his head." It's been very amusing to me that my whole practice for these many years has mainly been body oriented. It wasn't something I chose; it happened somewhat automatically.

I began meditating earnestly in early 1975. In May I attended a short mindfulness retreat, taught by an English monk trained in Thailand. He taught us, through a series of techniques that gradually increased in subtlety, to be aware of very subtle sensations that with training could be felt in any part of the body. These sensations were soothingly blissful to experience. Time went quickly, and I had no problem gearing myself up to practice. These sensations and the accompanying bliss were very satisfying to me.

I knew these sensations didn't correspond to anything I had previously known. Also, they were like the tip of the iceberg; they were accompanied by a feeling that the body was hollow but full of moving energy.

When this energy moved into a new area, I experienced sensations such as tingling.

I had previously read Hindu books about *kundalini*, the so-called serpent energy that moves up the spine through the body. I had seen pictures of the chakras, lotuses of various colors and sizes, oriented around a hollow central axis, with Sanskrit letters on them. It was a little too much for my skeptical scientific mind to accept, and I dismissed this whole tradition without a second thought. But here I was now experiencing processes very reminiscent of those mentioned in the kundalini texts.

Three things happened at this point.

First, I became ill. This illness has lasted for years. It has always appeared to be linked in some way to a deepening involvement with these energetic processes. My health problems continue to the present.

Second, I continued to experience inexplicable sensations in various parts of my body while meditating that have dominated my practice to this day.

Third, I developed a strong interest in the formal practice of meditation that uses the internal energies, especially in the systems of practice that have been developed in Tibetan Buddhism. I read everything I could on the subject and did everything I could to learn these meditations from the lamas I met in the east and later in America.

These systems of meditations are generally classified as *dzogrim*, the stage of completion or perfection. Dzogrim is always juxtaposed with the previously discussed kyerim. Dzogrim has several meanings. When doing a deity practice and completing the mantra recitation for that session, the environment, deity, and seed syllable all dissolve. One then rests in the resultant state. The practice of dissolution with the subsequent resting is one use of the word *dzogrim*.

Dzogrim also refers to a very extensive system of teaching and practice that one engages in after completing a deity practice. It has two main divisions. "Dzogrim with signs" is the practice based on the body's energetic system. "Dzogrim without signs" is resting in the buddha-nature and is the same as mahamudra or dzogchen. I will now discuss the former, dzogrim with signs.

A major tenet of the Buddhist tantric system is the belief in a *vajra body*, an energetic body that is somehow related to our grosser body of flesh and blood. The vajra body has three main components—*tsa, lung,* and *tigle.* Tsa (Skt. *nadi*) are the energy channels that run through our body. The most important is the central channel that runs through the center of the body like a central tent pole. There are two smaller parallel channels and numerous branches that form the *chakras.* The functions of the chakras are explained in the commentaries and have very little correlation to the meanings commonly ascribed to them in new age parlance.

Lung means "breath," "wind," or "air." It is the same as the Sanskrit *prana* and the Chinese *chi.* It is the subtle aspect of the breath that flows through the channels. Tigle (Skt. *bindu*) is harder to define. It literally means "drops" and refers to subtle energetic essences. We inherit the red tigle from our mother and the white tigle from our father at the time of conception. There is a strong connection between tigle and sexual energy. One analogy I've heard is that tsa are like channels, lung is like the currents that flow through the channels, and tigle is what is moved by the currents.

The main practice of tsalung is *tummo.* Tummo literally means "wrathful female," but is most often translated as "inner heat." Through posture, breath control, visualization, and some sense of the view, a great ecstatic heat that is extremely helpful for realization is generated in the body. The main exercise for tummo is *bumchen,* or "vase breathing," a kind of breath control. When performed as one's main practice, it is often accompanied by a set of physical exercises known as *trulkor.*

The bliss and heat generated from doing tummo has one primary purpose. It is a powerful means for stabilizing buddha-nature. Although the practice has many useful side effects—bliss, keeping warm in the cold, and many miraculous powers—one should never lose sight of this connection with rigpa.

The principle involved here is "the inseparability of mind and energy." Even as beginners we can be aware of the reciprocity between our breathing and our mental state. When our breathing is rough, so is our mind. When our mind is serene, the breath is gentle and smooth.

This principle continues until enlightenment. Every mental state has a corresponding energetic configuration in the vajra body. Even the other realms have their energetic configurations; when energy flows in specific ways, we will experience ourselves in vats of molten metal or enjoying the great pleasures of the gods. All our conceptual mental states and negative emotions come from our internal energy running amok. So if we use these forceful methods to control our energy, our mind has no choice but to relax into its own nature. There is simply no fuel remaining for conceptualizations or obscurations.

Another explanation of the purpose of these practices is that since the nature of the mind is great bliss, to meditate on bliss puts us in a state that is closer to this realization. Because it is such a rigorous practice, tsalung utilizes the ambitious, active nature of some practitioners to reach a state of mind that is profoundly effortless and relaxed, rather than stifling that vitality.

From my years of study, I am quite convinced that when practiced properly, tummo is really a most rapid path to enlightenment. Unfortunately, it is difficult to practice properly—the qualifications of a good tsalung practitioner are hard to attain. First, one must be able to sit in painful postures for long periods of time. Not much fun, but most of us can do this if we are willing.

Second, we must be able to control our breath for long periods of time. This is something that develops over time. Third, we must have clear visualization of the deity and her channels. This also takes a long time to perfect. The student must be willing to accept a lot a hardship, including abstention from sexual activity or release.

Acquiring the right external conditions may be difficult, too. It should be cold and quiet. If we aspire to do trulkor, we need the appropriate room and gear, and we need to be far from any neighbors.

Kagyupas will typically teach tsalung only to participants who are in three-year retreat. Some Nyingma centers are a little more relaxed, offering occasional courses in tsalung. Many people can generate a small amount of tummo(no, just a general warmth in the belly that's not tummo) heat fairly easily, but the real experiences of tummo are quite difficult to attain. If you truly aspire to these practices, prepare yourself for a long period of hardship.

So here we are, our ordinary beginning self. How are we to relate to our bodies as we practice? What does Tibetan Buddhism have to offer us if the traditional approach is beyond our present capabilities?

I've heard stories of beginners asking their lamas for some kind of introductory physical discipline to aid their meditation. The most frequent response is "prostrations." Prostrations do seem to have a yogic effect on the body in addition to their devotional benefits. Some lamas have introduced other beginning physical practices to their students: Namkhai Norbu Rinpoche and *yantra yoga*, Tarthang Tulku with *kum nye*. But in general, Western students are left without a physical side to their meditative practice that they find meaningful and effective.

Many practitioners use techniques from other systems, such as tai chi or hatha yoga. Alternatively, we might use more passive forms of body work, paying someone else to help us to open up. My problem with this is that I always feel like I'm cheating by going outside the Tibetan system. On the one hand, it's difficult for me to admit that there's a lack or a shortcoming in the way that Tibetan Buddhism is offered to us here. On the other, I'm not completely sure of the benefits or effects of these other systems. My meditation teacher is a buddha; my acupuncturist decidedly is not. Do all systems nicely mesh, or can someone open me up in a way that will create obstacles to my Buddhist practice? I think these are important questions for most of us, since there is so much available to us here in America. We might be foolish to neglect powerful techniques already available in our culture; we might also be foolish to experiment with the wrong thing.

When through their diligence and devotion people apply themselves to practice, they might become aware of processes happening inside their body. It is easy to become fascinated by these experiences; it is also easy to overemphasize their importance. Not every sensation of warmth is tummo. That's where study can be useful. However, there's not much material available on the Tibetan view of the physical process, especially for beginners. But these processes are discussed at length in other systems that are accessible to us.

In the Chinese Taoist view, one tries to circulate one's chi in a loop up the back and down the front of the body. This is called the microcosmic orbit and is believed to be a great aid to meditation. It is the basis of both the internal martial arts and acupuncture.

In the Hindu system, a powerful energy called kundalini lies dormant at the base of the spine. Through practice and the transmission of energy from a master called a *shaktipat*, this energy is awakened and begins to move up the spine, opening the chakras. This is also believed to be a great aid for meditation and is the basis of hatha yoga and other Indian meditations.

In the West, as I previously mentioned, many people believe in "body armoring," where negative patterns have become frozen into the musculature of the body. Releasing this armoring aids psychological growth while also easing stress and helping with all the stress-related symptoms.

How do all these conflicting systems fit into the Buddhist tantric view? There are no simple answers to these kinds of questions because many of the lamas themselves are not sufficiently knowledgeable about these other systems, and an accurate translation of the concepts and experiences is difficult. I've often tried over the years to question my teachers. What is presented below is what I have managed to piece together. Even so, please do not accept it as the final word on the subject.

The Tibetan view is similar to the Hindu view. Both systems describe central channels, chakras, etc. Hindu practice can be dangerous, however. With an inexperienced teacher, the energy can sometimes be prematurely awakened, which can produce unpleasant and negative physical or mental side effects. This is referred to as kundalini illness. Practices from the Hindu system are often publicly taught that from the Tibetan perspective require years of preparation.

The microcosmic orbit is not spoken of much in the Tibetan tradition. I've asked many lamas about it but have generally received only vague answers. Some of the visualizations that accompany mantra recitation seem to imply a connection—there is a circulation of light that resembles the Chinese version. I've never heard of any problems occurring when Westerners mix tai chi and Tibetan meditation. In fact, several lamas do it. Acupuncture, however, can be draining. When treated by the wrong person, you can feel very low in energy for quite a while after a treatment, so please be careful.

When I've explained the Western belief of body armoring to my lama, he accepted it readily and felt that both Vajrasattva practice and the more advanced tsalung practices would deal with it. He had no problem with the concepts.

Several things can happen when the energetic processes start kicking in. At best, everything will happen smoothly. Blockages will open and the mind will settle down. The practitioner might not even notice that a process is happening.

Less gentle, the practitioner might sway or feel warm during practice. Sometimes, he will feel inexplicable depressions, anxiety, and restlessness.

Worse might be strong shaking or searing pain. If you read Krishnamurti's biography, there's a lengthy account of the years of agony he endured. Mentally, the mind can approach schizophrenia, although I've never seen it happen. I have seen people become mentally ill while practicing, but I'm not sure that it was related to an energetic awakening. I feel that those people were already unstable to begin with and that their practice may have been more intense than their ego structure could handle.

Westerners are confronted with two choices: We can devote ourselves exclusively to the Tibetan path. If it seems neglectful of our physical processes, we accept that as part of our path. We might prefer that to the danger of mixing paths.

The other option is to mix our practice with some other physical discipline. As I've mentioned, tai chi seems the safest. Gentle hatha yoga is also probably okay; just make sure that you're not dealing too strenuously with the kundalini energy, and that you find a teacher you can trust. Western exercise, aerobics, jogging, weight training—it is unlikely that these will have much of an effect on your inner energy. It is also unlikely that they will hurt anything either, and they will help to keep you healthy.

Of course, you can try to learn tsalung. You'll probably find it difficult to receive the teaching and even harder to maintain it.

I've always found Western body-work useful, although I've heard an occasional bad story. Cranial-sacral work has worked well for me as have other forms of manipulations. If a part of the body is simply not in the right place, the energetic blockages will open only with the greatest of difficulties. I feel that it is worthwhile taking the risk of having someone who is skilled gently move things into place. Frankly, I can't imagine the difficulty of releasing these misaligned tensions without any help, relying only on practice.

Sometimes medicine will help. I have had incredibly good results with homeopathy. It seems to work on a very deep energetic level, and with the right remedy, deep tensions can be released. Probably the same is true of Asian medicinal systems such as Chinese, ayurvedic, or of course, Tibetan. For all these, it's important to find a skilled doctor who is sensitive to the energetic aspects of his or her practice and is aware of the changes that can occur in meditators. Be careful and examine wisely your potential doctor, or any body-worker for that matter. I've also had good results with acupuncture, but I know that it can be very draining, especially with an inexperienced doctor.

Conventional Western medicine scares me. It can probably cure your diseases, but I doubt it can possibly have any positive energetic effects. On the other hand, if you are under medication for psychological problems, please don't stop your medication without consulting with your doctor. Although meditation has the potential to cure all mental anguish, we shouldn't jeopardize ourselves in this way. Eventually, your practice will be of great benefit, but be cautious.

The relationship between psychotherapy and meditation has been the subject of many books. Releasing psychological blocks can certainly have a profound energetic effect, if one is open on that level. In theory at least, it seems to me that once one has made a connection with the Dharma, therapy should become redundant. Meditation should do it all. I've seen it with myself and with my students. When I first started teaching, a student of mine was able to stop taking Prozac and to end a $400-a-month therapy involvement. Buddhist teaching and practice can be very powerful! But as I just mentioned, please be careful.

If you are currently going to a therapist, how does he or she feel about your interest in meditation? If your therapist isn't sympathetic, I would recommend finding a new one. If you don't have a close relationship with a meditation teacher, a therapist might be useful just for talking things out and discovering blind spots in your personality. They can also be very helpful in the case of very specific problems, such as raising children, that Buddhists don't discuss often. Once again, if you have serious problems, don't abandon professional help without consultation. How does your Buddhist meditation teacher respond to your seeing a therapist? If he objects, are his objections reasonable?

It's important to stay healthy. It's also important to work on the energetic level. But please remember two things: First, never separate your desire to improve your body from your quest for enlightenment. Perfect health will never last. Your body is simply a vehicle for enlightenment. So although your various practices and disciplines should improve your health, that is not the point. The point is that a healthy body makes it easier to meditate.

Second, be careful whom you trust. An authorized Tibetan Buddhist teacher is part of a 2,500-year-old tradition. Even then, there can be problems. But where are the checks and balances with your yoga teacher or therapist?

Included within dzogrim are the practices of union. The tsalung practices are related with the second, the secret empowerment; the sexual practices are related with the third, the wisdom empowerment. Because of our interest and because of the associations that have developed around the word *tantra* these days, a few words on sexual yoga and on sexuality in practice in general would be appropriate.

You can probably go down to your local video shop and get a video on "tantra." The term seems to have come to mean the prolongation of intercourse through the use of techniques such as visualization, breath control, etc. While this may or may not be Hindu tantra, it certainly isn't Buddhism. In Buddhism, *tantra* is synonymous with the Vajrayana, and does not refer to any one practice, especially a sexual one.

As I just said, Buddhist sexual yoga belongs to the third empowerment practice. Thus, it is based on a certain degree of proficiency in the practices of the second empowerment, which are, in turn, based on a certain degree of proficiency in the practices of the first empowerment, and so on down the line to the practices of ngondro and the four thoughts.

I've been practicing Tibetan Buddhism almost twenty-five years. I have never received any usable teachings on sexual practices. I've only heard and read about them in brief. I have certainly never done them. Tibetan lamas think that Westerners are sexually crazy. If you want to alienate a lama, try requesting teachings on the sexual practices.

If your interest or initial involvement in Tibetan Buddhism has been with the hope of learning these yogas, I would say your chances are very, very slender. If you are a woman, you might have an opportunity to sleep with a lama. It does happen. To be authorized to practice the path of union is another matter. Buddhist tantra is linear, very step-by-step, and we have to start at the beginning.

Ladies, please be aware of men who hit on you with a line about practicing tantra. Even if they're older students or have the name "lama," chances are that they are only looking for sex. Do not be naive; do not allow the gentleman to break his vows and go to hell. This misuse of the precious teachings is extremely harmful both to the perpetrator and to the overall reputation of Buddhism. Older students and teachers should be trustworthy; it's the very foundation of our path.

It's fine if we have desire; nobody is forcing us to be celibate. It's fine if we want to have a meaningful and supportive relationship. What is not right is deceiving yourself and others about your level of practice. If you do, you shame yourself, your partner, your teacher, and all of Tibetan Buddhism. There have been so many scandals; each one weakens our ability to trust our teachers and our tradition.

With that rather stern warning, how can we integrate our sexuality into our spiritual practice without going to dangerous extremes? Let us examine the options.

The first is celibacy. Celibacy is usually defined in the dictionary as meaning simply to be single; I think most of us use this term to mean a life where we abstain from any voluntary sexual activity. We could be living in the world, as hermits in retreat, or as ordained monks or nuns in a monastic environment. We could be perfectly celibate, having no release whatsoever; we could occasionally masturbate; or if we are men, we might experience release in our sleep.

There are many advantages to celibacy. The most obvious is that being free from the entanglement of relationships and especially children, we have much more time to practice. Not only do we have the time, but our minds are also calmer since we are not thinking about our partner, children, or going out on Saturday night. In theory, that should get rid of most of our thoughts right there! Also, if we are skillful, that sexual energy will be available for practice. We will experience it energizing our body and as a source of bliss. We are fitting candidates for tsalung practice, where perfect celibacy is required. Others will respect us, and it will be easier to obtain sponsors and conducive conditions for practice.

The most obvious disadvantage to celibacy is if we are too full of lust to practice. Or even sleep for that matter. Instead of feeling calmer, we become obsessed. The only things we can visualize are attractive members of the opposite sex. We are prone to make unwise decisions in that state.

Occasionally, masturbating works. I met someone who masturbated regularly through a three-year retreat. At the end, his lama was very pleased with his meditative accomplishments and even said he had attained some special powers. We can also learn to circulate the sexual energy upward, away from the genital area. This technique works better for some than others. It's also better to remove oneself as much as possible from anyone or anything that will give rise to lust. It was much easier to be celibate in the East, for example, where the women were always modestly dressed and certainly not available. There were no *Playboy* magazines, cable TV, or any other provocative media, although that's now changing.

There are many dangers to celibacy. Keeping the sexual energy in can help our practice, but it can also be overwhelming, causing many kinds of energetic imbalances. Lamas will sometimes tell their blocked-up students to have sex because they are having energetic problems with their practice.

We might have old emotional issues that make celibacy attractive to us, despite the obvious hardships. I would guess that for those of us who tried to be celibate while still young, some of these issues were lurking in the background. We might have fears of sex, fears of intimacy, rejection, etc., all of which make celibacy seem appropriate. However, it doesn't work that way. One cannot maintain repression or denial and meditate at the same time. It's like trying simultaneously to go east and west. Eventually, all these old issues will come out.

If you're seriously contemplating a celibate lifestyle, ask yourself if it's likely these issues exist. The only thing that will make them go away is confronting them, not running away from them. This doesn't mean you shouldn't be celibate, but you should know what you are getting into.

I tried to deny my sexuality for two decades. Now that I'm sexually active, I'm much better off. Even my meditation has improved through the integration of my sexuality with my practice. But there are no hard and fast rules. I've noticed that middle-aged men and women who have experienced sex and relationships fully can lead celibate lives with less difficulty.

Another serious danger is that we can become emotionally cold, from a lack of love as well as from the difficulty maintaining the discipline. If this happens to you, try to find love in other ways, perhaps through your spiritual community or your devotion to your teacher.

Nothing opens us up or puts us as close to our buddha-nature as love; the teachings all agree on this. So if there is no love in your life, you are at a serious disadvantage in your practice. If you find your attitudes becoming rigid, this is also a mistake. I used to feel all noncelibate practitioners weren't serious or committed; now I recognize this attitude as simply a projection of my own unease.

Most of us will be sexually active laypeople. How can we use our sexual activity on the path? Obviously, we shouldn't use sex to hurt anyone, neither your partner nor an involved third party. People are very aware of these issues these days, so this much should be clear. I believe fidelity is very important as is commitment. Please don't use the need or desire to open yourself or to heal as an excuse to hurt your closest vajra brother or sister—your partner.

Anything done with a loving heart is virtuous. If you love your partner and give pleasure to him or her as an expression of your care, that is a virtuous act. Its healing power is amazing. So many of us are stuck on the level of feeling unlovable, not being able to open to love, not being able to express love, etc. Lovemaking can then be a very powerful practice for dealing with these old issues. Where our hearts are blocked, so will our meditation be.

Also, we can use a healthy sexual relationship to heal our relationship with our bodies or with our ability to experience pleasure. If we're not "in our body," sex can bring us back in; believe it or not, we have to get back in touch with our body before we can transcend it. If we're dissociated from our bodies due to experiences we have had in the past, this again will cause a limitation to our meditation. Sex provides us with a situation wherein we can be keenly aware and observant of exactly how far we have progressed.

If we have difficulty experiencing pleasure, how can we be open to the bliss of meditation? We will feel it is wrong to feel this kind of bliss when we are sitting and will subtly block and, therefore, limit and contract the experience. Sex is not necessary in any of these situations in order to deal with issues of love, dissociation, and pleasure. The healing can take place solely through practice. That would be best. But in the name of practice we may also be avoiding dealing with these issues. If that is true, we may remain stuck for a very long time. Our sexual activity will bring all these problems undeniably to the surface.

Many of us feel some confusion about the relationship between pleasure and enjoyments, and true spirituality according to the Buddhist perspective. A major source of the problem is a confusion between pleasure, on the one hand, and attachment or desire, on the other. There's no question that in Buddhism attachment and desire are regarded as negative states. And what is it that we generally desire or to which we are attached? Pleasurable experiences.

Nevertheless, pleasure in and of itself is neither desire nor attachment. When we cling to pleasure, that is attachment. When we want to repeat it, that is desire. But the experience of pleasure per se is not itself desire or attachment. Therefore, it is possible to enjoy without these two.

A moment's reflection will reveal that not only are pleasure and attachment not the same, but they are in many ways antithetical. If we are enjoying the sunset or a chocolate ice cream, clinging to the experience actually diminishes the pleasure. We are no longer experiencing it; rather we are starting to get lost in our thoughts, feelings, and anxieties about the experience.

Are there any spiritual benefits then to experiencing pleasure? I feel that the benefits are in the very abandoning of attachment. If we apply mindfulness to our enjoyment, we can let go of the clinging. This will produce a kind of openness within the enjoyment that definitely has a spiritual component. Also, we can learn to let go of attachment in general. We see that it actually hampers our genuine experience, rather than enhancing it. We can learn about deep patterns of attachment and clinging and use our pleasure to purify them. When we return to formal meditation, we will notice an improvement.

Another benefit of enjoyment is that meditation is also often enjoyable. Our attitudes about pleasure in general will be reflected in how we relate to pleasurable meditational experiences.

Many people who are drawn to spirituality have some kind of resistance to pleasure and assume that spirituality considers the pursuit of pleasure to be harmful to our path. In a sense the pursuit is indeed harmful; however, as I've mentioned, the pleasure itself is not. With this kind of attitude of resistance to pleasure, one will have difficulty accepting the pleasurable experiences of meditation without some kind of negative reaction. If we can recognize our negative patterns toward pleasure through our ordinary experiences, we can later meditate in a much purer manner.

Wilhelm Reich and his student Alexander Lowen explored the psychological aspects of pleasure in their exploration of the function of the orgasm. Although I've not discovered a spiritual component in their work, I feel they have mapped out a very valuable area of growth. Most us must make the journey from neurosis to sanity and mental health before real spirituality can begin. Our sexual activity and our attitudes toward it can give us valuable clues for making that trip.

It's normal for us to want to experience as much pleasure as possible in our sexual activity. What stops us? It's our being too much "in our heads." The process of letting go of attitudes in order to experience a more satisfying orgasm is very similar to the process of surrendering to deeper meditational experiences. Orgasms are, I'm afraid, no substitute for practice, but as I've mentioned before, we can learn to recognize some of our habitual patterns regarding pleasure. We can apply what we have learned to our practice. Let's face it—most of us are not going to give up sex. Thus, if we are going to be sexually active, then it is important to use that activity as a way to aid our practice.

I had some very bizarre and intense obstacles with my energetic system that limited my practice for twenty years. Not only did they limit it, they made practice miserable. No one was able to help me. I must have gone to more than ten alternative healers and at least as many lamas. Not one word of useful advice. One week with my wife, and the symptoms miraculously disappeared! I will forever be grateful to her; I also learned a lesson about the path that I will never forget.

CHAPTER EIGHTEEN

The Path of Liberation

We started our exploration with some yearning for the truth, our buddha-nature. That yearning, based perhaps on some glimpse or intuition, led us to seek and hopefully find a teacher. Following the progression of this book, we will have found a teacher within the Tibetan Buddhist tradition, become involved in a center, received instruction, and have begun a practice.

As we become more involved and diligent with our practice, we cannot lose sight of our original intention—to apprehend our true nature. Many of us become like tantric hobbyists. We learn everything we can about the lamas, the lineages, the practices, the rituals, etc., but somehow we forget the big picture.

The big picture is recognizing and stabilizing buddha-nature. This is the whole point of Buddhism, tantric or not. As Guru Rinpoche has said:

> Do not resolve the Dharma,
> Resolve your mind.

> Resolving your mind is to know the one which frees all.
>
> Not resolving your mind is to know all, but lack the one.[15]

No matter how many lamas you've met, how many rituals you've mastered or mantras you've recited, it all boils down to one point—recognizing your buddha-nature.

The practices that deal directly with buddha-nature are called the path of liberation. The practices that aid us in this recognition and stabilization are called the path of skillful means. The path of skillful means includes such techniques as kyerim and tsalung that we've already discussed. The practices of the path of liberation are mainly shinay and lhagtong.

Practicing the path of liberation without skillful means can be very slow. We might be very attracted to the simplicity of the path of liberation; unfortunately, we don't have simple minds. On the other hand, to rely on skillful means without the path of liberation takes us nowhere since we lack the view. It is the combination of the two that gives Vajrayana its unique power. The combination is often symbolically depicted, sometimes by the two hands of the deity, sometimes by the deities in union. It's a point we are never to forget.

Generally, these two paths are practiced concurrently, with the practitioner emphasizing one or the other over time. We could be doing a deity practice and at the end dissolve the visualization. At that point we would apply the instructions we have heard on the path of liberation, either mahamudra or dzogchen. With time, the practices tend to merge as the path of skillful means approaches the path of liberation.

As I mentioned in the chapter on ritual, many Westerners feel more drawn to the path of liberation. The rituals seem too foreign. Many lamas seem to concur; mahamudra and dzogchen, the two main systems of liberation, are widely and systematically taught these days.

Kagyu Samye Ling in Scotland, where I did retreat, has an annual program with H. E. Tai Situ Rinpoche teaching mahamudra step by step. He teaches it as a one-month retreat during the summer; the participants make a commitment to do two hours of mahamudra meditation a day for the rest of the year. Every year they meet and receive further instruction. The last I heard, the response has been highly favorable. Other Kagyu lamas are following suit with similar programs at their centers. There have also been a few attempts to teach dzogchen in America in this kind of systematic manner.

Mahamudra is the system practiced by the Kagyu and other Sarma schools; dzogchen is most widely taught in the Nyingma. There is no difference in view between them, nor in the result, which is complete buddhahood. The difference between them is in which practices are emphasized. Within both, you will find some distinction between a gradual and a sudden approach.

In the gradual system, the practitioner works his or her way through a series of practices aimed first at focusing the mind, then at recognizing its nature. The sudden path is obviously more direct. The buddha-nature is pointed out early in one's meditative career. One then takes this glimpse as the object of concentration for stabilization. Of course, both approaches have their proponents and their merit. In my opinion, without some initial calmness, trying to recognize or stabilize can be very frustrating and agitating. However, if we wait until our concentration is flawless, we might have to wait a very long time and may never grasp the real meaning of Lord Buddha's teaching.

The main practices of liberation are *shinay* and *lhagtong*. *Shinay*, or *shamatha* in Sanskrit, literally means "calm abiding." *Lhagtong*, or *vipasyana* in Sanskrit, is often translated as "insight.") When people speak of meditation, they are generally referring to shinay. There are many possible objects for shinay. You can visualize a buddha in front or a sphere of light in your heart. You can follow the breath, add the *vajra recitation* to the breath, or hold the breath in the vase as in the tsalung practices. One can take thoughts as the object or the absence of thoughts as the object. When the mind itself is taken as the object, it is called formless shinay; this can quite easily be confused with the insight of lhagtong. The absence of thoughts can be confused with emptiness, the mind's clarity with luminosity.

The benefits of shinay are twofold. Obviously, the pacification of the mind is a benefit in and of itself. We are no longer torn by emotionality and discursiveness but instead abide in a state of calm, spacious clarity. The other benefit is that it prepares us for genuine insight. It is often said that insight happens in the space between thoughts. If there is no space, then there is little hope for any realization. Through our various practices, that gap should widen and become more frequent. Then, of course, we have a greater chance for insight.

There are also some dangers. Mistaking the experience of shinay for one of genuine insight as I just mentioned is very common. One needs a teacher and some study in order to avoid this pitfall. Secondly, the mind can become too spaced out. There are traditional stories of meditators remaining months or years in a noncognizing trance, wasting their time and exhausting their merit. I doubt that that's very common nowadays; what I see instead is people losing the ability to drive and nearly getting into accidents because they are engrossed in opening their minds but losing clarity, awareness, and mindfulness. Since I've been teaching, this is the only real danger I've noticed in my students. If you have a tendency to space out or to be too open without boundaries, don't indulge like this in your meditation. Instead, you must emphasize the clarity and mindfulness and make certain that you feel grounded, especially before operating dangerous machinery. When in doubt, don't mix activities like driving with your meditation.

The opposite would be to have too much focus without any spaciousness. In that case, we're simply trying too hard. This can make us rigid and uptight and eventually lead to energetic imbalances and psychosomatic ailments.

Shinay is not only a practice; it is also the resultant state. Some teachings teach nine stages before the full attainment of shinay, the more meditative traditions usually teach three. Tsele Rinpoche, whom we first met in chapter 4, explains these three very clearly:

> At first, the mind seems more agitated, with even more thought activity than before. Sometimes between thought activity, your mind remains still for a short while. Do not regard such thought activity as a defect. Although up to now your mind has always been thinking, you didn't recognize that. This point, of recognizing the difference between thinking and stillness, is the first shamatha experience, like the waterfall off a mountain cliff.
>
> After maintaining the practice like that, the thought will be mostly controlled. You become gentle and relaxed; both your body and mind become totally blissful and you don't feel like engaging in other activities, but only delight in meditation.

Except on rare occasions, you remain mostly free from any thought activity. That is the intermediate shamatha stage, like the gentle flow of a river.

Later on, after practicing with undistracted endeavor, your body is totally blissful, free from any painful sensation. Your mind is clear cognizance free from thoughts. Not noticing the passing of day and night, you can remain unmoved for as long as you are resting in meditation and you are unharmed by faults. The manifest disturbing emotions have subsided and you have no strong clinging to such things as food and clothing. You have conditioned superknowledges, and various kinds of visionary experiences occur. The manifestation of these numerous kinds of ordinary qualities is the final state of shamatha, which is like an unmoving ocean.[16]

It's encouraging to me to think that we only have to go one step on the path before we reach a state of blissful mind and body. It seems worth some exertion and hardship to attain.

If we wait for that oceanic final state before we begin lhagtong, we will probably have a long wait. But the calmer the mind, the easier will be the investigations that follow. Lhagtong begins with a series of questions for the student to answer, such as "What color is the mind?" or "From where do thoughts arise?" The student is pointed in the direction of looking directly into the mind. The point here is not to analyze the question intellectually until a conclusion is reached but to gain experience through penetrating investigation. As I mentioned in a previous chapter, the student repeatedly reports back until receiving confirmation and attaining certainty.

Perhaps at no other stage of our practice is the teacher so crucial. Drungchen Kunga Namgyal states:

The purpose of having a spiritual mentor who knows the path to liberation is to have someone who knows how to remove the obstacles on the path and remove the veils of ignorance. There are those who fail to speak to their mentor even though they have many things to ask. Due to both the conceit of having fine realizations or a sense of hopelessness, some conceal what is happening, thinking, "There's little reason to speak, for you don't tell the mentor about such things." Due to the mind being carried away as if by a hallucination, some think, "There is nothing even the spiritual mentor can do to help me in such things." Others think, "I must present an amazing report of realizations, not these specific questions that I have." All such attitudes are utterly useless.

Get answers to the questions you put to your mentor; then, after coming outside, it is you, the student, who maintains the training at the level of your own present practice. So keep that firmly in mind, and get ready to report.[17]

This process can take awhile; even after rigpa has been glimpsed and acknowledged by your teacher, one can make subtle distinctions and entertain valid doubts.

With time, there's a shift from investigative lhagtong to resting lhagtong. That is, as doubts become clarified, one simply relaxes into rigpa; investigation becomes less necessary. It sounds nice to talk about relaxing into rigpa or into effortless meditation, but if the view has not been correctly ascertained, it can also be dangerous. Milarepa said this about effortless meditation:

Concerning the practice of non-correction, one should understand three things: If wandering thoughts and desire-passions are not corrected, one will fall into the lower realms. If bliss, clarity, and non-thought are not corrected, one will fall into the three realms of samsara. Only the immanent self-awareness needs no correction.[18]

Also, the investigative and the resting meditations can be balanced into one practice. These are all techniques to be learned from one's teacher.

Realization of buddha-nature proceeds in clear, recognizable stages. The most common teaching is on the four yogas of mahamudra; the reader can find many books on this subject. Those of us who are not full-time contemplatives will probably have to be content with momentary glimpses. In time, these glimpses will increase in frequency, duration, and quality.

Many lamas say that this is the age of dzogchen. Indeed, these teachings are gaining popularity in America. They are being taught openly in a way that has never been done before. During one public teaching I received, the lama said that the teachings he was in the process of giving were given in Tibet only to those who had completed about fifteen years of retreat. I have never really understood the rationale behind this transmission; many other Nyingma lamas have continued to keep the dzogchen teachings quite secret. When I asked Gyatrul Rinpoche, he said that if there is one person in the audience who understands, then it is worth it.

There are many classifications of dzogchen but the two most common are *tregchod* and *thogal*. *Tregchod* means "to cut completely"; by resting in the nature of the mind, we completely cut our delusion. *Thogal* is the more esoteric or secret of these techniques. It is a system of yogic practices involving posture and gazes that produces extraordinary results if the practitioner is able to conjoin them with the view. *Thogal* is the main practice that leads to the attainment of the rainbow body.

Fruition

Our original inspiration has taken us along some very unusual and profound paths. We have met great teachers; we have made commitments and sacrifices in our application of the teachings. We have found the pinnacle of Lord Buddha's teaching, the Vajrayana, especially the practices of mahamudra and the Great Perfection and have started to apply ourselves with some diligence. What are the benefits, the fruition, of following such a path?

"Buddhahood in one short lifetime"—how often have I heard that! Fast results with little difficulty. Well, it certainly hasn't been my experience. Perhaps this short life is not the right one!

The Buddhist path is clearly delineated. If you study and are honest with yourself, it is easy to figure out how far you've come, what's coming up soon, and what you have to do. Different systems of practice will also have their different roadmaps. In Mahayana we talk about the five paths and ten *bhumis*, or grounds; in mahamudra, we talk about the four yogas; and in dzogchen, there are the four visions. Ngondro and kyerim also have their unmistakable signs. A little study will show where we are on any path, and somewhat more effort will enable us to make fairly accurate correlations between these systems.

The problem with these systems is that close examination will reveal that we haven't gone anywhere. Despite the "Buddhahood in one life" hooks, as the years roll by, none of the signposts pop up. For ambitious people like myself, it can be quite discouraging.

Let's examine the earlier stages of the path in more detail. The Mahayana path begins with the generation of bodhichitta. Even that would be quite an accomplishment. Imagine letting go of selfishness and living a life dedicated to others.

The path also begins with a sincere weariness with samsara. This in itself is also quite an attainment and a sign of having successfully contemplated the four thoughts. It's difficult not to think of the Dharma as something that will make samsaric life more pleasant, rewarding, or bearable rather than something that will completely uproot the ego and any fixation we have with normal life.

Hence, we know where to start. Bodhichitta for others, weariness and renunciation for ourselves. If we don't start here, our claims to later fruit seem rather pointless.

When we begin meditation, there are the three stages of a waterfall, a river, and an ocean. These were mentioned in the last chapter. Even the experience of the river is said to be eminently satisfying. There are also three experiences that arise when meditating: bliss, clarity, and nonthought.

Bliss does not necessarily mean ecstasy. It can be pleasure, comfort, joy, mirth, etc.—any happy experience caused by our practice. Clarity can include supernormal knowledge, but it can also mean an increase in the lucidity of the mind. Nonthought is obvious—in the absence of thought the mind becomes open and spacious. Any one of these three experiences is accessible to the beginner; but clinging to them can be very dangerous.

Michael Hookam, a Dharma teacher in Oxford, England, has a slightly different presentation. He borrows from the dzogchen tradition in which the ultimate nature of the mind is said to be empty, luminous, and compassionate. As practitioners we approach emptiness through spaciousness, luminosity through clarity, and compassion through sensitivity or responsiveness. This classification gives the student a good idea of what to expect—increased openness, clarity, and sensitivity arising through diligence in our practice. I use this classification often while teaching.

Nonetheless, even with all these different classifications of experiences, there are those who, due to the busy-ness of their lives, will have a hard time even generating a little bliss, a little spaciousness. What about them? Is there any hope for them? Does Vajrayana have anything to offer such people like these, or would they be better off following a different path? I feel this is probably the major question we must ask as Vajrayana enters our culture. What can it really offer? Does it have any use outside the hermitages of Tibet?

I have given years of thought to this question, and I must answer "yes"; otherwise, I would not be writing this book. As a matter of fact, the techniques of Vajrayana are so profound that they may be the only ones that work in such chaotic times and for such disturbed minds. And they are profound at all levels of the path.

If there's anything the reader should have picked up by now, it is the supreme importance of the teacher-student relationship based on honest communication. With a relationship like this, where we really have an opportunity and a willingness to present our experiences to the teacher, meaningful growth is always very possible no matter at what level we are. I have noticed that even the older, more traditional teachers will relate to their Western students very directly in one-on-one situations. They will listen and give appropriate guidance. Next, the techniques must be understood and then honestly and correctly employed. We should not grasp at higher teachings simply because they are higher. We should be willing to admit we are beginners. By so doing, positive results will follow.

Imagine that single mother, that busy student, the middle-aged father. What can they really expect to gain from their involvement in Vajrayana? The Tibetan word for buddha, *sangye*, means one who has purified everything that can be purified and has perfected all good qualities.

This can provide the key: We can examine what the sincere but busy Western practitioner can expect in terms of negative characteristics abandoned and positive qualities increased. We can use terminology that is more "Western" and speak of "healing and growth."

In my own thinking, I've been trying to understand what healing means in Buddhist terms. To me it refers to the wounds we bear perhaps from childhood or from previous lives, that cause us continuous discomfort in the present. They do so because present situations always remind us of those past circumstances and evoke a habitual response. If you were beaten as a child, when someone is nice to you now, you may be suspicious because it reminds you of the circumstances that would precede your beatings.

This woundedness, this neurosis, is what is meant in Buddhism by "ego." This is a very tricky word because we use it with all its Western connotations and as a translation of Asian Buddhist terms. We must always be aware of the context in which we use the term *ego*. If we are dysfunctional in any way because of our inner landscape, from a Buddhist point of view this is having a big ego. And of course, this is exactly what Buddhist practice addresses.

I think that as Westerners we are almost blinded by our inner phenomena. Sometimes we are barely aware of the outside world. So the first stage of Buddhist practice, no matter what the technique, is to detach awareness from the fascination with our "problems." Healing in Buddhism is cultivating egolessness.

By becoming conscious of these patterns, they can be released, since they bear no relation to what's really happening in the present. Simple Buddhist practices such as mindfulness are extremely effective in training us to recognize and let go of negative patterns as they arise. However, Vajrayana takes it a step further. Through powerful practices like that of Vajrasattva with the flow of nectar, and even more aggressively with the body-oriented practices of tsalung, one actually invades the territory where these wounds reside, since as we discussed in the last chapter habitual patterns are implanted in the energetic pathways of the body. We are no longer passively waiting for whatever is there to arise and then be released; we are aggressively forcing more and more of these things to come to the surface.

In addition, the powerful symbolism of kyerim and rituals gives us even more incredible techniques to use for healing. Peaceful deities can pacify our wounds; wrathful ones can take the rage that is repressed and transmute it into awareness. With either type, we can also feel empowered to do what truly needs to be done to effect the healing. When one understands how to do these techniques, the healing benefits are endless.

When I look at my own woundedness, what I see is the five poisons, especially rage and fear. Hence for me, healing my wounds is no different from purifying the five poisons. Nothing purifies the five poisons more quickly than Vajrayana.

It is often stated that Vajrayana practice is for intelligent people with strong defilements. That fits us to a tee. It's not that we have to be pure before we can be Vajrayana practitioners. The more I understand the Vajrayana, the more I realize that it's the perfect system for our times— the best system for dealing with the extreme negativities of our minds.

Let me give a personal example. Recently, I've been plagued by intense periods of depression. Sometimes I can hardly get out of bed. I've applied many techniques, such as mindfulness and tong-len, but they are usually only barely able to touch it. The last time it happened, though, I generated myself as a wrathful deity. Through that power, the depression uncurled itself and became rage. Yet, because I maintained divine pride, I was able to go deeper and deeper into that rage. Eventually, I broke clean through. And I realized that no other technique would have been nearly as effective in dealing with intense depression and its hidden rage. I was extremely grateful and in awe of the omniscience of the enlightened ones for developing such a system. I realized also that no matter how funky I feel, Vajrayana is there for me. A perfect refuge.

If it works for me, it can work for you. The keys are understanding the techniques and being willing to apply them.

Part of the healing or purification that takes place is in the transition from identifying with the ego to the development of egolessness. Many people are afraid to drop the ego; others misunderstand and do it incorrectly. Therefore, I think it's important to spend some time on this key issue.

In the West, the term *ego* is variously defined. My dictionary equates it to the self. In Freudian thought, the ego is contrasted to the id and superego as one of the components of the personality. We all have some general or intuitive understanding of what the term means. We can speak of people having big egos, weak egos, or healthy egos. None of these is exactly what is meant by ego in Buddhism.

In Buddhism perhaps a more accurate term than ego would be self-image. The self-image is a mental event that contains a little picture of ourselves. When someone insults us, we think, "How could they say that to ME?" That "me," with all its associations, is what is meant by self-image. Here the "me" is someone special, who couldn't possibly be reprimanded justly. In another circumstance, a different self-image may appear to the same person. After spending another lonely Saturday night, we think, "How could anyone ever like me?" All these different "me's" refer to the same person; however, the images are very different.

We have many, many of these images. Which image is activated at any given moment depends on the external trigger. What they all have in common is that they are mental events, something that appears in our minds. We have only one problem here—we completely buy into these images. We identify with the various "me's" in the above examples, rather than regarding them in a detached manner as just another mental event. If we are able to observe their arising with detachment, the various self-images lose their power and slowly dissolve.

When we begin to do this, we might feel a considerable amount of fear and anxiety at first. The ego evolved as a way to deal with the chaos of being; dissolving it opens us to the fears that accompanied its original emergence. Letting go feels like death. Actually, it *is* death—what dies in the release is the same as what dies when we physically die. But remember, in Buddhism the moment of death is also a moment of pure enlightenment for those who can recognize and use it. The fear and anxiety is simply more thought that we can let go. However, without the support of a teacher and a spiritual community, it can be quite difficult to walk through the fear.

When we let go of these images and their attendant fears, we begin to experience spaciousness. When we identify with the self-images, our minds are contracted; as we let go, our minds open up to their vastness, which approaches the true or absolute nature. With time, this vastness actually becomes inviting; it no longer makes us feel as if we are dying.

We've experienced it enough to know that we can open up, survive, and be better off for it. Identifying with our self-image no longer feels safe and comfortable; it feels claustrophobic and stultifyingly boring. This is a major and important transition in our practice: when we reach this point in our practice, we have "gotten it"; our progress will be smoother and our commitment stronger.

Many people fear egolessness because they fear they will become dysfunctional. But let's look at the lamas we know: They left Tibet as penniless, starving refugees, adapted first to Indian and then to Western culture, and are now engaged in an incredible range of truly beneficial activities. Hardly dysfunctional. What I recommend to people with this view is this: Give up 10 percent of your ego, 10 percent of your thoughts. See what happens. Are you better or worse off? No one yet has said worse! Having done so, we can trust that slowly giving up the other 90 percent will be beneficial.

Almost all of us associate egolessness with a state of nonassertive wimpiness because of the way this term is commonly used in the West. People who have that predilection are probably drawn to the Buddhist teaching due to this misunderstanding. We let people walk over us and say we are nonattached. We don't assert ourselves to get what we want because we think we have no desire. I was like this for decades, and I can assure you this is complete nonsense.

This comes from confusing ego with self-image. The nonassertive personality has a very strong self-image of being powerless and weak. He feels he will be crushed if he asserts himself. To compensate, he develops a philosophy that exhorts non-assertiveness and passivity, that confuses nonassertiveness with desirelessness. This is big ego. This is strong self-grasping. This is wrong—it is not good Buddhism. I've never met a wimpy lama. They are hearty, earthy people who enjoy themselves while actively engaging in the world and accomplishing a myriad of beneficial activities. They are never afraid of standing up for what they believe.

One test you can give yourself is this: If there is something you want and you don't pursue it, is it because you truly have a different set of priorities, or is it that you simply feel unable either to pursue your desire or to succeed? If it is the latter, it is a highly defiled mental state that must be purified. It's wonderful to give up desires or not to retaliate when abused, but these should be choices made from a position of strength, not the limited responses of a crippled being.

So a sense of weakness is a self-image to which we cling. It can and should be given up. When we give it up, we will experience spaciousness and we will feel stronger. We don't have to become aggressive jerks; we simply want to reach a balance where we are free to act appropriately. This newly developed strength will greatly encourage you in your practice. You will feel much better because of it; you will also have valuable resources for continuing on your journey.

Another typical mistake that I feel was more common ten or twenty years ago was to equate egolessness with a pre-egoic, childlike state. There's something to be said for the open, innocent playful qualities of a child, but this line of thought become a rationale for indulgent behavior in the name of spirituality. Thinking, "I've transcended good and bad," while acting harmfully is obviously wrong thinking.

Similarly, some people never develop healthy boundaries because of their woundedness. As a by-product of this lack, they may be open to nonordinary states or experiences. They may feel quite developed. This is a very important point, because if people like this aren't careful, practice can make them schizophrenic. They already have the tendencies. It's great if you can talk with fairies; however, it's not the point of Buddhist practice, and you might find that by engaging in the Buddhist path, you might have to abandon feeling you are special due to your ability. You may even lose that ability.

One thing I've noticed is how annoyed lamas become by people's "phenomena." They certainly don't feel that you are special if you are having visions or amazing dreams. They want you to purify your five poisons. So this kind of openness derived from a lack of boundaries may come from having a weak ego, not from egolessness.

The point here is that our practice cultivates a strong, healthy ego (in the Western sense) as we dissolve our self-images (our egos in the Buddhist sense). Although this appears contradictory because of the ambiguous use of the word *ego*, it is not. Why? Because the qualities of a healthy ego come from a deeper, more intrinsic part of the mind than the self-image. As the various self-images are discarded, positive qualities that are innate to our nature emerge. These qualities will give us the appearance of having a good, healthy ego, but they do so without reinforcing self-images that contract the mind.

Please feel that you can practice the Buddhist path of egolessness without becoming a vegetable! When practiced correctly, meditation will make you stronger, more confident, and better able to deal skillfully and compassionately with the world.

Deity practice is one of the main practices of tantra, and perhaps the crucial instruction in deity practice is maintaining the deity's pride. When we think of this, it can give us a clue about what sort of changes or growth we can expect as a result of our practice. Consider the above discussion of egolessness. It's hard to imagine a wrathful deity being overly self-effacing, wimpy, or masochistic. What other qualities can we expect to develop in our practice? And the "we" here means the ordinary Western lay practitioner, not some idealized super-disciple.

We can develop a sense of meaning and value in our lives. Most people do not possess these, and so they substitute endless grasping at "stuff" as a poor substitute for the natural richness that is ours to claim as Vajrayana practitioners. Once again, consider the deity's world—the mandala, the silks, the jewels. We do not have to search outwardly for such things; they are intrinsic to the meditative states of being that we can contact. At the very least, we will have a sense that our life has a purpose and direction even when encountering difficulties.

We will have more confidence about facing death. Most people don't even like hearing the word. As tantric practitioners, even if we don't possess realization, we can still generate some confidence. We can do a short *phowa* retreat that will almost completely assure us that we can be reborn in a pure land. We can do a practice like that of Amitabha that will also help us to cultivate the causes for rebirth in a buddha-field. Through our devotion to our lama, we feel that his presence and blessing will help us when we die. The practice of tong-len can be a great aid in dealing with the suffering we most likely will experience as we approach death. I mentioned earlier the peace and joy that simple, older Tibetans transmit when one sees them in Asia, which is so very different from the gloom I found in even a well-appointed senior citizen community here.

Meditation can bring many useful benefits to our body and our relationship to it. We can heal ourselves of illnesses by purifying the underlying causes, whether karmic or energetic. If we remain ill, the practice of tonglen can be very useful in transforming our illness into a vehicle for growth. One of the main signs that our mind is calming down is an increased lightness and suppleness of the body. This experience is even possible while doing the Vajrasattva part of the ngondro; in the texts lightness is cited as a sign of success. This newfound lightness and suppleness can be your constant companion and a reminder of the benefits of meditation.

As I mentioned earlier, many of us are not "in our body"; we are "in our heads." Meditation, especially Vajrayana practices like deity meditation, can heal that sense of separation and alienation. Imagine yourself as a deity. The deity has a body, one with a fascinating form doing provocative activities. Visualizing the complete body of a deity brings our awareness throughout our body, bringing us out of our heads and in harmony with our bodies. So this sense of oneness with the body accompanies the growing lightness and suppleness.

We become nicer people. Through the practiced of lo-jong, we sincerely endeavor to be kinder. Through purification, our aggression and arrogance become pacified. Through giving up self-images we no longer have such strong agendas with others and can, therefore, be more open and skillful when dealing with them. As we become kinder and more skillful, it will come back to us. People will like us better and we will not get so embroiled in confrontations and disputes. It will be easier to get our way as we act more skillfully.

We will have fewer attitudes and judgments about other people and our environment. Because of this, we will get along with others better and will easily be able to adjust to any situation. We will be more flexible and able to adapt to seemingly contradictory roles in the family or at work because of not identifying too strongly with any of them. I always find it amusing how fussy so many "spiritual" practitioners are about food. Although there are many good reasons to have a sane diet, perhaps it's also good not to be so rigid and to learn to enjoy what's available.

One of the hardest things for me to give up is my negative attitudes toward others. I've realized that behind this is my own fear of social inadequacy; it's soothing to know others are floundering as much as you are and that you can get your friends to agree with your appraisal. But this kind of negativity, no matter how insightful it seems, is just an unhappy mind. Both lo-jong practice and the teachings on pure perception have helped me overcome this negativity, and I feel more open and loving for having done so.

The most famous benefit of meditation is, of course, calmness and relaxation. Chökyi Nyima Rinpoche says that if one practices for half an hour for one year, one should definitely feel the mind growing calmer. I feel that's a reasonable investment of time. Calmness permeates all of one's life. It's something we all value and admire in others. We all know of the many benefits of relaxation—people spend fortunes going to resorts to relax. If you persevere in your meditation, you can have all the benefits of that holiday in Acapulco for free.

In the chapter on devotion, I mentioned the subject of autonomy. Autonomy is not the same as having a big ego. It is more like having sound limits. In all kyerim practices, we generate a wheel of protection or a vajra fence. It's obvious that our tradition believes in having healthy boundaries. All the problems that come with boundary issues will be eliminated as the basic problem is addressed. People won't walk all over you. You will have a sense of your own strength and worth, and you will be able to say "no" when appropriate. Once again this can easily be understood in terms of the deity's pride. This practice is an invaluable technique of dealing with so many issues that plague the average Western practitioner.

Practice gives most people a sense of greater acceptance and humor in their lives. Self-condemnation is simply one more negative thought. As we see through these negative self-images, we become amused by our negativities rather than being repulsed. What an interesting display! How funny are these endless thoughts that pop into my mind every time I try to meditate!

Even a small glimpse of buddha-nature gives us a profound under-standing of the Buddhist view. We no longer merely think, trust, or spec-ulate; we know. That confidence is also invaluable; it's an anchor around which the rest of our life can settle. We are never fooled quite as much by dualistic appearances as we were before.

Finally, a close relationship with a high teacher confers the benefits I mentioned in the beginning of the book. Having such a relationship also puts everything in one's life into perspective. There is no substitute for that kind of unconditioned love, omniscient guidance, and great blessing.

The point I want to make perfectly clear here is this: You may never get to enter into long retreat. You may be hopelessly neurotic. You may never even vaguely approach the profound experiences that we so often read about in books. Nevertheless, there is a world of inconceivable value for you in the practice of Vajrayana Buddhism, just as you are. Much of that value comes from Vajrayana's very uniqueness, the profundity of its many techniques. Find an authentic teacher, practice intelligently and diligently, and these benefits will be yours.

➤ A P P E N D I X ◄

The Future

I'd like to conclude this book with a brief discussion of my feelings about the future of Vajrayana in the West.

I recently read a book by an American lama in which he suggested that the ritualistic side of Tibetan Buddhism would not survive in this country and that Vajrayana would come to resemble its Theravadan and Zen siblings. Although I understand his position and the yearning of many of us to "just sit," I hope the above discussion of the benefits of Vajrayana has convinced the reader that the greatest benefits for Western minds often lie in the deity or ritualistic side of Tibetan Buddhism. Without the deities, Vajrayana reduces to Mahayana. I believe that in these crazy times we need the very strong medicine of tantric techniques; nothing else can really combat the strength of our negativities. Even if we're not perfect tantrikas, there is always something in Vajrayana that can help us. There's so much to choose from.

Buddhism has always changed when it has moved from one country or culture to another. America couldn't possibly be any more different than Tibet, and we may feel that those differences imply a vastly different spiritual path. We can sit around and speculate, but if we try to change it ourselves, even with the best intentions, it becomes "Bruce-ism" or "Mary-ism," no longer Buddhism. This is an extremely important point. We may be accustomed to a great deal of freedom in many areas of our lives, but a spiritual path has its own coherent logic and its own lineage of blessing and transmission. Imagine telling your surgeon, "It's okay to cut me up, but I don't want you to cauterize such-and-such veins." That would be simply crazy. Yet Westerners seem quite happy to do that with Buddhism. "I like this part, but I don't like that. Let's throw it away. It's not really Buddhism." That results in there no longer being a lineage of blessing and transmission. It has been killed by our good intentions.

Only enlightened beings can really change Buddhism. We can see that now in His Holiness the Dalai Lama as he tries to address some of the cultural problems of Westerners. I read one of his discussions with gay Buddhist leaders in which they were trying to gain acceptance even though the traditional teachings condemn their sexual practices as non-virtuous. He has the wisdom, power, and authority to change matters like these; once again, we don't. Chogyam Trungpa Rinpoche was also quite an innovator; but he was also quite an enlightened being.

With time, Westerners will become enlightened. They may not radically transform Vajrayana; they may simply be able to teach in a more easily understandable form. There is an internal logic to Vajrayana that becomes clearer the more one studies it. We would like to think the parts with which we have difficulty are an expression of Tibetan culture and of no use to us here. In truth, they are an expression of the deepest insight and understanding into ultimate truth. Knowing this, it becomes harder to imagine it greatly changing. For instance, termas, the hidden teachings of Guru Rinpoche, are teachings that are discovered when they are appropriate to the time and place. His Holiness Dudjom Rinpoche was a modern terton, but there is nothing I've discovered about his treasures that is particularly revolutionary or modern, even though they have been widely practiced by Westerners. His termas did not introduce any radically new practices for our times.

I imagine that with time we too will change a little. Our children will grow up with concepts that seemed strange and alien to us now. Buddhist ideas have already begun to infiltrate our culture, making it easier for Westerners to approach the real thing.

Nonetheless, there seem to be some changes that may be inevitable. There will most likely be a moving away from ritual to formlessness in practice. This has already been predicted, but as I just mentioned, I fear that if it goes too far, many of the benefits of tantra will be lost.

Fewer people will become ordained; there will be a greater emphasis on lay life. The great danger, of course, is that there won't be enough people developing the depths of meditation to maintain the tradition. In that case, we will always be dependent on foreign teachers. Also, many of the outer forms might be lost, such as the details of rituals that only full-time practitioners have the time to learn. So many of those who are now ordained have such a difficult time. They aren't supported by the laity and must often work. They are not able to isolate themselves from the distractions and temptations of worldly life, and they often end up doing more center work than actual formal meditation. These days, ordination may often not be a good option for one who wants to lead a contemplative life.

With the emphasis shifting to the laity, aspects of the layperson's life will become more respected vehicles for growth and transformation. Romantic relationships are now emerging as such a focus. Work and child-raising are others. Situations that give rise to negativity are also situations where we can learn about ourselves in ways that we never could in a traditional cloistered environment. They always provide opportunities to step out of the ego and to act mindfully, lovingly, and skillfully.

For the vast majority of people in Tibet, sex was either a ordinary act often compared to eating a meal, or a highly sophisticated yogic technique for a very select few. In the West, ordinary people will use the incredible power of sexual activity as a method of transformation without being bona fide tantric practitioners.

The profound insights of Tibetan Buddhism will become integrated with more ideas from Western disciplines. We are already seeing this in many ways. Dream researchers acknowledge Tibetan Buddhists as the experts in the field. Cognitive scientists have an annual meeting with the Dalai Lama. Many Buddhists are therapists, and the meeting between Western therapeutic thought and Buddhism has been compared to the meeting of Christian and Greek thought centuries ago. Buddhists will converse with the contemplatives of Western religions and with physicists on the nature of the universe.

In the past, Buddhism always spread through royal patronage. When the king converted, the kingdom converted with him. The king became the main patron of the monastic system. This will not be the case here in the U.S. There are no kings. Buddhism will always have to compete with a healthy Christianity, scientific skepticism, and mindless materialism. As Buddhism grows, we as Buddhists may start to experience animosity from one of these groups, which may lead to a kind of persecution or at least to an adaptation of defensiveness on our part. But as I've visited the older, more established centers and have met with many of the older, more accomplished Western practitioners, I have no doubt that Tibetan Vajrayana Buddhism has already truly and deeply established itself here in our country and in the West.

Notes

Chapter 1

1. Arya Maitreya and Acarya Asanga, *The Changeless Nature*, Karma Drubgyud Darjay Ling, Eskdalemuir, 1985, p. 30.
2. *Ibid.*, p. 32.

Chapter 2

3. Longchenpa, *Kindly Bent to Ease Us*, Part One, Dharma Publishing, Berkeley, 1975, p. 78.
4. *Ibid.*, p. 76.
5. Tsang Nyon Heruka, *The Life of Marpa the Translator*, Prajna Press, Boulder, 1982, p. 92.

Chapter 4

6. Tsele Rinpoche, *Empowerment*, Rangjung Yeshe Publications, Kathmandu, 1994, p. 15.
7. *Ibid.*, p. 31.
8. *Ibid.*, p. 32.
9. *Ibid.*, p. 32.

Chapter 7

10. Longchenpa, *Kindly Bent to Ease Us*, Part Two, Dharma Publishing, Emeryville, 1976, p. 58.

Chapter 14

11. Jamgon Kongtrul, *The Torch of Certainty*, Shambhala Publications, Boulder, 1977, p. 123.
12. *Ibid.*, p. 128.

Chapter 15

13. Bokar Rinpoche, *Chenrezig: Lord of Love*, ClearPoint Press, San Francisco, 1994, p. 11.
14. Jamgon Kongtrul, *The Oral Instructions of Padmakara*, unpublished translation by Peter Roberts, Oxford, 1989, p. 6.

Chapter 18

15. Dudjom Rinpoche, A Dear Treasure for Destined Disciples: Pointing Out the Great Perfection, from Crystal Cave, Rangjung Yeshe Publications, Kathmandu, 1990, p. 119.

16. Tsele Natsok Rinpoche, Lamp of Mahamudra, Rangjung Yeshe Publications, Kathmandu, 1988, p. 39.

17. Karma Chagme and Gyatrul Rinpoche, A Spacious Path to Freedom, Snow Lion Publications, Ithaca, 1998, p. 97.

18. Garma C. C. Chang, Teachings of Tibetan Yoga, University Books, New Hyde Park, New York, 1963, p. 42.